Saying Goodbye to Our Mothers for the Last Time

Design: Smythtype Design
Cover art: Pastel drawing, titled *Moonscape*, by Carol Thayer Cox

ISBN-13: 978-0-9969686-7-6
Printed in U.S.A

Saying Goodbye to Our Mothers for the Last Time

A COLLECTION OF ESSAYS

Edited by
Carol Thayer Cox & William A. Harrison, III

LISA HAGAN BOOKS

This book is dedicated to all of our mothers:

Ann Ritchie McHugh
April 29, 1935—Clarkesville, Georgia
March 18, 2002—Atlanta, Georgia

Bernice (Bunny) Kay-Franklin
May 11, 1926—Bronx, New York
December 16, 2008—Ft. Lauderdale, Florida

Deanna Rita Larsen Ulrich James
March 16, 1938—Cincinnati, Ohio
October 21, 2005—Lorain, Ohio

Dorothy Rachel Carmichael
March 8, 1918—Lone Grove, Oklahoma
December 5, 1997—Duncan, Oklahoma

Edith Tabachneck Simonovitz
August 4, 1902—Tulchin, Ukraine (Russia)
November 9, 1976—Albany, New York

Eleanor Anne Finch Wix
April 29, 1927—Cavalier, North Dakota
February 5, 2007—Helena, Montana

Elizabeth Anne Maloney Dengel
July 7, 1922—Newport News, Virginia
April 4, 1978—Arlington, Virginia

Elsa Alina (Nivu)Koski Stack
June 22, 1907—Karstala, Finland
January 24, 1982—Tacoma, Washington

Elsie Adelaide (Jean) Male
January 23, 1916—Penge, London, England
December 30, 2001—Beckenham, Kent, England

Enriqueta (Ketty) Lebrón Vda. de Aponte
March 4, 1922—Guayama, Puerto Rico
July 6, 2010—West Palm Beach, Florida

Gisele Baroukel Miller
April 8, 1920—Oran, Algeria
December 23, 1997—Waterville, Maine

Helen Ricaby Stenstrom
January 5, 1913—Chicago, Illinois
November 27, 1988—Washington, DC

Helen Rowles Hansen
February 28, 1895—Wamego, Kansas
November 17, 1979—Sedalia, Missouri

Isobel Goodall Henderson Roberts
June 1, 1925—Shotts, Scotland
September 11, 2007—North Kingstown, Rhode Island

Isobelle Robertson Aitkenhead Beaujon
August 18, 1914—Glen Cove, Long Island, New York
July 21, 2003—Alexandria, Virginia

Juanita Smith Price
September 16, 1921—Salisbury, North Carolina
July 16, 1998—Fredericksburg, Virginia

Laurie Brown Johnston
December 8, 1904—Cleburne, Texas
February 1, 1981—Utica, New York

Lillian Straschun Cohen
April 28, 1913—Boston, Massachusetts
April 19, 2006—Brockton, Massachusetts

Louise Mary Jones Capps
February 19, 1914—Auburn, Maine
June 7, 1963—Westminster, California

Mabel Elizabeth Vaughan Jeffery
November 27, 1893—Junction City, Kansas
June 27, 1956—St. Johnsbury, Vermont

Margaret Walton Elliott
May 29, 1924—Petersburg, Virginia
November 1, 2007—Richmond, Virginia

Martha Florence Strong MacKenzie
September 21, 1891—Paxton, Illinois
March 13, 1959—Asheville, North Carolina

Martha Jane Stadtmiller Harrison
April 7, 1916—Blairsville, Pennsylvania
January 24, 2001—Newport News, Virginia

Mary Catharine Ritchie Farrelly
May 24, 1905—Philadelphia, Pennsylvania
June 28, 1991—Mendham, New Jersey

Myrtle Elizabeth White Alexander
May 25, 1916—Cabarras County, North Carolina
March 6, 2008—Raleigh, North Carolina

Patricia Ann Auernhammer Matthews
March 5, 1927—Saginaw, Michigan
December 13, 1979—Jackson, Michigan

Priscilla Watson Plautz
April 30, 1951—San Juan, Puerto Rico
September 11, 2003—Leonardtown, Maryland

Roberta Ruth Eye Brewer Nesselrodt
June 7, 1932—Franklin, West Virginia
May 21, 2006—Alexandria, Virginia

Rose Anne Cassidy Kearney
September 20, 1906—Carrickmacross, Ireland
February 24, 1999—Hayward, California

Ruth Gardner Hardesty Brittle
November 4, 1918—Ridgeway, West Virginia
February 3, 2007—Remington, Virginia

Ruth Shauck Bannerman
July 3, 1908—Silver Spring, Maryland
May 10, 2005—Silver Spring, Maryland

Sylvia Jessen Ott McGrath
October 26, 1915—Glen Ridge, New Jersey
February 28, 2005—Bowling Green, Virginia

Viola Johnson Hicks

March 2, 1909—Henderson, North Carolina

June 28, 1986—Henderson, North Carolina

Virginia Harrison Hews

January 9, 1929—Honolulu, Hawaii

March 23, 2007—Riverside, California

Contents

FOREWORD

Saying Goodbye to Our Mothers for the Last Time is a collection of essays about the process of losing one's mother. As a psychologist and educator specializing in death, dying, and grief for over 35 years, and as a woman whose own mother died more than 30 years ago, I am keenly aware of the power of stories in helping us through the dying and grieving processes.

Carol Thayer Cox and William A. Harrison have brought together the writings of 35 individuals who tell the stories of their mothers' deaths in their own words. For some, the death is recent; for others, the death occurred twenty or thirty years ago. The essays Cox and Harrison have gathered encompass this experience on every level: physical, emotional, psychological, and spiritual. The writers come from many different cultural, religious, and spiritual backgrounds.

The essayists write about what stands out most as they recall their mothers' deaths, and what is remarkable is that the essays together paint a picture of the entire process of watching one's mother die, suddenly or after an illness, of helping her on the journey, of saying goodbye personally or through ritual, and then of going through grief. Each essay is followed by pictures that bring alive the person who died and allow us as readers to feel connected to the writer and to his or her mother at a sensory level as well.

Many adults today do not know anyone who has struggled with the death of a parent and talked about it openly. Sometimes people feel that because it is the natural way of the world that your mother should die before you, it is unacceptable to feel the loss deeply and grieve openly. Many never talk to their friends or family about their grief, go into therapy, or attend a group with other bereaved people. I have had difficulty finding a book for my clients and friends that would provide companionship through the deep physical, emotional, and spiritual experiences that can be at the same time joyful, frustrating, and deeply saddening. This is just such a book.

In the pages that follow, you will find many of the truths of death and dying. The loss of a mother is a profound event in one's life. There is a sense for many adult children that they have lost unconditional love with this passing. We die as we lived, and very few of the mothers' personalities portrayed here changed appreciably as they were dying. Yet as we watch a loved one die, we must accept and grieve changes in their physical appearance as well as all the other changes in their lives. While a long period of illness brings about ongoing anticipatory grieving, the actual death is completely different. Grievers may feel anger, anxiety, guilt, or simply profound love. Many adult children are helped by the words their mothers spoke to them directly or indirectly, by creating rituals and reviving memories, by dreams or visitations that come soon or many years later, and by deeply held cultural, familial, or spiritual beliefs. Grief is often a very lonely experience.

Saying Goodbye speaks to those who are now caring for an ill mother and are unsure of how to make day-to-day decisions about death and dying; to those who are saying the final goodbyes or planning funerals and memorial services; to those who are confronting the grief they feel in a world without their mothers' physical presence; and, finally, to those who still feel sorrow years later. Because many of the writers come from creative or artistic backgrounds, the essays themselves are filled with lyrical language, poetry, and artwork that communicate to the reader through images as well as words. Many of the writers also come from mental or physical health backgrounds and write through those lenses. Regardless of their background, however, what shines through is their very human responses to the loss of their mothers.

The personalities of the children and the mothers in these essays are revealed in a myriad of ways: through each individual's approach to illness, death, and grief and in the unique expressions of every writer. Some essays will speak to the reader because the experience echoes his or her own, and this will feel soothing and supportive, while some essays may have less of an impact on a reader whose experience was very different. Still others will help the reader to think through end-of-life decisions, events, and emotions in new and innovative ways.

Each of these stories deeply embraces the relationship between mother and child and addresses the changes that occur as death approaches. Not surprisingly, the relationships described in these pages are not perfect. There are ones of tremendous closeness, others less so, and some with much negativity. In most cases, even when the relationships were fractured, the writers talk about being brought closer to their mothers, at least in small ways, toward the end of life. All of us can recognize our own relationships and mothers in these pages, and that is what makes this book so compelling and necessary.

I hope you will read these essays as I did and re-examine the death of your mother with understanding, comfort, forgiveness, love, joy, and humor. Because people are living longer today, many of us will experience the deaths of our parents in later life. As one of the essayists, psychologist Katherine Williams, notes, "the process of mourning involves working through layers of rich and often paradoxical memories, eventually incorporating the essence of the person who has died into one's current sense of oneself."

The essays in this book reflect that process richly. In these pages, I hope you will find a wonderful companion.

Elizabeth Turner Haase, Ph.D.
Psychologist in private practice
Washington, D.C.

Preface I

My first experience with mother loss occurred when my grandmothers died, one when I was in high school and the other when I was in college. I didn't live near either of them. My parents, like so many of their generation who had lived through one or both world wars, had become accustomed to accepting loss and moving on. Thus I never witnessed much grief beyond my grandmothers' funerals, so their passing had little impact on me.

However, I remember quite vividly when I came face to face with the vicissitudes of losing a mother. I was in my late twenties. My friend John Lamph, an artist and professor of art, received news that his mother had died of a stroke. There had been no warning; he was in shock. John was a quiet man, a lithographer who worked meticulously on his art. The day he learned about his mother's death, he went into his studio and painted for hours. Angrily striking huge sheets of paper with stroke after stroke of black paint (using a broom as his implement), he did one abstract work after another, staying up all night. He did 100 Franz Kline-like creations, which he subsequently called his "stroke paintings." I saw how raw his pain was. I also understood, without exchanging words with him, how transformative the creative process had been. He was able not only to express his rage, but also to contain it. Although exhausted, he emerged changed from his experience; he was calm again. There were several of those works that he liked well enough to exhibit.

It is only now, in retrospect, that I can appreciate how John's episode might have been the inspiration for this book. It was then that I realized how profound it is to lose the first person you have known in life, the person who has known you the longest and who holds memories of you from your very beginning. Whether the parenting was nurturing, mediocre, or damaging, you still experienced her as your mother. Biological or adoptive, regardless of what transpires, there is a bond between mother and child. Mother loss, no matter when it happens, is a pivotal event in someone's life.

If John's loss was the initial seed for this book, it didn't become apparent to me until a few more seeds were planted. I guess I needed a garden to get my full attention.

When my friend Peggy Heller and I decided to create a book about art and poetry called *Portrait of the Artist as Poet*, we weren't sure where our journey would take us. We had no idea who would be in our edited book, nor what they would want to say. However, once we extended our invitation and the poetry started coming in, we noticed there was a recurring theme about mothers. Sometimes it was about being a mother or wanting to be a mother; other times it was about losing a mother or losing a child. This subject was seen again in some of the art and essays. It was synchronistic that Peggy and I both lost our mothers while working on this manuscript. The grief expressed in many of the poems in this book touched us each deeply while also providing comfort by bringing us together in a collective sorrow about separation and endings. At the same time we were heartened by all the creations in that volume that are so life affirming. More seeds—I think I was beginning to notice them breaking ground.

In the fall of 2006, I was attending a business meeting at a national conference in New Orleans. My friend Linney Wix was sitting nearby. I observed her respond to a message on her cell phone. Within moments, Linney's face appeared grief stricken. I followed her out of the large ballroom and sat next to her on one of those long couches that line the hallways of big hotels. We remained there together during the next few hours. Linney had received a message from her sister regarding her mother's decline in health. Her intuition told her that her mother's days were numbered. I listened empathically. My mother had just died the year before, and Linney began to ask me questions about what it had been like for me to go through such a process. I really don't remember the specifics of our conversation, but I must have tried to tell her everything I experienced while my mother was dying—things I had done and things I wish I had done differently, my feelings and my fears. I think perhaps this was the first time anyone was willing to sit and listen so intently to the intimate details of my mother's death. The telling was therapeutic for me. I had the benefit of reflective distance, though. Winnowing through my memories, the chaff fell away, leaving the grain as my offering. I tried to instill confidence and trust that she would get through this and be okay.

Linney's mother died within a couple of months. Later, when Linney was reminiscing about our talk, she wrote to thank me. She said, "I'd not have made it through, feeling like it was as good as it could be, if we hadn't sat for the hours we did outside of the conference rooms in New Orleans.... It helped me in finding some of my end words, that we would miss her, that the space she filled would be empty and just how sad that really is.... Your words and love were with me the whole time." Now the seeds were becoming seedlings, and the idea for this book was born. I credit Linney for bringing to light an awareness of the need for a book such as this.

It never ceases to amaze me how the universe cooperates when I say, "YES." Everywhere I went, I met people, strangers even, who wanted or needed to talk about the death or impending death of their mothers. For instance, while in a take-out section of a restaurant, I encountered a middle-aged man who had ordered a large bag of French fries. His clothes looked crumpled, as did his dejected expression. I smiled at him and said that I understood that these fries were the best around. Clutching the bag of fries to his chest, he told me tearfully that he had just come from the hospital where his mother was in serious condition. The doctor had informed the family that there was no hope. To cheer her up, he was taking her these fries, her favorite food. This is one of many mother loss stories I began encountering on a regular basis. People tend to talk to me anyway—on buses, planes, and trains, wherever. But suddenly the subject seemed to revolve around mothers.

I need to relate one more seedling story, one that blossomed into the title of this book. My husband and I were attending an opera at the Kennedy Center, and a woman about my age was sitting next to me. During intermission, all the people around us had vacated their seats, so we started a conversation. This woman, whom I will call Mary, told me that she had just returned from Oregon where her mother lived. About a month earlier, her mother had requested the presence of all of her family. Having a terminal disease with no prediction of how long her suffering would go on, her mother had decided on physician-assisted suicide. Mary told me she was surprised how gracefully she and all her sisters had accepted their mother's decision. No one tried to talk her out of it. When it came time to leave, everyone who lived far away said a final goodbye. Mary thought she was at peace with it, until the time got closer to her mother's actual death. She realized that she had to go back and "say goodbye for the last time." When I heard those words, I knew I had the title for the book I had been thinking about editing. I actually gave Mary my contact information and invited her to write an essay, but unfortunately never heard back from her. Her task, however, may have been complete. She confirmed once again the compelling need for people to tell their stories about their last days with their mothers.

As one of the first baby boomers, I'm learning every day or so about the mothers of my friends who are either ill, in nursing homes, in hospice, or dying. Since there are so many of us, our generation is probably the first to have had the benefit of knowing that what we are going through is not uncommon. That's been the experience of baby boomers throughout our lives. But in this case, just knowing that other people are losing their mothers doesn't really help us get through it ourselves.

Particularly in our western culture, dying is rarely talked about and there is little to prepare us for that moment. When people die, we talk about who they were, what our relationship was with them, and what we want to remember about them. That's all well and good, but we don't often share with one another what really happens when the death occurs. And those are the memories that linger.

I began to wonder, what if we, who have lost our mothers, could talk about our experiences, even the painful ones, without worrying about how uncomfortable it might make others feel. Couldn't our stories help prepare those who will be facing their own separations from their mothers? Now, I realize there's no way any of us can ever be prepared for such a major event in our lives like the death of a mother. Each situation is unique. But there may be some things we can think about beforehand that might help us be mindful of what to expect or what we might like to do if we are present at our mother's death. Or if our mother dies unexpectedly, it might help to know how others were able to deal with it. How they were able to say goodbye, whether by their mother's side or not, is not something people readily tell one another.

So I sought prospective authors to write about something very intimate. Rather than write about the life of his or her mother, I asked each person to write about the death of his or her mother and thus the end of a known relationship. People learn from other people's life stories. This is why short stories, fairy tales, and myths have always been so popular. We find a main character to relate to in the story and vicariously experience the trials and sorrows as well as the celebrations and joys. Stories help us tap into these archetypes of life and death that are part of us all.

Initially, I had asked only women to write essays, emphasizing the mother-daughter connection. I am grateful to Paul Hansen, husband of one of the authors, Mimi Farrelly-Hansen, for requesting an opportunity to write an essay for the book. It was then that the book became much more than my vision, and I began seeking essays by men. Shortly thereafter, I invited Bill Harrison to be my co-editor, which has resulted in a collegial partnership that has enriched the editing process considerably.

While working on this project, we have received feedback from a number of our writers further affirming our belief that this book has a purpose. What first astounded me were the synchronicities that occurred around the timing of the invitation to write an essay. One person received the letter on the day of her first motherless birthday, and she proceeded to write all day. While meditating, another woman heard her mother speak to her after years of silence. A few days later when she opened the letter I had sent her, she gladly wrote the essay to help her discover what unfinished business she might have with her mother. It was not unusual to hear that a writer had recently dreamt about his or her mother about the time the request arrived in the mail. And then we were often told how therapeutic the actual writing had been, even though challenging. People thanked us for giving them an opportunity to express what sometimes had been held inside for a long while. They thanked us for the increased understanding the writing afforded them.

Although not the book's focus, the complexity of mother-child relationships is conveyed, along the spectrum of delightful to difficult. What surprised us were the ways in which humor sometimes weaves in and out of these stories of grief. We also were moved by the variety of creative means people use to deal with their mourning. This book takes a lens to the transition from life to death, zooms in on that event, and witnesses what people did, how they said goodbye, and how they fared afterwards. These are the stories that ache to be told, that capture a picture of what happens when death disrupts our ways of being and changes forever what we have always known. These are the stories that will guide, warn, encourage, and inspire others to know that they, too, can cross that threshold when the time comes for them to say goodbye to their mothers for the last time. It will also be a gift to those who have already lost their mothers, as these stories may provide solace and perspective.

Carol Thayer Cox

Preface II

The book you hold in your hands is the creation of Carol Thayer Cox, or at least it was to start with. The idea and subject matter were hers; just about all of the contributors are friends or professional contacts of hers; she worked out and drafted instructions that were sent to those who agreed to submit a contribution, and these guidelines served to keep the authors focused on the subject as she conceived it. After the essays were submitted, she communicated with the writers about questions that needed answers, the sometimes-delicate matter of editorial judgments, and the minutiae of mothers' and authors' names, biographical information, and photographs.

But it came to her, after contributions started coming in, that she should ask me to be co-editor. From the outset, I understood the generosity and faith involved in this invitation. We did not really know each other very well at the time, but as we started to collaborate, it quickly became clear that we were an incredibly good team. And as we worked on the essays that follow, laughed and cried over what we were reading, and discussed matters of organization and expression that would improve them without doing violence to the intentions, voice, and perceptions of our authors, the book gradually became mine as much as Carol's—mine, that is, in the sense that my affection for the writers, investment in the content, and commitment to the vision and purpose of this collection came to equal hers.

This is an important book. The death of one's mother is inevitably going to constitute a turning point in our lives. For those whose mothers are still alive, reading these essays might help to make the inevitable a richer, deeper, more satisfying experience. And since our relationships with our mothers continue and can change even after their death, for those who have suffered this loss, reading about what others' experiences were like can help us to better understand and accept the events and the nature of this attachment.

It hardly needs to be said—and yet it must be said—that mothers and our relationships with our mothers, however much we might want to idealize them, can be complicated, sometimes to the point of being distressing. Readers will find it inspiring to see how some of our contributors have contended with such difficulties. And it might be instructive to read about others' regrets and to hear their "if only" wishes.

Readers might also be aware of a vast range of authorial tones and styles, from the rather scholarly to the intimately conversational. Each one turns out to be exactly appropriate for the relationship and the events described, as well as for the writer's message. Similarly, the authors' revelations are muted or blazing in their honesty and forthrightness.

Every essay in this collection contains at least one important lesson, injunction, or observation (and some of them several) that has the potential to alter the course of our relations with our mothers, our ideas about funeral arrangements, or our tactics for coping with this loss. Some essays will speak to a given reader more than others, of course, but each one of them is worth reading, and I would guess that anyone will find some particularly riveting. As we get older, consideration of insights gained from these essays could affect the attitude we adopt toward our own mortality and so make this difficult time more satisfying for us and for our children.

I would like to echo for readers something Carol said in her instructions to contributors: each of these essays—and the book as a whole—is a gift to readers. If you are willing to think about the subject of the death of your own mother (and clearly you are, since you have picked up and opened this book with its provocative title), you are sure to find, as I have, a wealth of gifts to mull over, digest, and inspire you.

William A. Harrison, III

Ann Ritchie McHugh

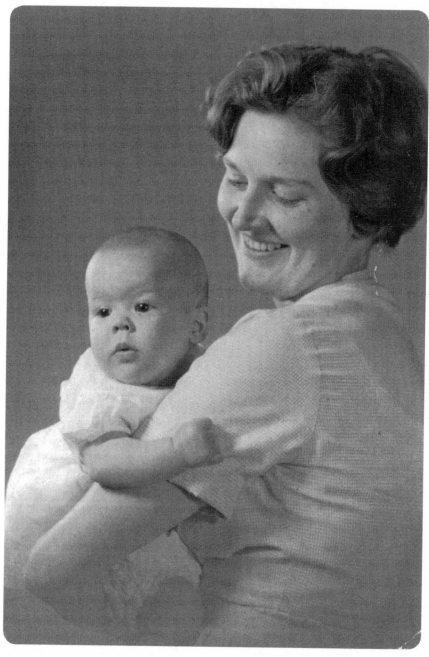

Mom (36 years old) and I (4 months old) in May 1963

Yellow

by Ritchie Robertson Two Bulls

Ann is wearing a bright yellow shirt as she rocks gently in the comfy, pad-ded rocking chair she had given us when our daughter was born. She is alive. She has good color, a round, pleasant face with an easy smile. It is a regular day. Ann has flown from Georgia to California to visit us like so many times before. As she sits, Ann begins to blow up a yellow balloon for my children, Grant and Reed. She blows with facility. She takes in air and blows into the narrow entry, filling the cheerful-looking balloon to capacity.

That was it—the dream I had waited for. I wanted to see her. I needed to experience her again, to receive a message. How was I supposed to do this thing of living in the world without her? What might she tell or show me that would assure me of a secure identity in the face of this profound, untimely loss?

Ada Ann Ritchie was a vivacious, engaging, and beautiful woman of Scot-Irish descent from southern Appalachia. She was raised by loving par-ents and grandparents in Demorest, northeast Georgia, with her younger sis-ter Helen Sue. Ann, a bubbly, friendly, and very outgoing woman, was fair-skinned with hazel eyes and auburn hair. She had studied studio art and art history in college in Virginia, where she met my father. She and my father raised my two brothers and me. They divorced after 25 years of marriage, while I was in college. Both remarried and moved on amicably. Mom was later widowed. She loved adventure, traveling, the arts, learning, entertain-ing, and being with people. Home was always filled with art, music, and won-derful smells, as she loved to cook. She adored her family. After my brothers and I left home as young adults, our mom would call us back for celebrations and simply to gather together, keeping her promise to have us visit her in her home at least once a year. She also made trips to see us regularly.

It was nearing Christmas 2001, and both of my brothers and their families were planning to visit Mom for the holiday. Mom had been with us in California at Thanksgiving after making a trip to France with friends and leading a pilgrimage to the Washington National Cathedral. She had gotten a bad cold and was trying to rest and get over it before family arrived, she said that day on the phone. Mom and I talked frequently by telephone once my children were born. My respect for her had grown exponentially after I began the humbling experience of parenting. And, I needed her support. She was always in my corner. I had no idea that this was the last time I would hear my mother's voice. It was Christmas Day when she commented in quiet concern that she couldn't seem to stop coughing.

Her coughing was not unusual. Mom had been diagnosed eleven years before at the Mayo Clinic with a rare autoimmune disease called relapsing polychondritis. Basically, her body was attacking and destroying its own cartilage, resulting in a floppy windpipe. For years this meant somewhat reducing her level of activity, sleeping with a CPAP to help air going in, using inhalers and some oral steroids, and going on antibiotics when getting an upper respiratory infection. Mom walked more slowly as a result, and she had to stop talking when coughing spasms came on. She learned to take a rest every day. Relying on her strong faith, she learned to live with this unpredictable disease. And she lived positively and fully, delighting in adventure and people.

After Christmas, Mom's health concerns became increasingly serious, and she was taken to the hospital by ambulance. A bronchoscopy revealed that the disease had progressed markedly, destroying more and more cartilage, even on the top of the left lung. It was hard for Mom to breathe, and she couldn't seem to kick this cold. When I called the hospital to speak with her, the nurses returned to the phone, saying awkwardly that Ann did not want to talk. This happened each time I called. While it stung initially, I had experienced so much of my mother's unconditional love over the years that I knew it was due to her illness, the compromised airways, and nothing else. A lifetime of unbridled love assured me of this. In years past when Mom would have brief coughing episodes on the phone, she would stop talking and I would try to ramble on, entertaining her with stories of her grandbabies and our family.

Mom was taken by ambulance from the small hospital to the Emory Intensive Care Unit in Atlanta, where she had a tracheotomy and spent some time on a respirator. The pulmonologist, having seen only one such case before, explained that there was no known treatment for her condition and that trying to put in stents to keep airways open would likely be futile, since there was little to nothing for the stents to hold onto now. The outlook was unpredictable and grim. Our mom elected to try the stents anyway. She was a strong, brave woman who still had things to do. She had three young grandkids and a fourth one on the way! She had just moved back home to Georgia and bought a house, intending to take care of her elderly Aunt Clifford. She was planning more travel and pilgrimages to the Washington Cathedral, had joined an Episcopal Church in Clarkesville, was connecting with cousins and childhood friends, and was happily equipping her home for lots of visits with her beloved family and friends.

Progress was minimal, but Mom was able to come off the respirator and move out of the ICU. My second trip to see my mom was when she was in the rehab hospital, still using a tracheotomy and requiring much attention from the respiratory therapists. I spent time decorating her hospital room with cards, photographs, and her grandchildren's artwork. I played DJ with her favorite CDs: classical music, sacred choral music, and Broadway tunes. I picked up where she had left off reading *Harry Potter* and read aloud to her. I swabbed her dry lips, washed her face, washed and combed her hair, and with the help of a cousin removed her acrylic nails; I massaged aromatic oil into her feet, held her hands, and talked. I talked. This was so odd. Mom had always done the talking, at times to my great irritation. I had often thought she could carry on a conversation with me without any of my input. She had to work very intentionally on listening. Although I knew she valued my thoughts and opinions, I understood that she just had to work extra hard to make space for the words of others and to temper her excitement. She was incredibly garrulous, enthusiastic, and powerful, a born extravert and leader.

Initially I felt uncomfortable having to take on a new way of being with Mom. She had never been silent before, at least not for long. Even her coughing spells had not lasted. Now she mouthed words to me, about 50 percent of which I could understand. These communications were mainly around her physical needs. I pushed my introverted self into giving her family news, talking about the Episcopal Church, remembering events and stories. I found it strange at first that my mother did not want to look at the piles of cards coming in or hear the prayers and words that her many friends and relatives sent. I wondered if these stirred up emotions and anxiety that she could not afford to express. Crying could result in choking, and she already worked so hard just to breathe. She couldn't take food by mouth, lost 45 pounds, and could no longer walk due to weakness. Because of her severely compromised state, she didn't qualify for physical therapy. Hospice could not be ordered, because no one could say for certain that she would die in six months. She could persist like this for a few years. As if Mom's beliefs were coming through me, I remember assuring her that whatever happened we would deal with it; I was not promising her false hope for recovery. We would make our way through; all would be well even with death.

After almost two months of hospitalization and in the midst of the hardship, a wonderful day arrived in February. It is a day I will never forget. I was at the hospital with my mom when the first photographs of her fourth grandchild, William, came. I had the honor of showing my mother the photos of my brother Wesley and Catherine's second child. Enormous smiles covered Mom's face, accompanied by the sweet shaking of her head that conveyed her utter amazement of it all. This child, with his little spark of light, resembled my brother as a baby. His arrival blessed us and reminded us that life would continue. As surely as death loomed, life bloomed as well.

When I left to return to my husband and children, 5 and 2½ years old, who were on the West Coast, I didn't know that I would not see my mom again. It was true that her body was shrinking away, even failing and mattering less and less. But her spirit continued, and it was big. As I

6

went through security at the airport, I stared at the blurry guard who was politely asking me to remove my shoes. He asked me several times before it registered. I stumbled my way onto the airplane and sank into my seat. Head down, I cried steadily and silently for much of the flight, feeling my heart breaking.

It was on March 18th when my brother Wesley called, calmly informing me of our mother's passing. Asphyxiation. Even though all of us, including relatives and dear friends, had taken shifts being with Mom every day and advocating for her care in the hospital over the three months, no one was with her when she last breathed. My first response to the news of her death was great relief. She had been withering away physically and required skilled nursing care. I had been with her recently and had told her I loved her and that we would be okay. I felt I had done all I could and I did not have regrets. She was released. My mother was a devout Episcopalian and had put herself in God's hands years before she died. Physical and emotional suffering was over. I felt peace for my mom. I could see her go.

Mom's legacy was crystal clear. I knew that she wanted me to take better care of myself and enjoy my life more, to value my family and to laugh more, to strengthen my belief in a power greater than myself, and to trust in that. I knew that she loved me completely, despite every moment I snapped at her, and that she forgave me for everything along the way. In the midst of the peace at her departure and the clarity of her wishes for me came the overwhelming ache of sadness. I was certainly ready to see her released from her physical predicament. I was not, however, ready to be without her. I honestly could not comprehend such a world. Who was I now? How could I be who I think I am? It was an identity crisis unlike any other in my 39 years. My mother knew me in ways no one else on earth did or ever would. I began to feel the onus of being a mother to my children: a mother without a mother. I could not fathom a life like that. I had to find my way on a road I did not choose. It seemed that I no longer had something to push against, which resulted in my having to grow up, finally.

For the days, weeks, months following Mom's death I waited for a dream, a vision, or some form of visitation from her. I felt impatient and desperate about it. I wondered with frustration why nothing was happening. I prayed fiercely for her to appear to me. She did not. I began talking to her sometimes, as I did my daily solitary walks around the Rose Bowl. I noted that I felt close to her when at art shows, museums, church services, concerts, holidays, and when cooking in my kitchen. I bought myself a shirt in one of her favorite colors: cantaloupe. I bought small gifts for my children on her birthday. I allowed myself to take naps. I quit praying for her to appear. I did not stop wishing for it, though.

Then one night that short dream came, more like Mom just passing through. Yellow. She was wearing yellow and blowing up a yellow balloon. Here was my vibrant, cheerful Mom breezing through to blow up a balloon for my children, taking pleasure in simple things. Simple. Bright. Ordinary. Maybe the balloon was for me, too.

Ritchie Robertson Two Bulls *resides with her family in Minneapolis, where she works as an art therapist at the Minnesota Indian Women's Resource Center. Ritchie is also the Volunteer Coordinator for First Nations' Kitchen, a program providing organic, healthy, traditional Native foods to the community. She enjoys singing, art-making, cooking, and traveling.*

Bernice (Bunny) Kay-Franklin

My mother and I on the night of my Bar Mitzvah celebration, May 1969.
She often remarked that this was one of the happiest memories
for her and our family.

Hanging Chads, Buoys, and Clay: Finding What Was Never Lost

by Michael A. Franklin

They had warned me before I entered the intensive care room to brace myself. Uneasy about the unexpected details awaiting me, I inwardly propped up my apprehensive bones, doing my best to accept the story of illness four steps ahead. As I crossed the threshold of her small fishbowl room, I immediately knew that the final slide of my mother's decline had arrived. As I dreamed my way into her room, encountering this first bookended marker of her dying process, the obvious signs of deterioration confirmed that my own process of bereavement had started. I saw my mother under the sheets, the sights and sounds of the machines breathing and feeding her. Silently hovering in the corners of the room was a text written in hospital talk that startled me. On a continuum from a completely comatose state to fully awake, my mother was somewhere in the middle, intubated with breathing and feeding tubes, ashen, and unable to make direct contact.

My mother was admitted to the hospital on Election Day. She was also from the infamous "hanging chad" county in Florida that set in motion the election defeat of Al Gore. After that debacle she swore she would never miss another election. I am told that she was rather irritable with the emergency room staff, insisting that she wait to be admitted so that she could go vote. A fierce Democrat, she was basically kept alive by her disdain for the Bush administration. Mom was depressed in her later years. As her body increasingly failed her, there was still one reliable strategy to get her back to her old fiery self. All I had to do was ask about George Bush or

Dick Cheney and she would spring to life. It was as if the two defibrillator paddles of Bush and Cheney had shocked her back from her melancholy state. Even with dangerously discordant vital signs in the emergency room, she still wanted to perform her civic duty. And although she did not make it to the polls, she did see Obama win. In fact, that was our last phone conversation. Together, long distance, we saw the world change.

A few days later, yet without any firm diagnosis, she continued to decline. Overall she remained in the hospital for a total of six weeks, transferred from a general unit to the ICU, and finally to the Hospice unit. I tried to be with her as much as possible, flying in from Denver several times towards the end of a busy semester at the university where I work. Since my mother had birthed me into this world, I wanted to help her release her body and love her into the next realm. I also wanted to protect her. Like an impassioned sentry, I sat by her side shielding her from the well-meaning parade of doctors and their five-minute visits. When a new doctor entered her room, I would ask, "Which part of the body do you represent?" And since there were many doctors from various practices, the daily procession consisted of new and unfamiliar faces.

With the exception of three doctors, I witnessed over and over again how difficult it is for medical personnel to make meaningful contact. The medical system did not allow these physicians to slow down and see the subtleties of my mother's condition. I spent ten- and twelve-hour days with her, watching her slight movements, trying to learn her non-verbal language of embodied pain. Honing in on her many facial and body cues convinced me that she was hearing me and that she was trying to communicate through the veil of the thick fog that seemed to cloud her drifting awareness. Part of my self-ordained role as sentry was to interrupt the automatic routine of the doctors and try to interpret her state to them. It was difficult to get them to hear me. Finally I had to insist that they consider me a relevant part of their team. As an artist and art therapist, I regard myself as a highly trained observer. My mother's life depended on these skills, and I was fervently committed to using them on her behalf. In fact, my observations helped the doctors to make a significant diagnosis resulting in her receiving the proper medications.

Every rattling moment was precious. My mother's bleeding, clenched hands; her silent, panicked expressions; her arms, black and blue from the dialysis sessions; as well as the chance to gently stroke and massage her soft skin and comb her brittle hair—these memories remain as indelible snapshots of fading time. My partner Jo, who works with Hospice patients and their families and was a student at Naropa University, taught me about a phrase by the founder of the university, Chögyam Trungpa Rinpoche. He spoke of how a vulnerable heart breaks and opens to love, which became a comforting lifeline during this time of uncertainty. My heart kept breaking and opening. At times surprised and ambushed by these unexpected, cascading emotions, I welcomed the gift of vulnerability that continuously emerged, leading me straight to the subject of love. Dying, death, and the resulting sensations of loss are really opportunities to connect with and excavate these layers of love. My relationship with my mother was complicated. The strata of our history appearing before me were laced with deposits of emotional intricacy, yet in the end I had dropped deeply down into my unyielding affections for her. I did my best to feel into and welcome these painful yet valued emotions.

We locate ourselves in the world by those we love. Existing beyond the borders of our own bodies, these loved ones act like reliable buoys, signaling back that we are seen, known, and loved. There is a sustaining care that I felt and still feel from my mother. Although we often expressed our care for each other through struggle and disagreement, our core experience was deep warmth for one another. We both knew that she was a sustaining force in my life. Mothers and motherhood are a mystery to me and, I dare say, to many men. The experience of carrying and birthing a baby into the world creates a form of unflinching maternal bonding that transcends any conflict. Clearly, fathers carry and manifest their own version of this story. And although I am not a father, I am a son fortunate enough to have had an adoring mother who now needed my help.

Death is like birth in reverse. Instead of pushing life into the world, there is a quality of letting go in order to enter the next realm. My dear mother fought against this time of releasing from the tight grip of the body.

For weeks I tried to help her with this transition, to hold and stroke her head, wash her face and hands, protect her, clean her, talk to her, listen to her subtle messages, cry for her, and hopefully serve her during this next phase of pilgrimage.

After the first four weeks of her six-week hospitalization, it was clear that it was time to move my mother from intensive care to Hospice care. While I was happy to leave the extreme environment of the ICU, I was also confronted with thoughts of finality, which were made increasingly clear to me as I helped roll her gurney bed to the correct floor and into the Hospice unit. As we crossed this threshold, like wading across the river Styx, I realized that I, too, was transitioning to yet another threshold: I knew that the final passage of my mother's life was now inevitable. Compared to the relentless sights and sounds of our previous three weeks, the Hospice unit was surprisingly quiet. It felt prayerful, like the sacred grounds where the hardworking dying could finally rest. Conflicted, I welcomed the calm and yet resented this undeniable truth.

Each night I folded my non-compliant body into an impossible hammock of chairs, maintaining my post. During the quiet of these last nights, crying spells would come upon me like an abrupt weather system forcing its way through the landscape. I prayed as this rain fell. I also chanted sacred mantras I had been taught as a way to clear the pathways that blocked my acceptance of my mother's final passage. What we thought would take a day or two ended up being an eight-day process. As her agitation increased, so did her doses of Ativan and Morphine. Each day she bounced back and forth between protest and drug-induced rest. I joked with my brother Barry that she was actually at a virtual Grateful Dead concert, stoned and happy. Humor helped, as did needed sleep.

Eventually I had to seize time for myself and rest. Taking a break from bending my body like Gumby into the hospital chairs each night, I returned to my mother's apartment to catch a few hours of sleep. On December 16, 2009, at 5:50 a.m., the call came that her breathing patterns had shifted, signaling that her final exhale was near. I dressed as quickly as I could, arriving at the hospital ten minutes after she had passed. I chanted more of the sacred sounds to her released soul and newly cast-off body. I washed her, kissed her, and felt thankful that the cold had not yet set in. As I stroked her hair, she still felt the same, warm and sweet. I could not help but love her even more as my tears distorted my increasingly opaque vision. She was gone from her body, the soul released. Soon my brother Barry arrived. Together we each took one of her hands and whispered as best we could our final farewell.

I sat with her for about three hours. Eventually the profound immensity of what had just happened as well as what now needed to happen left me feeling claustrophobic. I craved the experience of seeing and also being in big space. Barry drove us to his favorite place at the ocean, affectionately referred to as the "Major Ohm" spot. It was perfect. We walked to a point at the end of a rocky jetty. Ships were coming and going, amplifying the notion of is and was. In that moment my mother became both—deceased and eternal. Watching the ships easily cut through the water, I recognized that I had crossed into the life stage of orphan, into a version of alone lapped by grief.

There are many unanticipated gifts received from a difficult time like this. The two that easily come to mind are how death and dying grow us up and into the mysteries of life. The other is how the death of my mother brought me closer to other family members, particularly my brother. In many ways, since we live in different places, we do not really know each other. My mother's dying and passing allowed us to participate in this sacred event together. We rediscovered the intricacies and gifts cultivated by the other over the past decades. The tragic process of her fading away fulfilled a wish that she carried for many years: that my brother and I know and care for each other in our adult, albeit understandably separate, lives.

We got to confirm this emerging gift during the funeral. By chance, Barry and I discovered that we both love the bagpipes. More than any other instrument, they strike the quickest pathway in, entering the visceral place where tears are born. My family is Jewish, and as far as I know Jews do not do bagpipes at funerals. However, being the iconoclasts that we are, Barry and I secured the services of a seasoned piper. We asked him to leave his kilts at home, to edit out the churchy melodies, and play directly to the heart. We wanted him to use these beautiful, haunting sounds to uplift her spirit. As we had hoped, this piercing sound, like bright light, resonated and reflected the weightless spirit we were celebrating. As the bagpiper played, during these final moments before her interment, we dropped soil from Israel on her casket. She was now somewhere else, far away but also near, is and was. Although her form was gone, memory carries her deep inside. Through remembering, I visit with her, experiencing the gift of how a broken heart could open to a larger message.

A final note: At the funeral, the director of the chapel called me aside to view my mother's body in order to confirm that it was indeed her in the coffin. Together we stepped into the next room, which was empty except for the casket. The passageway between these two rooms, these two worlds, offered a poignant contrast between the crescendo of family voices in one and the complete silence in the other, life and death side by side. I slowly approached the casket, laying my eyes on the lifeless image of my mother before me. She was nicely dressed and her hair tolerably combed. Yet she also looked like an artificial version of herself. Her sanitized appearance, complete with thickly applied make-up, signaled that my mother was long gone from her body. I felt cautious as I approached, knowing that I wanted to kiss her cheek one last time. And yet I heard a strong inner voice advise me not to make contact with my lips. I disobeyed this assertive intuition and leaned in to kiss her one last time. As soon as I did, the icy chill of her skin assaulted my previous memory of when I last kissed the same cheek in her Hospice room. Then, she still felt warm and familiar. Yet in this moment of my final goodbye, the two sensations of warmth and chill, life and loss, confronted me. I literally needed to spit out the abrupt coldness that intruded.

A few months later I was working in the art studio with clay. There are many reasons why I love to work with this simple, ordinary material. As earth, like mud, it is cold to the touch. When the intentions of the artist are wedded with the flexibility of the clay to create spontaneous forms, shapes shift and new three-dimensional images appear. As this collaboration continues, the clay is then put into the transformative power of fire where it emerges hardened like stone. And finally, it lives in and holds space.

While working with the chill of the clay, which felt like cold skin, I was transported back to the scene of my mother in her coffin. I heard the same inner voice that previously told me not to kiss my mother's cheek now tell me to kiss the clay. I did. This time I was prepared and ready to feel the chill against my lips. I had made a fragile pot with extremely thin edges whereby the fragility of the clay is in direct dialogue with its flexible resiliency. Since I had been handling the clay, it had become warm. As has happened so many times before, the clay with its innate wisdom helped me to find resolution. The now warm skin of the clay body allowed me to transform this intrusive memory into a celebration of rebirth and renewal as the pot took on a life of its own.

This photo, taken when my mother was in her early 80s, is an example of the many playful moments we shared together. It reminds me of her precious presence, how much I miss her, and how happy I am for her wherever she might be.

Michael A. Franklin, *chair of the graduate art therapy program at Naropa University, has practiced and taught in various national and international academic and clinical settings since 1981. The author of numerous professional articles, he is the founder of the Naropa Community Art Studio, a project that trains socially engaged art therapists to serve marginalized community members through the studio arts.*

Deanna Rita Ulrich James (nee Larsen)

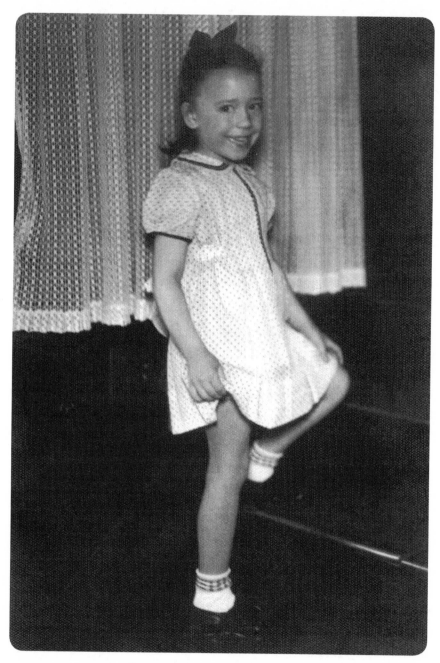

Deanna Larsen as a child of 6 or 7

Pictures of My Mother: An Artist's Experience with Loss

by Randall K. James

Deanna Rita Ulrich James (nee Larsen) passed over on October 21, 2005. She was 67 years old, and I, her only son and child, was 43 at the time. She had been struggling during the last several years with a host of health problems. She had diabetes, high blood pressure, congestive heart failure, and many other less severe physical maladies, all of which were in some way related to these three main conditions. A week or two before her death, she went into the hospital and was in critical care because of complications of these illnesses. At the time I was living in another state, about eight hours away.

I cannot say that the only reason we lived so far away was because of my rather strained relationship with my mother, but it was certainly a factor. I was made to clean the house for my mother and stepfather every week during the span of my adolescence and young adulthood. This deeply affected my relationship with my mother, and we were never really able to come to terms with these experiences. As a result, I was angry with her and my stepfather Nat, who is also deceased. While Deanna was, in many ways, a loving and wonderfully empathic mother and social worker, she was never able to resolve her own housekeeping behaviors that she learned from her mother. Apparently, she got the message that she was not good enough at cleaning, and so she stopped cleaning altogether after I reached an age to take over those chores. I resented her for asking, and she resented having to ask. The tension between us was quite palpable at times. Yet, this long-standing dynamic became meaningless as I gazed upon my mother resting in the Intensive Care Unit (ICU) after her kidneys almost stopped functioning. At that moment there was, of course, nothing I wouldn't do for her.

A week before I got the first call about my mother's condition, I had been working in my art studio on a series of collage and acrylic paint combinations. I spontaneously created three pieces literally days before I got the call about my mother's hospitalization. They were attempts to capture the contemplative mood I was developing outside the studio through the practice of meditation. The red vertical lines I used were new to my work and act to freeze or deaden the pictorial space. I have, interestingly enough, not used these elements in any other work. In retrospect, I have come to understand that these paintings were very much about my mother's imminent death. These three pieces seemed to represent or correspond to the three general phases I experienced in my mother's passing. The first one in the series, which was actually the last of the three created, has a yellow outer hue, often associated with knowledge or cognition. So I ascribe this painting to an inner knowing about, and anticipation of, the hospitalization and the seriousness of my mother's condition.

The second painting is smaller, and the main color tones are red and a deep maroon that suggest bruising. The strong, slightly angled horizontal lines cut across the large maroon circle (the body) and the smaller red circle (the head) that sits atop it. A larger horizontal bar is evenly positioned across the lower portion of the large circle and separates the very bottom of it from the integrity of the whole. A similar pattern is repeated with the top of the smaller red circle being set apart. Additionally, one of the horizontal elements has a pointed end and is reminiscent of a medical needle. This piece of art physically, more than the other two, reminds me of my mother. For these reasons this painting seems to represent for me her actual passing or death itself.

The third painting, which was actually the first one created, has the feeling of being a monument to something. The large and small circles are repeated, yet here they are separated from each other. The head is removed from the body and a lighter halo surrounds it. The red vertical stripes cover the entire width of the painting. The three red squares seem to recapitulate the three square paintings themselves, and when taken together with the vertical red stripes, suggest a finality or ending that is not present in the other two works. Blue and aqua tints that often reflect calmness and healing infuse this piece. Hence, I believe this painting foreshadows the events and experiences that followed my mother's death. In art we often get a glimpse of our future, but because of our time-bound habits of perception, we can only know it after the fact.

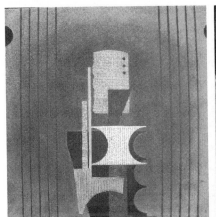 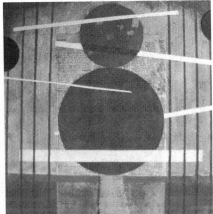

Three paintings in my "Canvas Collage Series"

Deanna had entered the hospital because her kidneys were starting to shut down. I traveled up to be with her within a few hours of getting the call, just enough time to make arrangements for the care of my then two-year-old daughter. The doctors and nurses were able to stabilize her within a few days, and in less than a week's time, I traveled back home to resume the work I was doing in the studio and to relieve both my wife and our friends who had rallied to care for our daughter.

A week or perhaps two passed before I received a second call. She was back in the ICU, again with failing kidneys, and with the addition of a hospital-acquired infection. Deanna had entered a coma this time and was not able to talk with me. She was placed on a ventilator and had a catheter and multiple tubes and devices attached to her, as she lay motionless upon the hospital bed. I sat with her in her room and visited with her for as long as I could. I must confess I don't think it was too long, a few hours perhaps; then I left to find some way to numb myself as the realization that she might not make it through this ordeal dawned on me.

As the only child, I had to make all the decisions for my mother's care by myself. I called my wife, and she and my daughter joined me within a couple of days. I also called the youngest of my three older stepbrothers, and he and his only son joined us at my mother's bedside during the next weekend. While this family support was immeasurably helpful to me emotionally, it was still I who had to make any and all decisions concerning her medical condition, which did not look bright. The doctors had once again stabilized her kidney functions, but they were only operating at about 20 percent. She remained in a coma while the infection raged in her body.

While Deanna did not have any advanced medical directives, she and I had talked on a couple of occasions about death and the manner in which she wanted to pass. From these limited conversations, it was fairly clear in my mind that she did not want to remain on life support. She preferred to pass naturally and with as little intervention as possible, unless the conditions were such that she would not make it otherwise. After consultation with the attending physician, it seemed clear that my mother's prognosis was not good, and despite some hesitation on his part, I decided that she would want the ventilator and other medical devices that sustained her life to be removed. Her kidneys were shutting down and her body was unsuccessfully fighting the infection.

Deanna believed that in a previous life she was a gruff and womanizing male with cruel and sadistic tendencies. She also believed that her relationship with my stepfather was in some way a compensatory or balancing dynamic. She recognized that her second husband was a male chauvinist, and if he wasn't cruel, he could certainly be indifferent at times.

Her belief in reincarnation influenced my own ideas about death and survival. There were two incidents involving the death of both my mother and my stepfather that are related to this concept. Nat believed strongly that one had to struggle in life. This was his experience in his life and in his death. Just over eight and a half years before Deanna's passing, he died of emphysema acquired from a lifetime of smoking. Interestingly, he died on March 20th, just four days after my mother's birthday, while she passed on October 21st, just four days before his birthday. Nat lost his physical and mental faculties over the course of many months and was transferred from the hospital to the Hospice facility when his doctors anticipated that his death was near. Yet, he tenaciously hung on to life. After exhausting the timeframe that Hospice allows, he was transferred to a nursing home where he survived another six months. The night before Nat died, I had a dream in which I was attempting to get him out of a hospital. He was in a wheelchair and I was pushing him all over the hospital looking for an exit, to no avail. I then had the idea that I would take him through the psychiatric ward, and we could get out that way. Well, this worked. As we passed through the psychiatric ward and reached the other side, he stood up out of the chair and declared that he was off to Europe to become a white male actor. And with that he was gone, and I woke up. The very next evening Nat died, just after Deanna and I had left the nursing home. What makes this particularly fascinating is that approximately four or six months later, the friend of a friend who plays in a musical band in Germany started to play a song called "Nat," which my good friend had written about my stepfather. While this may be viewed as coincidence, the synchronicity carries significant meaning and confirms for me that we participate in a larger arena of events that is unknown to most of us.

As my mother's health deteriorated and I decided that all medical interventions not related to her comfort should be removed, the doctors did what they could to stabilize her enough to comply with my wishes. She was transferred to Hospice care in the early afternoon. My wife, stepbrother, his son, and I stayed with her until late in the evening. She remained uncommunicative. I was, of course, emotionally and physically exhausted, so my wife volunteered to stay with Deanna. My stepbrother and nephew left for home, and I went back to my mother's apartment to rest. I pulled out the sleeper sofa and crawled into the bed. About an hour to an hour and a half later, I received a call from my wife. She told me that Deanna had just passed away and that it was peaceful. My mother's somewhat labored breathing had increased and then stopped. I was terribly grief-stricken and sobbing as I traveled to the Hospice. The staff said that they would take care of the details of arranging for funeral home pickup and other logistics. My wife and I went back to the apartment to try to rest.

The next day, after a semi-restful night's sleep, my wife and I attended to Deanna's funeral arrangements. She had expressed a wish to be cremated. We planned a memorial service to follow within a couple of weeks. Then, my wife and daughter traveled back down to our home while I stayed up north to tend to the rest of my mother's belongings and close out her apartment. Once again I found myself having to be responsible for my mother's physical environment. However, this time it was different: it would be the last time I would have to do so. This realization brought with it a sense of release, as if a heavy weight had been lifted from me. The burden of being made responsible for her things was at an end. I did not feel resentful, for I saw this as my duty, one I was glad to perform. Yet, the sense of having a weight lifted from me was unmistakable. That was not the only feeling I was experiencing. There was, of course, grief and sadness. But there was something more. I sensed a desperation, an almost panicky sensation, that didn't feel quite like my own.

I recognized that this panic came not from my current relationship with my mother, but from a prior incarnation of myself. Somehow losing her made it clear to me that we had been connected before, in a much different way, in a previous life. I came to understand that my soul had lived a prior life as a woman, and that this woman was romantically connected with the soul of the domineering man Deanna had spoken about. Feeling these experiences as not belonging to me, yet seemingly coming through the me that I know, suggests to me that the notion of reincarnation is not the static, one-life-at-a-time phenomenon that has been attached to this idea. It is a living dynamic between various aspects of a larger entity we call our souls. The more I examine myself, the more I realize that many of the characteristics I think are mine are actually elements or aspects of other lives that my soul is living. We are a part of these other aspects in one way or another, and they are a part of us. As we follow and learn about those vibrational threads that define the characteristics we experience as who we are, we simultaneously learn to detach from them, as they are not our own, and begin to participate in a larger area of experience, from which we have our origin.

As I was getting ready for bed on that first night alone in my mother's apartment, I lit two identical candles that were about twelve inches tall. I lit them to honor the passing of both my mother and stepfather. It must have been around midnight when I fell asleep watching the flickering candle-light, as thoughts of my life with my mother and stepfather danced, trickled, and thundered through my head. I awoke with a bit of a start around 4:00 a.m. to find that one of the candles had burned all the way down. The wick of this one had burned clear through to the bottom. Its twin that sat right next to it on the coffee table was only a quarter of the way burned down. There seemed to be no apparent reason why the one candle was consumed faster than the other. It was as if the candle had been burning for a full day and its twin only a few hours. I was naturally quite astonished by this fact. To suggest that this was the result of my mother's presence while I slept would, of course, be wishful thinking at best, and delusional thinking at worst; yet that is what I believe happened. I think it was a sign my mother gave to let me know she was still…present. As I write, I am reminded of conversations my mother, my stepfather, and I had about death. Nat would often say that when he died he would try to come back and "mess with the lights" or electronics in some way to let us know he was still conscious in the afterlife. In the intervening years between his and my mother's deaths, my mother and I would sometimes joke that Nat was playing with the lights or messing with the TV when something unknown would cause them to falter. I think the candle burning all the way down, while its twin did not, was Deanna's way of "messing with the lights."

The next several days were very difficult, and I found myself moving between states of sobbing grief and numbness as I sorted through my mother's belongings. Most of the furnishings I gave to Goodwill. Various pieces went to friends or family members. There was a small suitcase of old letters and photos that were of particular interest and importance to me. These were the letters Deanna had saved throughout her life. Some writings were from her mother and father, but most were between her and my stepfather Nat. These letters and the poems she had written after her retirement were the most important treasures I found, and they had a profound effect upon me as I took them into my consciousness.

After sorting through and cleaning out her apartment, I traveled back home and started to pore over these mementos of my mother's courtship with the man who would become my stepfather. I spent two weeks totally absorbing the content and learned more about the context of my early life than I had ever imagined. I discerned in these deep and profound letters penetrating character analysis and revelations of the interpersonal dynamics between my mother and stepfather. They revealed a courtship that was at once compelling and illicit. Most were written by Nat, who was an extraordinarily analytical writer. I was finally able to comprehend both of these individuals with greater clarity and objectivity and put to rest some troubling gaps in my understanding of those early years of my life.

The other thing that affected me deeply was a photo of my mother when she was a young girl. For many months after her death, that picture would reduce me to a sobbing wreck; even to this day I get teary-eyed as I contemplate and gaze at it. The layers of meaning for me are deep and complicated. I'm not even sure I can fully articulate them. They are tied up with our experiences of time and the vicissitudes of personality development.

This image seems to capture for me a state of innocence that I never knew in my mother. It is the innocence of childhood that gives way to the complexities of our adult lives. I am awestruck by the transformation of this young girl with her beatific smile into the woman that I knew as my mother: the overweight, depressed, and in many ways guarded woman that this young girl eventually became. Deanna was not a great woman in the sense of external accomplishments. But she devoted herself to the service of others—of understanding their lives and their suffering and of working diligently to help ease their circumstances. I think she did this because she, too, felt deeply the pain that life dishes out. She was, in that sense, one of the most courageous women I have ever known. She fought fiercely for the rights of others and against the injustices she encountered in her life.

The black and white and somewhat faded image also speaks to the relentless passage of time as we experience it. We are but specks in the infinite expanse of eternity; yet these seemingly tiny specks are capable of contemplating the vastness of All-That-Is and our relationship to that enormity. This one little photo of a young girl taken sometime in the mid-nineteen forties speaks to me of the paradoxes of our existence: the young and the old, the timeless and the time-bound, the joys and the sorrows of life. And it is from that young girl that I was given my existence, and then, in turn, my daughter hers.

Randall James is an artist and art therapist who works with a variety of clients and is dedicated to assisting them in making creative changes to lead happier and more productive lives. He is excited about exploring the connections among the advances in neurobiology, mind/body medicine, expressive art therapies, and the mystical insights of world religions.

Dorothy Rachel Medley Carmichael

Dorothy Rachel Medley in 1935

My mother and I in Tucson, Arizona, in 1964

Pretty Lady

by Donnelle Goplen

I left for Duncan, Oklahoma, as soon as I was able to arrange a flight. My 79-year-old mother, Dorothy Rachel Carmichael, had suffered a massive stroke and was not expected to survive. My husband and I had just returned from a vacation in the Caribbean when I received the phone call. I had two hours to pack and drive to the airport. After arriving in Oklahoma City, I drove the hour and a half to Duncan. It was the first week of December in 1997, and Christmas lights decorated the local parks, downtown area, and many private homes. My mother lay dying, so the festive holiday lights and music seemed jarringly out of place. I came alone to this vigil. I was my mother's only child, and I had come to be with her at the end of her life.

Duncan had always been our hometown. It was where my mother, grandparents, aunt, uncle, cousin, and many of my grandmother's other relatives lived during my formative years. My parents divorced when I was two years old, and I was left with my maternal grandparents, Vera and Watt Womble, who became my primary caregivers. We lived at 902 Bois'darc and 909 Bois'darc. I almost never saw my father because he was serving time in a federal prison for armed robbery. My mother worked as a waitress in many local restaurants: the old Wade Hotel Coffee Shop, the Chisholm Trail Hotel, several cafes on Main Street, and the old Sky View Night Club. She sometimes lived with us for brief periods between marriages and when she had nowhere else to live. She married three times and divorced twice.

Many memories entered my mind as I drove through the familiar streets that are named after trees and numbers: Bois'darc, Elm, Willow, Eighth, Ninth, etc. When I drove by the block where our house used to stand, I remembered my mother during the 1940s, how beautiful she was! She loved to laugh and have a good time. Mother was a party girl. She liked to drink and dance and stay out all night. She had lots of friends and liked to please everyone. I continued past familiar landmarks like our local grocery store where mother sent me to buy her cigarettes and the café on the courthouse circle where she worked a daytime shift and occasionally let me stop by after school for a burger. As a very young child, I recalled sitting on the floor rummaging through Mother's purse searching for her tips. She let me count and stack all the coins. When I looked up, she smiled at me through a haze of cigarette smoke. Lost in these thoughts, I almost missed the turn to the hospital. I quickly shook away the memory and pulled into the parking lot.

When I entered my mother's hospital room, I was surprised by her physical appearance. She looked so attractive and appeared to be sleeping peacefully. A week before suffering the stroke, she had gotten a permanent and a manicure. Beauticians from the community volunteered their services for nursing home clients. I sat by Mother's bedside as the nurses and aides appeared every half hour to turn her from side to side. Her blue eyes would suddenly spring open, but there was no recognition, no connection to anything. The hospital staff referred to Mother as "pretty lady," and it was surprising to me that someone who was dying could still look so lovely. When I touched her, I felt the ridge of a scar running down her arm. She had suffered years of physical abuse. I remember the pain, anger, and shame I felt when seeing my mother hurt. My stepfather drank heavily, and when he went on a rampage, Mother was often beaten severely. I loved her so much and wanted to protect her. I felt such hatred for my mother's husband. As a child, I had to endure these feelings in silence. Back then, there was no place for children to talk about family problems, especially those that felt so shameful and secret.

Today, many of my high school friends remember the 1950s as a time of innocence, security, and happiness. But it was not that way for me. I married very young, at the end of the eleventh grade. I quit Duncan High School and did not graduate with my classmates. I felt that I needed to get away. Soon

I had two sons. We moved to Texas and later New Mexico. I focused all my attention on raising my young sons. It was not until the late 1960s that I began to question the direction of my own life. I divorced my husband, got a job, passed a GED, learned to drive a car, and remarried. At the urging of a professor from the University of New Mexico, I started taking university classes. I continued my education with the support and encouragement of my husband. I made the Dean's List, graduated with honors, and received a bachelor's degree. I worked as a welfare caseworker and later in adoptions for the State of New Mexico and attended graduate school at night. I received my master's degree in counseling in 1974 and worked briefly for the Bernalillo County Department of Social Services. My husband was transferred to the Washington, DC, area, so we left New Mexico for Virginia. I eventually got a job with the Prince William County Community Services Board in Manassas, Virginia, a mental health center that helped families and individuals deal with difficult problems. I started work as a staff therapist, received many promotions, and finally, after eighteen years of service, retired in 1997 as Outpatient Program Coordinator for two programs, one for youth and adolescents, the other for the seriously mentally ill.

In this role, I helped many people deal with personal problems, but now it was time to face my own feelings and conflicts regarding my mother. Her physician indicated that it might take a week or longer for her to die. I sat with her every day. I began writing a letter expressing my wishes for how our relationship could have been different. I wrote about my suppressed feelings of anger, my frustrations, and my futile efforts to win her love and acceptance. I wrote pages and pages, getting rid of the bitterness and negative feelings. Writing the letter became an important therapeutic exercise. At the end of each day, I was exhausted. I learned that a nurse at the hospital made extra income by providing massages and would bring her table to the bed and breakfast where I was staying. I booked a massage for every evening of my stay, and it helped so much. Tears streamed down my cheeks as I received the comforting massage that helped in releasing some of the stress. It seemed to loosen the tightness in my chest and let the love that I had always felt for my mother flow along with my tears.

On the last day of Mother's life, I sat beside her and held her hand. A nurse came by to check her vital signs and told me that I had about ten minutes. If there was anything that I wanted to say to my mother, now was the time. I felt a moment of panic. Finally, I told Mother that I loved her. I was still holding her hand when she stopped breathing. I leaned over and kissed her cheek for the last time. I remembered her gentle blue eyes, her warm smile, and the love and forgiveness I felt linking us together in her final moments.

Donnelle Goplen *is a retired family therapist to severely mentally ill clients and their families. Presently she enjoys traveling in the United States and abroad, cooking for family and friends, reading every day, and working out several times a week. Her ultimate thrill at the age of 65 was skydiving, and she still can't believe she did it!*

Edith Tabachneck Simonovitz

Collage, approximately 2" x 3" (old playing card with ink, torn paper, photo, and watercolor) titled "Picnic: my mother at 25 with her father and mother." I made this after finding a cache of old photos—none of which I had ever seen—in my aunt's basement, more than thirty years after my mother's death. For me, her youth, her closed eyes, her dress-up clothes are startling and mysterious.

Dreams, Films, and Happy Endings

by Barbara Sobol Robinson

I.

I am awake suddenly and sitting straight up in bed after a dream in which my mother appears in a flowered hat. My real mother wouldn't be caught dead, as she would say, in a flowered hat. Any flamboyance she had was not for public consumption. Rather, she seemed to harbor a secret self. I was allowed to catch glimpses of the secret Edith who was my mother, the sparkling self behind the shuttered exterior.

It was mostly movies and television that united my mother and me. As a young single woman, Mom liked to go to the movies with her friends— her two first cousins, Edith and Rose. So when she married and had children (my sister and me), and we got old enough to go out, I believe we replaced the girlfriends as companions. My mother was socially shy and introverted; she would not go places by herself. My father, a sociable guy who preferred playing pinochle or otherwise schmoozing with his friends (also relatives), would go to the movies only if there were something playing he specifically wanted to see. My mother just went, and we were expected to accompany her. We saw a double feature almost every Friday night while my father worked late at the grocery store. I cannot tell you how many sunsets were ridden into by how many movie horses, or how many melting embraces I saw, or how many tearful goodbyes set to swelling music.

After a night at the movies, I would often dream. Once, when I must have been angry with my mother, I dreamed that I was standing alone at the end of a long pier at sunset as a ship carried my mother away, back to

Russia. Goodbye! Goodbye! In the dream I was heartbroken, although I suspect there was a passive rage at work in my sending her away.

Later, when television entered our household life (I was in high school), we all spent a few hours after dinner in front of the TV set. Then my father and my sister would move back to the kitchen table and talk late into the night. My mother and I would continue watching TV: *I Love Lucy*, Milton Berle, Sid Caesar, the news, the weather report. She knew the histories of the comedy families. She read the fan magazines and could tell me what the real actors were doing as well as what Lucy had said in a particular episode. After we all went to bed, my mother would occasionally wake up and wander out into the kitchen. I was a night wanderer, too, and sometimes met her there. We would have something to eat, and she would often report an odd dream, stimulated by images we had seen. The next morning she would repeat the dream for the whole family. I loved the stories of these dreams. My father was perplexed by this strange preoccupation of his wife. He would shrug sometimes: "Dreams, schmeams." He would really say this, genuinely puzzled and sincerely dismissive of her stories.

My mother was not born here. She came to America from the Ukraine when she was about eight with her mother and two older brothers, Izzie and Nate. They came to join her father, who had already made the journey and had established himself as an entrepreneur, a man with a pony and a wagon, who hauled ashes from the coal furnaces of the rich and middle class. Two other children, Sammy and Rosie, were yet to be born. My father told and retold how he came to New York from Prague by way of Marseilles, lying about his age to get a job on the ship. On the other hand, the earliest memories my mother shared with me were not of Russia but of living close to the Hudson River at the lower end of Albany in a neighborhood bustling with immigrant Jews, Italians, Irish, Chinese. She told me about families who would sit out on their stoops on summer nights. As if life started there...as if there had been nothing before that to remember, as if the long passage across a vast ocean had wiped away all recall of what had happened before.

She was a pretty little girl, shy and quiet at school. But at home she and Sammy were conspirators and mischief-makers. They rescued a discarded Christmas tree and pulled it, tinsel and all, past their mother, up to the attic, and displayed it from the front attic window. An outcry from the neighbors: "Mrs. Tabachneck! We never knew you celebrated Christmas!" I do not remember my mother ever telling me the rest of the story. Grandpa was sometimes violent, and the boys at least were raised to expect beatings for misbehavior. The girls were rarely or never hit but may have been ridiculed. My mother's rebelliousness and her subversive humor did not come out of nowhere, as she would say.

They all went to synagogue at the Pearl Street Shul. After 10th grade my mother, who was smart in school, dropped out to work in her father's new business, the gas station and corner grocery store. She stayed close to home; her best friends were always her cousins and her brothers. Later she learned secretarial skills, and she and "cousin Edith" went to New York. She fell in love, cousin Edith says (this may be a myth), with a fireman there who was outside the limits for permissible suitors by my grandparents' strict Orthodox family rules. Still later, she met my father, an ambitious, sociable, and handsome Czech who may truly have found her attractive, but who also was profoundly attracted to the whole upstate Tabachneck family. I never heard about love and never saw any affection go out from my mother to my dad, although I sometimes saw attempts on his part to be affectionate to her. My sister was born, the apple of my father's eye. I was born and my mother withdrew into what was surely depression for almost two years. My father imported his youngest sister, 18-year-old Flora, to take care of me. My six-month photograph shows a soft and chubby baby in a sailor dress, somber and unsmiling.

My dad made money, first as a grocer and later in the stock market. He bought the first of his many Buicks and formed a social circle of friends, colleagues, and brothers-in-law. We, the daughters, were driven to and from piano lessons and progressed from public to private schools as we grew.

My mother kept house, monitored our piano practice, accompanied us shopping, but in other ways began to disappear. She seemed to live in some isolation and in an interior world more than in the "real" world. The paradox was, as she slowly became obese, she more and more became invisible, withdrawing to the safer, unexposed interior.

She could sew and made outfits for her own daily life out of old clothes my sister and I had worn. She also made doll clothes and, over a period that seemed to be a year or more, made doll furniture out of old jewelry and other detritus of a middle-class life. If she seems eccentric, it was not flagrantly visible until her very last years. She did show up for school teas, synagogue events, every family party. Her dress-up clothes were *not* made of rags but carefully tailored by her brother-in-law Desi. As she became heavy, only he was allowed to address the issue of clothes for the real body in the real world: silk and sequins (by Desi) for what the world required, *shmatas* (sewn by her own hand) for housedresses. She did, I guess, what she needed to do to get along, so as to be left alone much of the rest of the time.

What am I forgetting? She was short (4'10"); she had (when I was in elementary school) thick coal-black hair wound around her head in braids and gold green eyes. She loved to walk and was afraid to drive. She smoked like a chimney. And she had a streak of deep cynicism, nihilism, atheism. My mother could be immensely funny and biting in her wit. She had the timing and the perfect double take of a true comedienne. It was the watching of those endless movies and sitcoms that sharpened her own view of life. Toward much of the world she was simply dismissive. But she was intensely loyal to a small inner circle, at the center of which were her dead father and her three brothers, all rough, smart, funny, coarse, wisecracking, self-deprecating Russian Jews. Toward the women—her friends, her own sister, and the women cousins she had grown up with—she was less forgiving. I remember her rolling her eyes and the words "That Ethel!" or "That Ruth!" followed by a stream of criticism about their child rearing, manners, dress, eating habits, social aspirations. I remember how well I absorbed it. In my fourth grade diary is a passage about my then best friend that begins: "That Cecil! She has no manners. She looked in our refrigerator without asking."

I was my mother's daughter. In the dynamics that developed in our family, my sister was my dad's and I was my mom's to raise. If she needed an audience for her dream stories, that was my job, to listen. If she needed to mentor someone in the dreaming and the telling of dreams, that was my role, too. I absorbed her posture toward the world, her interiority, some of her humor, and her creativity as well. Like her, I did little that was meant for the public eye—nothing that could or should be seen or appreciated or applauded, but rather written (poems), drawn (sketches), or thought (privately and stashed away in a drawer or in the mind). She did not want nor did I want much attention.

But oh, how I did crave *her* attention. And the movies, the long walks down Manning Boulevard at night under the huge elms and maples that lined our long street, those were magical times because I was her companion in her world. I think perhaps that was the closest to positive attention I received: to be in her aura when she was happy and included me wordlessly. You can tell, I think, that there was not much hugging, cuddling, or conversation. But to be close enough to the body that bore me was something that both satisfied my diminished expectations and yet stirred more longing, such that longing is a quality forged into my very bones.

II.

The more I try to write in such a way as to recreate my mother, the more I seem only to be recreating the relationship as I internalized it. I miss the mark often about the "real" person who was my mother; but the description of my internalized mother is accurate. This is the person—this fiction, this internalized image—to whom I need to say goodbye.

My mother began her descent toward death—the public descent, the one we knew about—when she fell out of bed one morning, dizzy and disoriented. It was 1976, and she was 73. She had been weak and tired, but she had been keeping her usual routine. She would get up, shower and dress, make breakfast for my father, and write out "the order"—a list of groceries for my father to bring home in the evening after work. She sometimes wrote a letter to me, entertained my sister's children, who visited nearly every day, and watched some daytime TV. And if it was spring, fall, or summer and if the weather was dry, she always got outside to mow a segment of our huge lawn with her electric mower. It was a common sight on our block to see my mother, dressed oddly in one of her homemade culottes, cigarette dangling from her mouth like a gangster's smoke, and connected to an outdoor outlet by a long and dangerous electrical cord that trailed behind the mower she pushed. She had a system and kept to it. She had been mowing the lawn this way for years with no visible change in the weeks before she fell.

The last weeks in the hospital are fragments of scenes and dialogue. She died very quickly, in a matter of a few weeks from entering the hospital that day. I was afraid to go see her but I went anyway. I flew up on the day she was to have exploratory surgery to examine the extent of the suspected stomach cancer. I got there just as the doctor came out to say that the cancer was inoperable. My uncle wept, my father said nothing. I remember being stunned and unable to feel my own feelings. I followed my father into my mother's room. I saw him touch her hair and heard him say something very softly. "My girl," he said. "My girl"—as if he were struck and plummeting backwards 40 years to a flash of love. It was the most intimate moment I had ever seen between them, and she was participating only from her deep, drugged state.

I came and went from her hospital room where I began to see her as gaunt, and I saw the bones of her father's face begin to define hers. She traveled in and out of a delirium, as people do on morphine. Once, she saw the heart monitor as a big wedding cake with candles on it (these were the spikes that marked the waves travelling across the screen). Once she saw me, did not recognize me, and asked, "Where are my babies?" Mostly, there was a lot of silence. I do not know if she and my father or she and my sister talked at all or whether they, too, simply endured the inevitable decline in silence. I do not know whether she dreamed, and if so, whether or not her dreams comforted her.

She died. I drove the three hundred miles to her funeral like an automaton. Weeks later I came back and stole her midnight blue crepe dress with the sequins from the trunk in the basement where my father had stored it and her robin's egg blue rayon housecoat—one gown, one *shmata*. Although I had thrown my ritual shovelful of dirt onto her casket as it was lowered, I never did say goodbye.

III.

MEDITATION ON BIRDS

My office window, six panes of old glass,
Good for meditation. If I sit in the grey chair,
I see, through the bottom leftmost pane,
The top of a tree
Always bare, summer and winter alike, and often
Filled with birds
Lined up on the horizontal branches,
Pigeons and sparrows, common and stark, who
Fly up alight startle return fidget
Attune and reattune, disturbed or calmed by wind
No bigger than a baby's breath.

Still still and still,
Then shuffle flutter shift shudder
Rise
And oh…Gone!

String of black birds
In the topmost branches of my tree.
Stay awhile, that
I might love you.

Being asked to write "On saying goodbye to my mother,"
I saw that I have never said goodbye to my mother, nor
To my dead son that sparrow
Or to my living breathing daughter, or
My life! As if it were the only one!

They say:

The child who
"feels felt"
by his mother is
the lucky child who
carries a charm
forever
in his heart.

Birds come, birds go
Birds strut darkly along the gutter outside the glass
Birds swoop away and down

I look up
Catch those wings
But mostly
The way I go
Is earthbound, one foot
In front of the other
Step by step
By step.
This life:
Log into ash by way of fire.

IV.

   According to current attachment theory, to *feel felt* by the mother is a basic emotional need of the child. Whatever gaze arcs across physical space to connect the eyes of the baby to the eyes of the mother, this intangible gaze and the responsiveness therein—the warmth or lack of warmth that informs it—comprise the building blocks of neurobiological attachment. It is called attunement or *the feeling of feeling felt* by the other.

For me, perhaps even as an infant but definitely as a young child—it was a leap of my still immature imagination that provided me the feeling of *feeling felt*. By this I mean that between my depressed mother and me, *the feeling felt* stopped just short of achievement. I felt intense longing for my mother, but could not often find the reciprocal spark. Whatever my mother could not communicate with words, body, or gesture, I think I may have projected or filled in imaginatively to comfort myself. I believe, too, that the tools I used to make those leaps—mostly humor, metaphor, and imagination—were paradoxically her gifts to me and were learned at her knee. The not *feeling felt*, the longing, I experienced as immense, and as things have a way of evolving, it is now both my weakness and my strength. My writing poetry, making art, and my profession as an art therapist are outgrowths of the modeling of my mother and the great effort I must have made to fill in or find and solve the mystery on my own. Forever infants, we humans are driven to explore and to touch the mysterious face of the mother throughout our lives.

In our final moments together, my mother and I recapitulated the quality of our earliest exchanges—a falling just short of direct connection. For me, the silent gap was bridged by intense, eventually unbearable longing, by turning away. For her, I do not know. Perhaps the losses of her own childhood and her own motherhood were amplified by illness and impending death. But we could not gaze into each other's eyes. For years she has remained internalized in this way—the projection and recipient of my inner child's desire.

In a dream, I am paying attention to some other child, and my son, about four, comes running at me and begins to hit me with a soccer ball. He is crying, angry. I grab the ball and throw it as far as I can.

As I write out this dream, I can feel my mother's presence within me still and the enormity of my unfulfilled longing. I have work to do in my dream world: Play ball with my son. Shout out to my mother receding on that ship. Demand that she play with me. Engage with ghosts! Here is a thought: the more I learn to and intend to engage, the more the relationship with my mother will change, even now. There is a chance that there will be another dream one day in which my mother appears, this time more comfortable in the flowered hat. It's something one might wear to a good funeral, one with plenty of loss and sadness, some humor, and no regrets—not a goodbye of unrequited longing, love, and rage, but a musical number. I can imagine a fine harmonizing of her voice and mine, each holding up her own part of the chord.

Maestro: A little light music please. A little Gene Kelly or Fred & Ginger. Thank you, Mom, and goodbye. My mother in a flowered hat exits smiling. Fade to sunset, glorious violins.

Barbara Sobol Robinson *has been writing and drawing since childhood. Now retired from public service, she lives with her husband in Washington, DC, and maintains a small private art therapy practice. While some of her writing has been for the profession, she is happy to have created a body of work that tells her life story in a stream of images and metaphors.*

Eleanor Anne Finch Wix

My mom, probably in her late teens, closing a gate in the wind on the family farm out in eastern Montana, where the wind never ceases to blow

A candid shot when I was struggling to shut the gate on the way to the ranch. Behind me — it was windy!

Mom's writing on the back of the photo

Dreaming/Dying

by Linney Wix

Four months ago in a dream I saw Oprah weak with grief. It was her first birthday since her mother's death. She was dressed in a bathrobe and leaning against the wall of a hotel hallway, immobilized by her mother-loss. Outside, I stood at the top of a high dirt cliff looking down to a faraway winding river. I wanted to walk down to the river but could not because I was afraid of the fast-moving and dark water. Today is my first birthday since my mother's death almost a year ago, and I am achingly unprepared.

When my mom died on Monday, February 5, 2007, my sister, my daughters, and I were with her. I had entered into her dying process almost three months before. It was November, and she had just moved to a retirement facility after selling her home of 45 years. I flew to Montana to be in the old house one last time and to celebrate her new home, a large light-filled apartment with expansive views of the hills south of Helena, Montana, her hometown. During the weekend Mom told me she didn't know herself anymore but couldn't say what she meant by that. She seemed spacey and disconnected. Thinking she was having trouble with all the changes the move entailed and hoping to activate connections between her mind and body, I massaged her head, and her back and shoulders. As always, she loved the deep touch of my hands and melted into the rubbing.

Later I realized I'd been so caught up in clearing out the last things from the house that I hadn't paid enough attention to her increasingly disconnected state. At the airport as I was leaving, I was shocked when her parting words were, "I wonder if we'll be together." I walked to the security line before returning to ask, did she mean in life? In death? "Both," she answered. This remark opened the door into the dreaded chamber where I would lose my mother. Two days later she was hospitalized with complications of diabetes that had resulted in strokes and hemiballismus, a condition characterized by uncontrollable jerking movements on one side of the body.

I've lived more than a thousand miles from my parents for three decades, so we did not have a daily relationship. Between the time she wondered if we would be together and the time she died, I traveled those thousand miles up and down the Rocky Mountains between New Mexico and Montana four times. On my second of the four visits, when I spent two weeks with her over the winter holidays, I was initiated into the grotesqueness of her affliction. My first visit early in December had found her remarkably well—free of movement and making strides in a rehab program. This time, however, the nonstop twitching and jerking of her left leg and upper left body were distressing to behold. I ended each day exhausted to the bone, and I wasn't even the one moving incessantly. While she rose each morning, Mom soon returned to her bed in search of rest and relief, which did not come.

The day after Christmas my sister and I began looking for an assisted living facility for Mother. We were lucky to find one with an available room and a director who knew her just across the field from her apartment. Mom had played the piano for the director's wedding thirty years earlier. We arranged a visit but Mom went to bed instead. Leaving her in assisted living on New Year's Eve was a step closer to losing her. While it seemed and still seems like the only realistic option, it felt as if this were an ultimate abandonment. On the way there she said she felt like a dog being put in the car to take its last trip to the vet.

I wish we had done things differently. I wish we had better prepared her and ourselves for the moment of parting. The staff had counseled my sister and me to choose a time to leave—like suppertime—and go. They likened leaving Mom to leaving a child at daycare. We took their advice and when the time came for supper, my sister and her husband and my daughters and I kissed her goodbye. We all just walked out. In leaving her, we were thoughtless. The next morning we would all depart for our homes.

We would not be coming back to visit as we would if we lived nearby, and we would not be picking her up at the end of the day as we would if we'd dropped her at daycare. She was rightfully stunned by our sudden leave-taking. Our actions betrayed her and us.

Three weeks later I flew in for a long weekend. I knew from phone calls that Mom was moving away from us. When I got her on the phone, which was rare, she had few words. It was clear that speaking had become very difficult. She was unable to swallow due to the ongoing "neurological incidents," and with the help of my sister had entered Hospice care just days earlier after telling her doctor that she wanted no interventions. Even so, I figured this had to be temporary; with effort she would come out of it. Not realizing that she had no effort left, I latched onto the line they gave me about how some people get discharged from Hospice. I was sure she couldn't be at this final way station already. How could my mother be dying? She had warned me in the summer that she wouldn't be around forever, but near the same time she had told my sister she felt ready for another ten years!

Such was the prelude to her death, the time of flying back and forth between my everyday work reality and the surreality of losing my mother forever. The time in between in airplanes, airports, and cars gradually helped me get used to the thought that she was actually and actively transitioning from life to death. Those hours of travel gave me time to remember my childhood wanderings on our Montana farm and all the times that I would return to the house to tell her what I'd found. They gave me time, too, to imagine into future days devoid of being able to call her and tell her of my adventures.

On this third trip, I spent my flight time preparing to speak with Mom. I knew she was determined to die. I had seen this in her wondering if we would be together, followed by her diminished capacity to take care of herself that had been caused by the strokes that took her first into rehabilitation, then home again, then into assisted living, and into Hospice care. All this seemed unlike my mother. I knew her as one who could win blue ribbons for procrastinating. On the plane I thought and wrote about how I wanted to talk to Mom and thank her, not just for everything she'd ever done and been for me, but also for waiting, while I was out of the country on sabbatical leave, to die. I wanted, too, to tell her how I'd miss her, how large would be the abyss of losing her.

Upon arriving I found her sitting in her recliner. She greeted me with a huge smile—even her eyes lit up. Has anyone ever been so glad to see me? She was unable to speak. I knew then that talking was now or never, that I had to tell her what I'd been contemplating on my way north. Seeing her showed me that there wouldn't be another chance.

I pulled her purple walker—still bedecked with the red ribbon we'd tied on at Christmas—up to her chair, turned it around to face her, situated myself on its seat, and leaned toward her. There was a pitched intensity to what I was about to do. I needed to be up close, to focus, and have her focus. I thanked her for not getting sick a year earlier. I told her there would be a huge gap in my life when she was gone. She replied softly and slowly, "I suppose so." Out loud I admired her determination and grace in choosing to die instead of hanging on to a life compromised. When I noted what a huge decision this was, she marched her fingers along her leg, as if to say, "chomp, chomp, chomp"—an expression she had always used when things needed to be done. I remarked that her taking this route was a gift to us, and she whispered it probably was for all of us, meaning, I guess, for her too.

It was the twenty-fifth of January, a Thursday. My words felt as if they didn't take long enough. They felt scant. Yet her words, spoken in slow motion, were far more scant than mine. I felt as if I had to pack a lifetime of words into this brief moment. I felt desperate, as if this would be my last chance. I was right about that. It was my final talk with her.

Later, as the afternoon grew dark, I asked Mom if there was anything she wanted us to know. Again very slowly and softly she said she'd have to think about that. I never heard from her on that question. Finally—and the weight of this question caused me almost to forget it—I asked if I could cleanse her body after she died. I sensed she was surprised but let me know that yes, this would be okay with her. I believe I said most of what I wanted and needed to say. I finished by letting her know that I would be looking for a sign that she had made the passage.

Dreaming/Dying

The next morning, Mom had a pretty good conversation with the Hospice social worker while I was in the room. She was able to respond to the questions, telling the social worker that most of all she loved my sister and me and her grandchildren, and that she loved music. Since talking was difficult, she merely glared at me—and my mother had a telling glare—to indicate her long disapproval and disappointment at my living so far away. I am uncertain whether she was able to forgive me.

Three days later when I headed back to Albuquerque, my grown son stayed on to care for his grandmother. My sister, who lived closer, would be there for much of the time as well. Were I better at trusting myself to make on-the-spot intuitive decisions, maybe I'd not have left. When I think of it now, my leaving made no sense. Mom didn't feel like getting up that morning, but when I asked if she wanted to get up before I left for the airport, she practically hopped out of bed. By then, though, there wasn't enough time to be together. I got her settled in a chair only moments before I had to leave to catch a plane in order to teach a class that evening. I stood in the doorway and turned to her. She blew me a kiss and I blew one back to her. There were no words.

That was Monday. On Thursday I got the last seat on the day's last plane out of Albuquerque heading north to Salt Lake City and then to Helena. When I landed just past midnight, it was six degrees below zero. My son picked me up and took me right to Mom's bedside. My sister was in the recliner—the same one from which Mom had greeted me just a week earlier. Mom was still. The room was still. It was clear that the eternal stillness of Death was on its way. I kissed her and told her I was there. Then I lit a candle near the small icon of Our Lady of Perpetual Help that I had brought to watch over her when our eyes could not.

When I entered into the stillness that enveloped that room, my sister and I embarked upon four nights and four days of being present with our mother in her dying. In my journal I wrote, "So, what did she do those final days? Except to move her legs enough to uncover her feet, she lay there rarely moving. Her eyes could see, it seemed, until Saturday when they turned very red and layered over with an extra film of glass-like mucus."

During our final watch, my sister and I rubbed her feet and hands with oil. We talked to her and to each other and swabbed her dry mouth. We sat with her as the morning light filled the room and as the evening shadows fell. My son left, and my daughters arrived. Sometimes, we walked in the nearby hills. We talked about what might happen at the actual moment of her death. We wondered if our mother could let herself die in our presence. We wanted to be with her. She had always regretted not being with her own mother at her death. Each night, my sister and I unrolled a small mat and slept together on it, right there next to Mom. Throughout the days, friends came to say goodbye. While it seemed right to leave them for their own private moment, usually I stayed, unable to move from my chair, watching and listening for ways to navigate this unfamiliar terrain with love. Each of us had times alone with her. She kissed every one of us goodbye. On Sunday, the third day, a gale blew up. Mom had always loved the wind, and I imagined that it had blown in to take her away. However, it was not yet time. It would take another day, four days in all.

On the fourth morning, my sister and I rose from our sleeping mat, had a bite to eat, and took a walk, feeling at loose ends. The day was bright and warm. As he and his wife had every day since November, Mom's minister and our lifelong family friend paid her a visit. Like one of the family, he pulled a chair up alongside Mom's bed, not to move again until it was all over. Once or twice his voice punctuated the silence as he remembered moments with his daughter during her dying four years earlier.

About eleven in the morning I went into Mom's room, opened the window, and found my place. Not long after, my sister came in, and then, one by one, my two daughters. Each found her place, and we waited. I sat at my mother's feet. Someone entered and suggested that I rub them. I declined. I felt she needed to be unburdened physically in order to take her leave, that my touch would have been an obstacle to her passage. At 1:30 in the afternoon Mom's breathing changed to the "fish out of water" gasping that the nurse had told us could come near the end. In those last moments I found myself cheering her on, saying to myself, "Go on, Mom. It's okay. You can do it!" At 1:38 she breathed in and did not exhale. The candle still burned and Our Lady still watched.

With the first anniversary of her dying upon me, I have been thinking a lot about last year at this time. Two nights ago I wrote these lines called, "Last Year, Four Nights":

Four nights on the floor
The two of us, sisters, listening
Together for the last breath,
The last breath of the one
Whose breathing we've known since
Before we had our own—
A steady, familiar in-and-out, surely
Strange to be listening for its end.
And through four nights it didn't end.
She couldn't stop breathing
Until the dream was dreamed.

In the dream, she and Dad hover above us,
Smiling together and remembering.
We are no longer grown,
we sisters
but small girls sharing our childhood rollaway.
Far in the future, as grown sisters
We curl together on a small mat
Listening for the last breath.
Above us, our parents
Come to check on us
Remember us little,
Love us
Always.

This was not my dream. It was not my sister's dream. It was the dream of Tanya, the director of the assisted living facility where Mom died, the one whose wedding she had played for. She dreamed this dream during our final night of deathbed vigil. Could it have been my mother's dream, dreamed through Tanya to be given to us in words, something for us to hold onto as we entered midlife orphanhood? Perhaps our mother could not die until, wandering, she found our father waiting, or until the dream of being with him and remembering us little was dreamed. Perhaps only when her remembering had been dreamed could our mother depart. Only when she had found our father and they could be together again could they see my sister and me grown and together in a way that we were together as girls, asleep in the rollaway, asleep on the mat. Then and only then was the way clear for her to leave us.

I was glad my sister had silently agreed to help with our mother's body because, once faced with the task of washing her body, I didn't know if I could do it. I didn't even know how to do what I'd asked permission to do. Knowing our wishes, the staff brought washcloths and warm water and then left us alone. We washed and rinsed and oiled our mother's body. Cleansing the body of the mother who first bathed us as infants. Washing the baby. Washing the body. Anointing the body with oil. Caring for the body, the first and last act. Washing, anointing, caring. All repetition of the birth-time washing, anointing, caring; hers a way of welcoming us; ours a way of bidding farewell as we prepared her body for the fire.

There was a memorial service. Our parents' minister and friend offici-ated, just as he had at our father's service thirteen years earlier. We wanted the music our mother loved—the post-World War II music she had played on the piano with such pizzazz. While a friend's mother said this was the only funeral she'd ever been to where she wanted to get up and dance, the music made it hard for me. Nobody plays Mom's songs like she did. Mak-ing it through one of her favorites, "Stardust," played by another's hands, felt endless.

Once it was all over and everyone had left, I had a few days to myself in Mom's apartment, the home she'd hardly gotten to enjoy. I felt a desper-ate need to take something home with me that would connect us. I wanted it to be a ring, but we weren't ready to go through her things yet. So I went to our favorite jewelry store in town, studied the stones and the settings, and right then and there ordered a ring with three small Yogo Sapphires, which are found only in Montana where everybody in my family of origin grew up. There is one Yogo for each of my children. At either end of the Yogos is a diamond—one for me, and one for Mom. I wear this ring always as a sign of our unbroken union. On the day I left my old hometown, I wrote, "On this, my last day in Helena, and one week past Mom's dying, it snows. It snowed last night, blizzard style. Last Monday, on her dying day, the sky was blue and the clouds wispy—at day's end there were angel wing clouds over the south hills. It was a good day for dying, it seemed—clear skies, no overcast, sun shining. The way onward seemed clear, so I opened the window to make it even clearer. The snow since has been a comfort."

Now, almost a year later, on my 57th birthday, I wait for the sign I asked her for during our last conversation. Is she not sending it or am I not receiving it? Nothing seems as clear-cut as I wish it to be. Several months ago during a bodywork session there was a moment when I felt my mother slip in through a very small, fingertip-size opening between my ribs to help my heart heal. Was that the sign? Was it Tanya's dream? Or my dream of Oprah? Is wearing our ring enough to bridge the great divide between my life and her death? Must there be only a single sign, or can all these experiences indicate that we are still together, in death as in life, just as she wondered at the airport?

On my first motherless birthday I am as bereft as Oprah was in my dream. Today there was no birthday card in my mailbox addressed in Mom's handwriting. Her annual phone call, complete with her singing Happy Birthday, did not come. For my almost unbearable first birthday without her, what I got instead was a letter inviting me to write about saying goodbye to her. Perhaps that invitation and my response—the sky is dark now and I've spent the afternoon writing—is one more sign. Perhaps this is Mom's way of letting me know that anytime now I can walk down to the river. The water is no longer too fast or too dark to enter. I don't have to be afraid. Perhaps it's her way of reminding me that there is, after all, a time for everything, and that now, even in my grief, the water flows.

Linney Wix, *like her family before her, lives in the wide-open and windblown spaces of the West. Daughter, sister, friend, mother, and grandmother, she practices in New Mexico as a book artist, art therapist, and professor of art education. She is author of* Through a Narrow Window: Friedl Dicker-Brandeis and Her Terezín Students.

Elizabeth Anne Maloney Dengel

My mother as a young woman

My mother (right) kissing me on my wedding day (1972)

Finding Peace with My Mother

by Elizabeth Eitt

My mother's ghost surprised me the other day. But that's what ghosts do. They rock our little self-absorbed world. She's been dead for thirty years, and she came back to gently conjure up the past. As I sat quietly and alone in meditation, a voice, her voice in me, our voice, rose into my awareness like a clear and perfect bubble.

"Are you sure you've made peace with your mother?"

This question clutched my throat, unnerving in its vivid simplicity. My peace was disturbed. The authentic work of meditation practice had begun in earnest, unearthing yet another karmic seed.

"That's over and done with," I heard myself arguing with this inner teacher, debating the calm intruder. "Go away. I've done that. I've done it all. It's finished." I found no initial curiosity about this ghost of an idea but rather the pounding rush to push it away.

Inner truth is a persistent shadow. It can make us question our complacency about the unknown, giving movement to the emotion of buried memories. Still and all, resistance can reign as a defense to the play of light on the death of one's mother, like a warrior queen riding the white horse of denial.

I continued to whine for days. I was giving justifications for my false sense of security; I was pleading a good and well-versed case to my deeper knowing and shutting my mother out.

I had written the "letters to mother" and burned them on the ritual fire while the moon rose up over the bay. I had gone to Al-Anon, lit candles, and prayed. I had processed her fall down the stairs on my watch by talking it out, writing it down, and engaging our family in conversation after her death, all for what I thought was closure.

Both my mother and I acknowledged the fact that she was a frail alcoholic in the final stages of cirrhosis of the liver, and I was a young mother with a four-year-old daughter and a three-week-old infant. I accepted the fact that I had little or no experience caring for the sick, but we reassured each other that this homecare plan was our best strategy, as we would be a team educated by her kind and honest doctor. He had made us aware of the probable eventuality of an "incident," given her physical weakness, and we thought we were prepared. When some of my older cousins and Mother's close friends accused me of being overly deferential to my mother's single wish to die at home, I called a family meeting. They were scared. I worked to understand their worries and concerns; they wanted me to change my mother's mind by changing mine.

I leveraged and persuaded on my mother's behalf as we sat around the kitchen table, where each of them had tossed around their problems with her over the years. They finally gave up and withdrew. I was left alone to figure it out through Irish determination and pure grace. My mother had always stood on solid ground with these important people. Now she was mining an unusually strong part of herself and thus flying in the face of convention. Her marriage to my father was short-lived, and I was her only child. Here was something—one final thing—that we were going to do together no matter what. I gave thanks to her for the opportunity that we had given ourselves to go through this intimate experience together.

I had forgiven her for leaving me and my baby daughters with the SHOUT of a sudden and traumatic death. Her stumbling fall down seven steps to the landing left her semi-conscious and bleeding from a gash in her skull. Who would have thought that blood could be so loud, that the flow of a delicate fluid could be so deafening?

All my life I had counted the steps in my home. Ten steps up, turn, seven more to the top. The four med-techs from the ambulance had to maneuver her down those last slippery ten while I waited at the bottom with my babies, ready to say goodbye to my mother for the last time. After she left, I must have been guided by a mother's intuition, adrenaline, and what can only be called a blessing when I gathered up my little girl and together we washed my mother's blood from the white nightgown I was wearing when she fell. The warm, sudsy water on our hands was alchemy, transforming our confusion and fear into a liquid embrace, if only for that moment.

I danced and sang and cried my way through the aftermath of my mother's death with my dedicated husband, my knowing family, and my wonderful friends. I had framed photos, made altars in her name, thrown dirt on her grave. Yet, for years after she died, I was angry. I stumbled and fell and picked myself up. I misbehaved. I lost my mind and called it back home.

"Are you sure you've made peace with your mother?"

Her ghost had been quiet for a long time, and yet the question persisted. Day after day, unsatisfied with old platitudes and easy explanations, wanting to get to the heart of the matter, my deeper self prevailed. It wouldn't take "yes" for an answer.

In my fifty-sixth year, my mother's age when she died with her head bleeding in my lap, she reappeared to my inner self, my true self. And finally, the pulsing stem of my flowering brain allowed the past to push its way into the present for another sincere examination. I held onto and trusted the idea that we revisit to heal. Giving up avoidance and the alienation caused by "having done it all," I surrendered to the possibilities that lay just beyond the edge of fear. I summoned my courage and could feel the old terrors fading, the controls softening, and a clear light with something like substance taking its place. Could this be my mother's new voice? My heart opened to this humming light where new life waited in her words of consolation and counsel. I reasoned myself to be quiet. I wanted to hear her clearly now.

My mother was a survivor. From her premature birth, when she weighed in at a pound and a half, to her early and ungraceful death, she lived. Her life may have been unfulfilled in many ways, disengaged and sad a lot of times, but she played and worked and helped others in the face of it. She gave of herself to her job of 25 years with dedication and skill, and to her family she gave a lifetime.

My mother did her best at providing for me a safe and honorable home surrounded by a big extended family, a love for animals, and a keen interest in people and their personal stories. She made sure I learned to enjoy reading, writing, and music so I could move and grow through life with rhythm and curiosity. She laughed easily, teaching me that a sense of humor is something to cherish. She trusted me to look death in the face, giving me the confidence to help others with their suffering. She helped me to know that good friends are food for the soul. She gave me a spiritual base.

I know that my mother loved me fully and cared for me deeply amidst all the mistakes and disappointments in her short life. I am easing into remembering the joys and sorrows in my relationship with my mother: the care she took dressing herself for work in the morning, the way she rested at the sink while doing dishes, her dependence on alcohol as a remedy for unhappiness.

My mother is leading me to understand how her life affected mine and reminding me to use both strengths and weaknesses to become more naturally who I truly am—without the pressing need for approval. And in this process I have been given a remarkable gift: my mother has become my official guardian angel, my benefactor, my guide. Was I beginning to hear the whisper of that healing all these years later?

When I feel doubt, I call on her. When a problem arises, she's my circle of shamans. When I have a desire, she is my golden genie. She's there now watching, and all I have to do is remember. I keep a bottle of the fragrance she used, and when I open the stopper, her incense fills me and gives me something to hold onto.

Many times I fall prey to regrets, anxieties, and disenchantments about our relationship, and I expect these unconscious emotional weights will continue to rise up to be released. When I identify with the spirit of discontent that smudged her daily life, it only serves to create distance between myself and others. And sometimes I feel the aching need to make up for something just beyond my reach. The difference is that she is here with me, offering emotional healing and spiritual guidance, stabilizing my true self with a heartfelt reservoir of creative energy.

At my mother's funeral, the priest came to the front row where I was sitting and took my infant daughter out of my arms. He held her high in the air for the whole congregation to see. My protective new mother's heart skipped a beat. And in a voice heard by the entire universe, he said that the infant symbolizes the real meaning of life as an ongoing process, a vast and never ending circle. He said that death is not an end but rather a beginning and that we can all begin again every day in the spirit of love and peace and happiness. He called us to look at the infant as the essence of resurrection and hope and to contemplate the preciousness of life itself. So there in front of a church full of people, my baby daughter in her bright green "onesie" with the red feet represented eternal life and healing. The spirit does indeed work its powerful mystery in unexpected ways.

The last thirty years have given me many life experiences that have led me to remember and also to forget my mother. Now on the cusp of the thirtieth anniversary of her death, I see my mission as one of conscious and open memory, drawing on her strengths, her sense of purpose, and her love of life. I want to leave my two daughters and my son with a constantly developing sense of connection as a legacy from their grandmother. I believe in her ghostly insight and the soothing message of encouragement carried across time from a thousand grandmothers before her.

As I continue on my long journey into personal growth and daily transformation, my wish is to remember her new voice as my voice and to use her guidance as my north star, seeing myself a little more clearly and loving more deeply, more fully, every moment of the rest of my life. This, I know, will take diligence, discipline, and a sense of adventure.

I find that making peace with my mother encourages me to make peace with myself.

Liz Eitt *is a polarity therapist with a specialty in yogic science and neurofeedback. She lives on a small organic farm in the county of King George, Virginia, with her husband, two dogs, and five cats. Her private practice is located on the farm.*

Elsa Alina Nivukoski Stack

My mother with me (Cissy) and my sister Linda on the right

My mother Elsa

Stroke My Curls

by Cara Lee Barker

A Farewell Gift

Writing about the experience of saying goodbye to my mama, I had no idea the places this journey of remembrance would lead me. My mother and I said goodbye for the last time on that crisp, cold day, January 24, 1982, before she took her last breath at Madigan Army Hospital. She was 74. Then, the day before my 36th birthday, my tiny family and I huddled together, feet half-frozen, as we watched her cherry wood coffin lowered into the gravediggers' hole, a yard or so beyond where we stood.

I should not have been surprised. Four days before her last breath, she told me, "I'll be dead and gone before your birthday." She was so certain of this fact that she directed my sister Linda to make a secret field trip to Gunderson's Jewelry store, off Broadway in Tacoma, and carry out a mission. Twelve hours after her funeral I opened my Mammy Yokum's gift. Inside the cobalt-blue velvet box, a simple gold hoop bracelet lay securely fastened, a bracelet just like the one my mother always wore. It was as much a signature piece for her as her single pearl earrings. Only mine had an inscription inside which read, "Always remember we love you, Mother." Just remembering these words today makes my eyes well up.

My mother had a way of always being thorough. But I think my tears, nearly three decades later, have more to do with her capacity to embrace whatever challenges she was given, without complaint, all the while making sure she was attending to her duty as a caretaker. What startled me at the time, however, was not only that she had the presence to say goodbye in such a memorable fashion, but that she had done it in a way so foreign to my sister and me. She had signed her farewell message "Mother." On her conscious passage into death, she transformed the very naming of herself from the personal "Mom" into the impersonal "Mother." Her essence was leaving its historical form. She was about to leave her earthly costume known as Elsa Alina Nivukoski Stack. Looking back on it now, I believe my mother was reminding us that her essence would remain behind through love. She knew it with 100% certainty. As usual, she was right.

Perhaps because so many anniversaries of her death, interlaced with my own birthdays, have come and gone, the looking back on our last goodbye comes down to an unraveling of sorts. What I notice is that the many colored threads of this tapestry return in reverse order—which is to say, I remember first the events that happened last. For the act of saying goodbye, in truth, was a process more than any single instant. Paradoxically, my mother's dying became the labor and delivery of my own becoming. Even though I believed I was my own person, the truth is that when she passed on, I began finding her very much alive in me: her sayings, her loves, her tendencies, and even her aging.

My biggest regret is that I did not know then what I know now. I feel as if I am growing old in a similar way, with one exception—my mother was not one to regret. She came from the school of "Just do the best you can. That's all the good Lord can expect." Today, when I reflect upon the complex facets of her farewell, it was just as much a hello. It brought us both beyond the edge of what we had known, the way we had of responding to the familiar in one another. There was nothing either of us could do but make a summersault into the unknown. Into the abyss we tumbled, a place where she greeted whatever lay beyond. My tumbling went smack into the disorientation that comes when we lose essential reference points. She knew naught what it would be to leave her body, and I was clueless as to what it would mean to go on without my mother, embodied as Elsa. And this is how we said goodbye. We did the best we could with what we had right up until the time she left.

An Unanswered Question

The question that remains, however, is this: Was there a certain moment of her death? Is there ever just one moment? Now, you could say that her final moment was when she said to the nurses, "I want to be raised up!" The nurses interpreted this to mean that she wished to be lifted from the horizontal position on that army hospital bed. They complied. Her osteoporotic neck subluxed (broke). Technically, this was the cause of death. What was not recorded about her death, however, was that not only had she predicted that she would die before her scheduled surgery that day for amputation of a gangrenous leg, but that she was a nurse anesthetist who knew she would not make it through surgery with a naso-gastric tube, given her osteoporotic state. So, was she asking the staff to assist her to leave early by snapping her spinal cord? Or, had she slipped into an altered state of consciousness that I had witnessed some days before, where she was experiencing dialogue with those beyond the veil? I'll never know. But the association that came to me at the time was that of the old Inuits who go off into the wilds to die when they feel it is their time. It has always struck me as uncanny.

The Last Lap

What I do know is that on that particular Sunday morning of her death, something very peculiar happened. For three weeks running, I had gone to the hospital shortly after dawn with a sense of the greatest urgency. Most nights I stayed until nearly midnight, because she did not want to be alone. Not that it was strict military protocol, but the staff knew I had been an Army nurse, so they cut me some slack. On the toughest evenings, though, I stayed in her room, sleeping either in the chair beside her or on the other bed if it was free. On our last night together, for some reason, though, the atmosphere in my madre's room turned nearly festive. My closest college friend, Penny, had smuggled in pizza and a small bottle of red wine. I think she knew my sister Linda and I were pretty well spent. Together, the three of us shared our memories relating to Mom, with my mother fading in and out of consciousness. Before we left, my mother called my sister and me to her side, took our hands, and told us that she had had a good life, that the two of us had been good daughters. The simple act of reaching for our hands remains memorable to me. For like my maternal grandmother, who was Finnish, she was neither demonstrative nor tactile. Writing these words today, I am aware that my hands retain cellular memory of the softness of her palms in mine. I do not remember any other time she reached out in this way, with the possible exception of when she grasped my hand at my father's death nearly a decade before, which actually took place only a few hundred yards away. There was an intentional clarity, not only to her words, but also to her tone, the character of which I am afraid I cannot convey with language. It simply was a just-so-ness that permeated the spaces between her words that I shall never forget. Her last words to me were, "I love you, Cissy. Thank you for teaching me to hug." I never would hear her voice again, except when she visits in my dreams.

A few moments later, as I walked through the long, khaki-colored corridors through Ward 19, where my father had died nine years earlier, something inexplicable shifted. The oddest sense of peace entered my heart. Anxiety somehow melted, leaving in its wake a deep, abiding calm. That night, I slept like a baby, feeling that all was well. When I awoke the next morning, for some reason that I did not recognize until years later, the need to rush to the hospital had vanished. I remember it was a clear Sunday morning. The sun was shining, the sky, a clear azure blue. Linda and I awoke, took long, leisurely showers. It was as if there was a force field that simply would not allow us to rush. In fact, we felt drawn to stop for a leisurely brunch, and afterward, dropped by the candy store to pick up some early Valentine's treats for the hospital staff.

Ten minutes later, as my sister and I walked toward Mom's room, we were met with an auspicious image. Mae, the nearly six-foot African-American nurse we had hired to provide extra care for our mother, was standing outside her door. Mae's right hand was extended as if to say "stop." As we approached, my heart began to sink. I heard Mae's words through a fog, "She's gone. She passed two minutes ago." Instantly, I felt the same internal cold I felt when my father died, and would feel again, eight years further down this same road when my son was killed. It is the cold of death. There was nothing to do.

I found myself moving, as if through molasses, directly to my mama's side. Instinct led me to reach for and hold her hand. Her body was still warm, every muscle in her face, relaxed. For what seemed like several hours, I held her hand, stroked her arm, spoke to her, sang to her—not the her that had inhabited this body, because my mother was clearly not in this husk anymore. Although I could feel the warmth gradually leave her physical form, there was, for me, a strong sense of her eternal spirit in the room. And it was to this presence that I sang. I suppose you could say that I was singing us both homeward. I stroked, I thanked, I prayed, as she moved into liminal space between life and death, and I moved into my own deepened relationship with the Great Mother.

A Contract Completed

Looking back on it, I believe I was keeping my end of an unspoken bargain I had with my mother throughout my life, perhaps before my soul chose her as my mother. She mothered me when I was a little girl. But as an adult, when she lost my father and many of her brothers, sisters, and friends, we became conscious partners on the grief walk through what Africans call the "Land of the Gray Cloud." In fact, ten years earlier when I was pregnant, my mother and I took a university course for nurses and physicians on "Death and Dying." Many times we discussed death, dying, grieving, life, and living. But, at the moment of her death, it seemed as though all of it had been a preparation for saying goodbye to my mother for the last time. Or, as T. S. Eliot puts it, "We shall not cease from exploration/And [at] the end...[we will] arrive where we started/And know the place for the first time."

Saying goodbye to my mother was part of our shared, ceaseless exploration. It seemed appropriate, too, because Elsa was a lifelong learner. Earlier that week, as I sat alongside her bedrail, each of us seemed at times preoccupied by our private reveries. No doubt, these times were preparing us for the road up ahead, when our paths would diverge. Perhaps, in part, it was the cadence of that drip, drip, dripping rhythm of her IV lines and the monotonous beeps of the monitors that helped us get into this trance. Periodically, I would check and re-check her signs, symptoms, and equipment, only to drift off again. These were simple yet complex moments suspended in the quiet. Funny how her words came back, coaching me as the midwife to her death, like a personal mantra, "There are no short cuts."

Full Circle

During her last few days, my mother returned to her native language from the place she called "the Old Country." In Finnish she repeated, "Kylla kissa kynnet loytaa kun pucehun kitta kiiped," which, loosely translated, means, "A cat will find her claws when she has to climb a tree." At the time, I understood that she was finding strength to confront her death. It did not escape me that she was telling me it was time to find my own claws, too. But what also interested me was that this saying was one of my maternal grandmother's. My grandmother, who died of a massive stroke at age 41, before I was born, spent her last ten days of life being cared for by my mother, whom she had nearly disowned for becoming a nurse. Grandma Paulina believed that nursing was tantamount to being a maid. As an immigrant, she thought this a family disgrace. Sitting with my dying mother, I realized, for the first time in a visceral way, how ironic it must have been for my mother to give her mother the very care my grandmother had thought so demeaning. What irony it was that this same grandmother was now rendered speechless and dependent on my mother's capacity for forgiveness, compassion, and care. For my part, I was dumbstruck with how brave my mother had been to follow her own destiny, despite its personal price tag, and to serve with love the very woman who had nearly disowned her for doing so.

I sat with my mother and I marveled. As she rested, and I prepared myself for her dying vigil, a kaleidoscope of memories moved through my awareness. I recalled how she seemed to have her own private struggle with the spiritual side of life. It was not until I visited Karstulla, a small Finnish village near Lapland, 14 years after her death, that I understood the spiritual solace she found in nature—be it by a river's edge, a mountain lake, the woods, or a garden—a solace she found at her deathbed. She had told me that these places were her church; the comfort they gave touched her as deeply as the hymn, "Be Still My Soul," from Sibelius's Finlandia.

A year before her final hospitalization, one night she said to me: "I wish I had your faith. I seem to relate to Job." It was only after her death that I found a notation she had made that said, "We make our plans and then the unexpected comes. And I ask at times, Why me? Why now? Why like this?" I do not know which plans she was referring to. I only know that she had always been a vital force, a rock of Gibraltar for so many others, and, over the last ten years of her life, seemed ravaged by arthritis, osteoporosis, and the hellatious side effects of medications to ease her physical deterioration, her massive ulcerations, too many to mention. I remember changing the dressings on her legs, and despite the wounds that penetrated nearly to the bone, she barely whimpered. I remembered looking into the infected tissue of my mother's body that was falling apart and wondering how she came by this strength. I recalled the first Finnish word she taught me as a toddler: "Sisu. Never forget this word," she told me. "This is your Finnish nature. Our people have grace under pressure. Never forget this. Sisu is your heritage."

I witnessed her Sisu in action, as she suffered the indignities that come to the elderly with hospitalizations, endless pricks, pokes, examinations, and doctors discussing their cases in front of medical students, as if the patient in the bed had no purpose save to serve as a teaching visual aid. The day before my mother's scheduled surgery, when her physician of many years, Dr. John W., came into the room, it was she who gave him a medical lesson. He had become like a son to my parents some years before, when my father's health began to deteriorate. As John walked crestfallen into my mother's room that afternoon, he slowly approached her side, his eyes avoiding her own. "Elsa," he said, placing his hand on her shoulder, "I don't know what to say. You go into surgery tomorrow. We both know what this means. I can't save your leg, and we know the results of surgery. I feel so bad. I have failed you."

My mother took John's hand in her deformed arthritic hands and said, with serious Sisu: "John, then you don't know the first thing about medicine! The medications and treatments you give are not what heal. You, John, yes you, are the best medicine. You have not failed me one bit. You have helped me heal." With that, this 40-something-year-old man fled from the room in tears, and she turned to me, saying: "Go be with him."

As I followed him into the hallway, where he sobbed, he said, "Your mother knows better than anyone that we doctors are socially and emotionally arrested at age 13 just to get through medical school. Your mother is taking care of me. I should comfort her, and it is she who comforts me."

They Are Here, All Right

By the time I went back into the room, my mother had slipped into another reverie. She was whispering in Finnish more and more and English less and less these days: "Stroke my curls, Mama. Stroke my curls." In the nearly 36 years that I had known my mother, I never remembered her asking to be touched in such a tender voice. I could see the face of a blue-eyed little girl shining through my mother's thinning skin. Apparently, she was visiting the Land of the Beyond more and more, so she was mistaking me at times for her mother and, at other times, her sister Tekla, who had died eight years earlier from leukemia. "Stroke my curls, Mama," she pleaded. As I stroked my mother's baby-fine hair, which seemed reminiscent of silver moonlight, I had never seen her look so peaceful. Just then, she smiled brightly, as if welcoming an invisible multitude into the room. I imagined these people would be her father; her grandmother and grandfather; her brothers Leo, who had died in France in World War II, and Arne, who had died of a stroke in 1954; and Carrie, a dear family friend who died in 1968. I listened. She spoke. Later, as she returned her gaze to me, I asked, "Mom, who were you talking to?"

"Well, them. All the ones who have come to take me home. Oh, that's right! None of you can see them yet, can you? But they are here, all right."

If there was one thing my mother wasn't, it was ungrounded. Neither was she poetic nor was she given to exaggeration. A strong, sensing, thinking type, as we say in Jungian parlance, she was given neither to hyperbole nor fantasy. She was a practical woman, a linear thinker. When my mother spoke, we did well to listen. She spoke only when necessity required it. Otherwise, she was more comfortable with silence. Perhaps this part of her nature made what she shared and how she shared on her deathbed that much more poignant. She gave the gift of her internal vision.

Eternal Return

Since then, when I recall my mother's communication after her death, it has been unique. I have learned that every death, like every life, is different. There is no right. There is no wrong. For a long time following my father's death in 1984, or my son's in 1991, I experienced a number of things that connected me to their essence. Perhaps this is because their deaths were sudden, unexpected, and traumatic in nature. Hers, on the other hand, was a gradual letting go. While they have all communicated in poignant ways since their passing, my mother's spirit communicates through my senses: the first spring forsythia and camellias; summer tomatoes on a vine, basil, pink roses, and yellow snapdragons; the lapping of waves against the shore at dawn; the moss of the forest floor in the evening. More recently, I have felt her presence in the wrinkles on my face and the morphing of my arthritic hands with each passing year.

But in the first pangs of her death, quite honestly, I felt as though I had dropped through the floor on which I had been standing. My mother was that ground. While I was relieved for the ending of her suffering (as well as the relief of ending those non-stop medical emergencies her last few years), I felt an ache in my heart that was beyond fixing. Blessedly, the passage of seasons, coupled with the continual unfolding of my own life, has brought me more and more assurance that the Great Mother-line is alive and well in my heart.

Over the years since I said goodbye to my mother for the last time, I have come to realize that the best way for me to honor her is to respect this precious gift of life that is with me today. The challenge, for me, is to tend to my own unlived life! As Carl Jung wrote, "...children are driven unconsciously in a direction that is intended to compensate for everything that was left unfulfilled in the lives of their parents."* My mother always wished she had taken a class on public speaking. Although she had enrolled in one, she never got to take it once her health failed her. Since that last time I said goodbye, I do what I can to honor my own voice. And so it is that my grandmother, who lost her speech, and my mother who longed to speak her voice in life, inspire me to stand up in the truth of my own heart and voice what I came to say. My hope is that in paying less attention to others' opinions of what I convey, I can live my own life more fully than each of my maternal ancestors was able to do. Then perhaps I can pass on the legacy of our mother-line to my own daughter, and she to my grandbaby, Talia Marie, with the hope that they may carry the longing of it forward in whatever way makes their hearts sing.

*Collected Works, Vol. 17, p. 191.

Cara Barker *works as author, artist, and Jungian analyst to discover the story beneath the story. By decoding the meaning of symptoms, dreams, and life-altering situations through the creative process, she helps her clients rediscover wellness, joy, and freedom. A much-loved featured contributor for the Huffington Post, Cara writes and paints in her group studio with her clients, daughter, granddaughter, and friends.*

Elsie Adelaide (Jean) Male

Mum and I in Bearsted, England, 1939

Mum and I in Arlington, Virginia, 1989

"Well I Remember How You Smiled"*

by Brenda Barthell

My mother was almost 4,000 miles away in England when she died. Geographical distance had always sheltered me from the death of loved ones and the formal rituals associated with dying. My father was killed in the last few days of World War II and is buried in a British military cemetery in Germany.

I was eight years old at the time, and my mother told me that he was "ill," a euphemism perhaps meant to protect us both. My uncle, her brother, had been killed at sea in the first few days of the war. We were living with my grandmother when she died, but as children we were not expected to attend funerals. I do remember being allowed to see the flowers before being taken to a friend's house where we would not be able to witness the grieving. When my grandfather died I was in Switzerland, and most close relatives have died since I have been living in the United States. Opportunities to say goodbye have not therefore been part of my experience, and goodbyes have been difficult for me ever since. I have even been known to avoid them.

Growing up, I never spoke to my mother about dying, especially about my father's death, because I did not want to be the cause of yet more tears. Clearly, I had taken on the role of protecting her as she had protected me. In later years, she was better able to talk about him, and tentatively I began to ask questions about his life. I wish now that I had asked more. In her last years, she broached the subject of her own death but often in a lighthearted way. "I don't envy whoever has to sort out my things when I'm gone," she would say. I believe this was her way of preparing us for the inevitable.

77

During one of our phone calls, she said that she had woken up one night and "seen" my father in the room. She hoped it didn't worry me. I told her that it was a normal phenomenon, but again, I wished I had asked more. How did he look? How did he seem? Did he say anything? She had talked in general terms about an afterlife and the possibility of reincarnation. She even doubted the existence of God at times, not being too impressed with the job he was doing.

Mum had been healthy all her life and seemed to feel cross that her body was finally wearing down. A month after the September 11th attacks, I had flown home for my nephew's wedding. My mother was by then using an oxygen tank and walking with a cane but still lived in her own home with the help of equipment that allowed her to function independently. It was distressing to see this deterioration. It seemed to have happened quickly, probably because there were yearlong intervals between our visits. This was not the same feisty mother who had been active in the community, who quilted, quilled, arranged flowers, traveled, and generally enjoyed life. It was obvious that I had to accept she was nearing her end.

Two months later, my sister called to say Mum was "not doing well," and schooled in euphemisms, I assumed this meant she was dying. I made arrangements to fly home the next day. Heightened security concerns had caused people to fear flying at that time, so it was easy to get a seat at the last minute. She was in the hospital and was surprised to see me. "How were you able to take time from work?" she asked. I tried not to hear any sarcasm in that question, and she may not have intended it. It was probably regret on my part that I had allowed my career and other commitments to take priority over seeing her more often.

I visited her in the hospital every day for ten days, and each one of those days I cried with her and for her. The only physical comfort I was able to offer was to rub her back when she complained of itching. My sister had been the one to take care of things after I moved away. Mum became tired of the constant medical procedures and asked that they be stopped, seemingly impatient with the business of dying. The nursing staff resisted these requests, but I arrived one day to find someone from palliative care at her bedside. I was relieved that she was being heard. A week later, Mum was still with us. I delayed my return home just in case the next visit would be the last, but I eventually decided that I needed to say goodbye. I told her that I loved her and that she had been a good mother to me. She wondered if she would see my father again, and I asked her to give him my love. It was reassuring to know that she might not be alone.

I came back to my home and my job and waited for the inevitable call. A few weeks later, my sister telephoned to let me know Mum had died in her sleep. I felt that I had already said goodbye to her but still felt numb. The next day I worked on a painting that somehow gave me a connection to her. As an artist and art therapist, I knew that creative activity could offer comfort as well as insight, and it did indeed calm and settle me. I worked intuitively on what became an abstract landscape, mostly in blue. This painting, "Meeting Place," now hangs where I can see it when I wake up in the morning.

Elaborate funerals and religious rites were not part of our family's tradition. The only grave is that of my father. The War Office sent us a photograph of it. Mum had decided to donate her body to medical science, and we heard that they were able to use her eyes, which I know would have pleased her. A few days later my sister called to let me know that her children felt the need to say goodbye to their grandmother in a more formal way. We agreed, somewhat reluctantly, and a memorial service was quickly arranged. My sister planned the service, and I wrote the eulogy that was to be given by an old acquaintance who had become a vicar in later life. My mother's friends from the Women's Institute asked that their hymn, *Jerusalem*, be sung. The last line refers to "England's green and pleasant land" which, for someone with divided roots, had always moved me and did so even more on that day. If we are measured by the friends we keep, then my mother was truly blessed. She may have died in a hospital ward surrounded by strangers, but at the memorial she was with family and friends, and I am grateful to my niece and nephew for insisting on this farewell.

Because my visit home was brief, decisions about what to do with her possessions had to be made quickly. We were dismantling the home in which my mother had lived for 62 years and also the home where I had grown up. It could have been an emotional experience, but it was done with efficient speed leaving no time for sentimentality. We even found welcome comic relief on discovering not one but five Bibles tucked away in a bedroom closet. It struck my sister and me as very funny, because our mother had not been a churchgoer, nor had she subscribed to any one religion. We asked family and friends to take whatever they wanted, and the rest of her possessions were donated to charity. I have her engagement and wedding rings, worn thin by this time, her collection of demitasse cups, and a few personal items that I could carry on the plane. I returned home and went about my routine. All that was left to do was the paperwork, which my sister handled.

In the years since her death, I have often thought about what I could create or plant in her memory. But what would a piece of granite or a rose-bush say about her? Would visiting it or tending it help me connect with my mother any more than I do already? Last year, there was an exhibit of my paintings titled "The Special Relationship," a reference to the connection between England and the US. It also represented a personal journey and one that connected me, not only to places that are dear to me in both countries, but to the people I had known. The emotional closeness that I tried to depict, despite the physical distance, was also reminiscent of the relationship I had with my mother. It is that kind of experience that seems to be a more fitting remembrance of her.

Even now, in my gestures and speech, I feel that my mother is a part of me just as I was a part of her. We had similar values, although we didn't always agree, and I believe I know how she would respond to certain circumstances. For a while after her death, I would occasionally feel the need to pick up the phone to share good news with her, but such impulses have faded over time. I would like to think that she already knows what it is that I want to tell her. She can come into my mind at unexpected moments, some that evoke sadness and others that remind me of how loving she could be. On the rare occasions that I am frying eggs and bacon, I recall my mother crying as she prepared the same breakfast for my father on the last day of his leave—and that would have been 65 years ago. Memories of her wiping my face with a cool cloth when I was sick surfaced when I was having a facial, my tears mingling with the luxurious lotion being applied.

I still have family whom I visit in England, but I have not been able to go back to the house in which I grew up. I heard that the new owners had chopped down some of the trees, and I want my memory of the way it was to remain intact. So, too, do I want the memory of my mother's smile to stay with me, rather than the impatience with which she wanted to leave this world.

*A poem by Walter Savage Landor, 1775–1864.

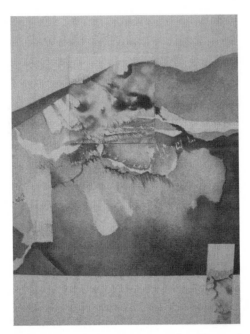

"Meeting Place," watercolor, 10 x 14 inches, December 2001

Brenda Barthell *practiced and taught art therapy in the Washington, DC, area. Now retired, she has pursued a longtime interest in painting, and her abstract works have been juried into solo, group, and corporate shows. Much of Brenda's art alludes to her divided roots, her attachment to this country and to her native England.*

Enriqueta (Ketty) Lebrón Vda. de Aponte

I am standing on the left; seated is Nenen (my father's uncle's wife who brought him up and who was like a mother to my mother); my sister Dalia and my brother Elpidio are on the right; my mom Ketty stands behind us.

Mami's Unfinished Business

by Nilda I. Aponte-Lebrón

"*Levantarme,*" she did say that, "*levantarme,*" it was very clear to me. She did not manage to say *quiero* (I want) before the *levantarme* (to get up), but her determination implied her strong desire as her lips trembled, laboring to form the words. I sensed that she willed her body to get up. She wanted someone's help; she had fallen many times before and would get up again. My eyes welled; this time we could not, would not, get her up. In my mind I implored, "Let go *Mamita,* you have to let go now so you can rest, be at peace, go with Papi." Oh, why does she hang on? That was the way I found my *mami* at the West Palm Beach Hospice when I arrived on that balmy July morning from Virginia. She was visibly agitated at my presence, trying to show me she was still here. I was so grateful I had not arrived too late.

I was the middle of three. My brother Elpidio was oldest, then I, then my sister Dalia, three years younger. When our father passed away in Puerto Rico in 1992, my mother went to live with Dalia in West Palm Beach, where my mother's last surviving sister and her only son Harry also lived. From that point on, Dalia devoted her life to caring for my mother. Both Dalia and Mami were very active in a Baptist Church, just as we all had been while in Puerto Rico.

Since 1979, I had lived in the Washington, DC, area, where I went to work as an attorney for the federal government, while my brother remained in Puerto Rico with his family. When I received news that my mother had a stroke, I lived with my partner Deb in Alexandria, Virginia, where my son Herb and his family also live. My daughter Nina chose to reside in Puerto Rico after college, and she lived there with her husband Samuel and her six-year-old son N'Gosi.

We had celebrated Mami's 88th birthday on March 4th, knowing it would be her last. She had suffered a stroke in February but had made somewhat of a comeback, but with obvious diminished capacity. My father passed away eighteen years earlier. Because I was absent, the grief for his passing was long and full of remorse. I could never forget or forgive myself that at the last moment I chose not to be there.

Although objectively I was the most "successful" sibling, I was also the "black sheep," and probably proud of it. During my first year of college, I came to the conviction that if there was a god she would prefer I base my behavior on my own sense of morality rather than on the fear of her existence. Later, I chose to adopt the humanist faith of my husband's family and their progressive political leanings. My father even once wondered if I were an *independentista* (an activist for Puerto Rican independence from the United States) and a socialist.

My feminist agenda that had started long before I met my American boyfriend was a constant annoyance to our traditionally male-oriented Puerto Rican family. My first open rebellion occurred when I was twelve as my mother came to tell me one Saturday morning while I was making my bed, "From now on you will make your brother's bed as well." "What!! Is he crippled?" It was spontaneous outrage. I shocked even myself at how disrespectful I was. But my mother simply walked away, and nothing else was said. About ten years ago I asked her, "Did your mother tell you to make your brother's bed?" When she said yes, I understood why my mother would ask me to do such a thing even though she should have known how I would react.

When I became an adolescent and I began to consider my own future, my mother's subservience to my father caused me to think less of her. Later, when my two children started preschool, I told Mom I was going to law school. She said I had no reason to, my husband had a good job with the government of Puerto Rico, and I should just stay home with the kids. I said, "Well then, what do I do when they leave home to have their own lives?" "Then you travel," she answered, precisely as she had done. I went to law school. Clearly my mother felt she had failed me as a role model. And I in turn had little use for her motherly advice.

Once my own nuclear family moved back to the States a few years later, my husband and I separated, and I went to practice law in Washington, DC. I then announced to my parents that I was a lesbian and would become active in the gay rights movement. That year my parents forgot my birthday. They apologized the next day, but my estrangement was complete. The love that was still there was hard to give and take. We still kept all the formalities of family, but I sought my support in the lesbian feminist community.

Many years later, I went to visit my father, who was seriously ill in a hospital in West Palm Beach, where my parents had gone to visit my sister. While there, a cancerous tumor was found in his esophagus. It was in that hospital that he told me he loved me. I guess I had thought he didn't love me! I cried a lot over this, but not in front of him. He lasted five more years and died of a heart attack back home in Puerto Rico. After that I cried every day for six months as I realized my loss and regret. Then one morning while crying at work, I felt my father's presence. I heard him say that I must stop grieving and go on with my life. I sensed his forgiveness.

Once I knew my mom was leaving us, I spent every weekend I could visiting her and my sister Dalia, who had devoted those eighteen years to caring for her. Deb and I also took a golf vacation for a week in West Palm Beach so we could be with her every evening. My mother had been in slow but sure decline since my dad's passing, and throughout I was aware that she was very disappointed in my lifestyle that was so different from her own and the way she had brought me up. I was a lesbian and an atheist.

From time to time I felt the need to let my mom know what my feelings were about religion. Every Sunday I visited, I knew she wished I would attend church with her. The one Sunday that I did, I felt her hopes were high that I would continue. Although I had gone just to please her, I am glad I went that one time, because the visit was revealing about who my mother really was. My first reaction was shock and surprise. My mother was a leader in her church. She was also eloquent in prayer and felt quite free to express her opinions. There was great reverence for her, and she was everybody's grandmother. In this Latin American congregation, where most grandmothers had stayed in their home country, hers was an important role indeed. I became anguished at the thought that all those years she never revealed these characteristics, and I concluded that my father's presence must have repressed her; it took his passing for her true self to emerge. My father, whom I adored, did this. I felt aggrieved for Mami.

On one of my visits after my mom's first stroke, I violated a promise to myself not to discuss politics or religion, when I responded to a comment made by a woman from her church who came to visit. This woman stated her certainty that Mami would eventually be with all her brothers and sisters from church, because they all believed in Jesus as their savior and the Son of God. I responded that when Jesus preached that we should love one another, he meant everyone. I could not accept that only those of certain beliefs were blessed. I said, "Buddha, Mohammed, Confucius, and Lao Tzu were all also sons of God." When I remembered that my mother was present, I added that I had not forgotten all the values I had been taught and that they were being passed on to my children and grandchildren.

As she contemplated her passing, I suspected Mami felt an urgency to get me back to her church, the only path, or I would miss out on eternity. Several times I told her not to worry, that I was going where she was going and that we would be together with Papi. Each time I said it, she only gave me a puzzled look. What I couldn't explain to her was that I had always believed we have eternal souls, though I am still more inclined to believe in the "universal unconscious" or a "holographic universe" than in an anthropomorphic God. I could not tell her that I was convinced that Papi had appeared to me and told me she would suffer a stroke and would come to be with him within the year. So, near the end, there was considerable tension and confusion between my mother and me at the same time that I felt closer to her than ever. I took every opportunity to hug her, kiss her, and tell her, "te quiero mucho mamita."

Then the last day of June the stroke came. My sister called. She had found Mami Wednesday morning with her torso on the floor and her feet on the bed. Dr. Brito, her primary care physician, and my cousin Harry, also a doctor, immediately came to help. They advised that Hospice could stabilize her. Mom's stroke left her unable to swallow. This, and the fact that she had a pacemaker, high blood pressure, and diabetes, made it inadvisable to treat intravenously an accompanying abdominal infection that had plagued her for several years and was diagnosed as active again. Only palliative treatment was recommended. Dalia, my brother Elpidio, and I agreed this was the best course.

Deb and I made arrangements to fly to West Palm Beach the next day, Thursday morning, July 1st. Herb, my son, would be coming in on an afternoon flight. My daughter Nina and her son N'Gosi had arrived from Puerto Rico the previous Wednesday for two weeks in the States, one with us and one with her dad. Rather than going to Florida, she had stayed behind in Alexandria with Herb's wife Diane to help with the children. I had given her this excuse not to come, and I knew she welcomed it. She was holding on to a hurt, a perceived wrong that made her feel unloved and judged by her *abuela*. Nina had long ago said that all was forgiven, but not really. I was resigned to the fact that she would not say goodbye to her grandma.

When Herb approached her bedside, Mami's eyes seemed to be trying to focus. "Herb is here," I said. She already knew. He hugged her, kissed her forehead, and stroked her hair as he spoke softly. "Nina stayed to help with the kids," I said. Elpidio's daughter and her two children had been there since Wednesday. From the moment Herb arrived Thursday afternoon, Nina was the elephant NOT in the room. Herb visited once more, Friday morning, and then headed home to Virginia to be with Diane and their three boys.

My mom wouldn't go, and the doctors had stopped making predictions. By Saturday she seemed to be beating all odds. Was she waiting for Dr. Brito—or for Harry's wife Susi, who was also out of town? Or, was there someone from her Senior Center she expected? As we were making these speculations, my siblings were not saying what they really thought.

Shortly after my arrival at the Hospice, the visits from members of her Baptist congregation started. They were from Honduras, Uruguay, Dominican Republic, Puerto Rico, Cuba, and so on; quite a number of the

Latin American countries were represented among the visitors, but they all showed their admiration and love for my mother. Her influence and presence would be missed, it was clear.

On Saturday a large group from the church came. By then Mami was not responsive and was expected to go any minute. I witnessed the impossible once more—she seemed to be singing, following each hymn being sung, her favorites as requested by my sister Dalia. She at times pursed her lips together, even showed her enthusiasm by directing her mouth and chin toward the group. How very Puerto Rican a gesture! Knowing she would hear me, and seeing her so determined to be involved in the singing, made me want to show her that I was also; I sang the hymns I had not sung in years with genuine enjoyment. I hoped Mami would feel the emotion I displayed singing and that I would be with her eventually and not at that other place. Perhaps this would help her let go, yet I knew she still believed she had more to do. Nina was still missing.

On Monday afternoon I got a call from Nina. She had an evening flight that would arrive just after midnight. After spending some time talking with Nina, Herb offered to arrange and pay for a roundtrip ticket so she could say goodbye to her *abuela*.

After Nina's divorce from her first husband, Elpidio told her she was not welcome in his home, and Mami told her she could not stay at our empty family home in San Juan because she said that a young woman cannot live alone. Perhaps my mother and my brother assumed that she would do as any other young Puerto Rican woman would do and go back home to Mom or Dad in the U.S. (Mami had expected me to return home to Puerto Rico when I separated!) But Nina had resolved to stay in Puerto Rico; she had long decided that was home for her. So she suffered hardship, feeling alone and abandoned, and she blamed those who would not help.

Several times my mother had spoken to me about the fact that my daughter refused to welcome contact with my brother, although both were in Puerto Rico. When they met at family events, she was cold and barely civil. Mami thought I should help mend the estrangement. She also complained that Nina never called. I explained that Nina felt hurt, that I had tried to mend things, but that my brother and my daughter each felt the other was "at fault" and should apologize. I could not insist with either one. I knew this was really hard on my mom, but I found it difficult to explain that there was a lot of pain involved, some having to do with her. She finally dropped the subject with me, and my brother was annoyed that I felt he should make the first move; Nina felt the same way. So things went on like this for about ten years!

When Nina announced she was coming to say goodbye, I realized Herb's comforting, listening, or whatever had helped; Nina had finally crossed the threshold of true forgiveness. She arrived just after midnight. I witnessed this important moment as she approached Mami. First she asked for forgiveness and forgave my mom for the past. Then she read a prayer and said more words of comfort. I was so moved that I could hardly listen, but I knew Mami heard. She had been waiting for this moment.

When we got back to the hotel, Deb, Nina, and I ate some comfort food and drank wine together, floating down from the emotional experience. We slept well and were ready for breakfast early the next morning. We sat down at our usual table, waiting for the arrival of my brother and sister, who had met us at 8:00 a.m. for the last few mornings. As they neared the table Nina got up, approached Elpidio and hugged him. He said, "I love you, Nina." And she responded with a bigger hug. It may have been ten minutes later when my sister's cell phone rang. My mom had passed away at 8:07 a.m. We all felt she had witnessed that hug of reconciliation and was able to let go.

Mami's life was celebrated first in West Palm Beach. We heard heartfelt testimonials from many of the people whose lives she had touched, including a young woman who said, crying, that she was truly influenced by her to finish school. Her husband, who could not be present because of job responsibilities, had given my mom his karate trophy, because he claimed that he would not have earned it without her influence. My mom had proudly displayed that black belt trophy in her home. One man stated that her advice to him had saved his marriage; a woman spoke of my mother's recommendations as to how to discipline her children.

There was more eulogizing in Puerto Rico, where a fourth grade classmate remembered her. Most of my mother's nieces were present with their husbands and children. One woman had been my mother's friend since their husbands served in Korea. I recall my mother's incredible support for her and her three boys. The people from the church from Puerto Nuevo came, and their warmth and support for our grieving was genuine. Mom had made her last visit to Puerto Rico to be present at the church's sixtieth anniversary a year before; she had been one of the founders. This time at the burial site I was calm and composed because I had no regrets; my grieving was more private and gradual than it was in February 1992, when my dad passed. I rejoiced that they were together again after eighteen years.

Now I understand why such a wonderful human being was so quiet about her true self. She used her influence with my father behind the scenes because she was adamant that he was the head of the family. She did not stand up to my sassiness because she would not suppress my own spirit! And I know that she loved me and mostly admired what I did, whether she understood it or not. Mami, now I know that in so many ways I am a lot like you.

Nilda Aponte *is grandmother to four beautiful boys. She earned her retirement as a civil rights attorney for the federal government. Her efforts as a feminist in Puerto Rico in the '70s led to the amendment of the Civil Code, giving equal rights to women. She lives with her wife in Florida.*

Gisele Baroukel Miller

My mother at our family lakeside camp in Maine where we spent all our summers. Photo was taken in the 1950s.

My mother and I in Brazil in 1973

The Face of a Dying Woman

by Wendy Miller

"Do you think that is the face of a dying woman?"

What does the face of a dying woman look like? Does she look like she
is dying? Perhaps we have an image from films or novels, or from observing
someone dying in Hospice care. But, if that is not the case, maybe only in
hindsight can we see death in the face that appears before us—a weakness,
a glance, a grayness. We have images, but what is the actual experience of
seeing the face of a dying woman?

This is what I remember as my mother was dying. I thought she was
recuperating from her cancer. She was fighting for the energy to live, and
she was doing a damn good job. She was supposed to have surgery on her
spleen that would boost her immune system and help save her life. But
when the doctor saw her walk, finally, at the last possible hour, he realized
what we all could see but were not willing to say. She couldn't walk. She
could hardly move.

"Whoa," he ultimately said. "We need to stop here. Going ahead
with this surgery could kill her." Would he have done that if I hadn't just
innocently asked him whether he had seen her walk? Wouldn't we have
assumed that he had seen her move? But she had come in, beautiful as always, pushed by Dad as she sat on a swivel office chair. Everyone was always captivated by her presence. How could we have known that we were
looking at the face of a dying woman?

Or could we have been conscious of it the day we all gathered for
Thanksgiving at our family home? My sister Sara was setting the table in
the dining room with gorgeous plates, splatterings of purple and white,

along with small copies she brought of Sandra Martz's book, *When I Am an Old Woman, I Shall Wear Purple*. Mom stayed in the den and was like a guest for the holiday meal in her own home. That was certainly a first. She had been the organizer, the cook, the planner, the creator of the holiday joy that we all had known for years upon years, 47 for me to be exact. We have photographs from that day and she looks beautiful and happy: she is sitting on the couch; one by one, it seems, each of her grandchildren came to sit with her, hugging her closely.

Now I look at those pictures, and I wonder how I could not have known she was dying. Her smile is only partially there. Her aura is only faintly present. She is half gone from herself and from us. I was blind to it then but see it so clearly now. Would I see the same thing in these photographs if she hadn't died four weeks later? Maybe, but I don't think so.

The first night of Chanukah, the phone rang at exactly 3:50 a.m., but we thought it must be a wrong number. It rang again. My husband Gene picked up the phone. I heard him say, "Oh, Howard, I am so sorry." I grabbed the phone. Could that voice be Dad's? It was a voice I had never heard before—a depth, a despair: "I lost Gisele. I lost Gisele tonight, and I don't know how it happened."

I cannot remember much after that—screaming, crying, talking to Dad, calling my older sister. She had already spoken with him and had called Paula and Peter, dear family friends who lived nearby, to go be with him. He had been to the hospital and had come home. How could all that have happened already? I tried to call my younger sister Julie. She was away in Tahiti. I had to find her. We are Mom's three girls; we are one. I had to move through hotel people in another language to connect to her; I put the phone with her on it next to the other line with Dad on it so they could speak to each other. What was I thinking? How could I imagine they could hear one another? Of course they couldn't. I was crying between them. I was outside myself, beside myself. "I'm beside myself," my mother used to say. What does that mean? Beside my mother was all I wanted, all I could conceive of—to be beside my mother. Remembering the image of the face of a dying woman causes pain that runs through your system—with such sharpness, such force—that all the platelets rearrange themselves, and cellular knowledge sends jolts of new positioning without ever warning the neighboring tissues.

An Image Speaks: The Pattern of Arrangements

LIFE:
The grand maker throws down your pickup sticks,
and that arrangement is the constellation of your family.
You live, breathe, move within that constellation,
and it is your own.

DEATH:
The grand maker picks up the sticks,
whose arrangement is the constellation of your family,
and throws them down again.
The colors are the same, the numbers the same,
but they are no longer touching and lying in the places
that they have resided in as home
for their entire existence.
In that moment it takes to die,
it is all changed forever.

"Tell me, Doc, who, what, where, when, how?"
As soon as our plane landed in Portland that next morning, Gene and I and our three-year-old daughter Eliana rented a car to drive the hour and a half north to my family home. Immediately, they dozed—it was so early in the morning—and I detoured to the doctor's office. Before going to see my dad, I went to the Maine Cancer Center. I had to. I knew the exact question that would be driving my dad crazy, and we had to have an answer.

I was acquainted with Mom's doctor from appointments, from visits, from family conversations together. It was Dad who really knew him best. He had accompanied Mom to all of her appointments, but we had also gone with her during treatments in the summer and on our visits. This doctor was familiar with our family. We knew his nurses and his office staff. I entered the office alone. Right away, the condolences started from one nurse after another: "I just saw her yesterday. She looked so beautiful!" It was what everyone said about my mom. Sick or well, she was always beautiful in body, mind, and spirit.

No one expected her to die. "She was just here yesterday afternoon. Her blood numbers were good." She had delivered her holiday gifts, Belgium chocolates, of course, only the best chocolates ever. The nurses went to get Doctor Tom for me. We went directly together to an exam room. I wanted to know how she died, why she died, when she died, what she died of. We began in tears. I said, "Was there anything more Dad could have done? Should he have taken her to the hospital sooner? I know that is what he is asking himself." My heart ached for him.

"The only difference it would have made is that then she would have died at the hospital or in the car getting there. And he would have felt worse."

"But this is what that rude doctor told me in the hall in September," I retorted. He said that she would not be able to fight an infection, and it would take her in three hours. How I hated him. How angry I was at him for being so vocal, so intrusive, and so arrogant. "You, Dr. Tom, diffused my anger and told me that he was the type of doctor we would want to have."

I realized that my anger often gets in the way of my listening. It is a family trait. I wanted to believe that my mom would still be here, and that guy would still be a jerk. But perhaps we should have listened to him. Perhaps if I had, I would have made Dad listen to him, and perhaps and perhaps, and in the end, maybe we would have been better prepared.

Dr. Tom said, "She had nothing to fight a bacterial infection. It came on very quickly and it took her just as quickly. She died with your father. We both know that is what they wanted."

"But, if..."

"I know what you are asking, but there wasn't anything anyone could have done."

"Her heart just stopped."

"Her heart let go."

I cried with Dr. Tom. I cried the whole way driving to my home. Was it multiple myeloma that took her? No. Was it the illness or the treatment for the illness that took her? No. Was it supposed to be like that? No. Was it her heart—a weakness in the genetic history of the hearts in her family of origin, like her mother's heart, her brother's heart? No. Or did the infection stop her heart? Yes, apparently so.

What is dying anyway? What is the meaning of this moment that changes all moments? What happens afterwards?

Later, much later, I created a painting that gave me some solace. Using oil paint, I crushed the colors down to the last piece of each oil bar, trying to find the place where souls go. I had no other thoughts while doing this; I just painted until there were no colors left. As I emerged from this trance-like state, I saw that I actually had painted an ethereal landscape. I believed that was where my mother was, and it was very comforting to me.

"I want to be with my mother."

From the moment I entered the den of my family home, and throughout the week, all I remember is how hard it was to walk, to talk, to swallow, to sit, to stand, to move, to do anything. If Dad got up from his red chair in the den to walk down the hallway to use the bathroom, I got up. When my sister Sara arrived, she did the same; if Dad moved, we moved. We moved as if we needed each other, as if we had the same pair of legs. All my relatives came. Lots of people came. People came for days. I only remember some of it. I remember Gayle Ann, my cousin and childhood friend, coming into the living room during one of the short Shiva evening hours we arranged, and there I was lying on the white living room couch. She kneeled on the floor beside me, hugging me. I never even got up. She said, "We grew up together. So, when I think of my mother, I think of your mother. Our homes were like one." Her words comforted me.

Dad, Sara, and I would go together to the service; Julie and her family were stranded in Tahiti for five days. How could we have Mom's service without her? How could we move as one, without our whole family present?

We wanted to wait. But Jewish people do not wait; they bury very quickly. Dad had already broken tradition. He had made the funeral home hold her body in town, waiting for us to go see her together, so we could see her, touch her, say goodbye, before transporting her to the Jewish cemetery folks in Portland where she would be prepared for burial.

I never thought about any of that preparation at the time. It was just what my family did, what Jews in Maine did. I never thought about our choices until later, when throughout the years of my anger at losing my mother, I found out that my friends made different choices. They washed their mothers, or they prepared them for burial. They buried them with special items or notes or whatever rituals they chose to perform. These were not my thoughts or even wishes at the time. I just wanted to see my mom. But I have no regret about not doing those things. I like that my mother was prepared for her burial according to the conservative Jewish rites of tradition. Growing up in Algeria, a Sephardic Jew in an orthodox home, Mom was given at least some semblance of the ritual and respect, blessing and purifying, that contained a piece of her heritage, albeit Maine style, but her heritage for these past 53 years.

At the funeral home that next morning, with all of its official tone, properly suited men, red velvet steps, red brocade on the walls, we were brought into a room to await her. The man would bring her to us—my dad, my older sister, and me. Alone, together, we waited as they rolled in a table laden with a long black bag. Zipped up to her head, inside a black bag, there was my mom, beautiful, as always, white-gray and pale, not her olive skin, a quiet sleeping face. Was her face peaceful? I can't say such a thing.

I can say that it wasn't long enough to be with her. It seemed to me that very quickly, too quickly, my dad and my sister said, "We need to go now...that is enough." The implication was that we had to let them take her to Portland, as if there were a rush or a timeline. They left the room, and I was to follow, but I didn't want to. I did not want my mother to go and for it all to end so fast. I wanted to touch her, to kiss her, to stay alone with her. I wanted to be with my mother, not with the details of what was to be done with her. But I was afraid to break stride, break off, break out of the "we" movement. It was as though we were glued together, and my desire, contrary to theirs, was wrong. I couldn't even voice it. I swallowed it and walked out quietly as I was told.

It wasn't until years later, sitting in the room with my dad after he died, that I apologized to my mother for ignoring my intuition at the expense of my heart. At his passing, when my older sister told me it was time to go, I took care of myself, saying, "This time I need to stay until I am ready. I can't bear the years of anger again. I am okay, you do not need to worry about me, and I will come soon."

"Where is Nanny now?"

Another problem of these days of deepest darkness, the Shiva days that were supposed to be the Chanukah days of light, was how to explain what was happening to my little girl when I was so distraught over the passing of my own mother. She could see the pain that we were all in, her mother, her poppy, her cousins, her aunts, her daddy. I kept trying to think of ways to help her understand what it meant that Nanny had died. How do you make concrete such an experience for a little person?

"Where is Nanny now?" was her question. People told me to tell her, "Death is kind of like a big sleep." Well, it doesn't take a therapist to know that is not the right thing to say. "She is with God," was another suggestion. "She has gone to heaven." But, if she cannot understand death, how could she understand God or figure out where heaven is? She went to Nanny and Poppy's big bed and watched lots of Barney and Elmo. I worried that our words were meaningless to her.

Then, as little people always seem to do, she answered her question for herself. She called me to come with her into the bathroom, an intimate place. She felt safe there. "I haf a kestion," she said. "Is Nanny a fairy now?" I stopped and thought for just a second, not quite knowing how to respond. I wanted to cry, but I'm sure I smiled. Such a beautiful image took me by surprise. I looked up, and in a flash, I realized she had named it better than any of my adult relatives and friends.

"Yes, sweetheart, your nanny is a fairy now."

"Is she my fairy?"

"Oh, yes, she is your fairy now. She loved you so, she would do anything she could to be your fairy, now and forever."

Less than a year later, we were in a small park near the condo that Nanny rented for those end-of-winter weeks when a Mediterranean woman absolutely needs to get out of Maine. There, on Marco Island, Florida, was Nanny's replacement for Algeria. Eliana, whose nickname was Yannie, ran around from the swing to the teeter-totter, falling into the sand. At one point, I called her, and, as she ran to me, she stopped, turned around, and went back to the swing. "What are you doing? Come on, Yannie, let's go." She put her hand out as if she were holding hands with someone.

"Mom, wait! My Gazelle is cold." Then I heard her say, "Come on, come with me." She had an imaginary friend, a rabbit, she said, named Gazelle. I realized that although I never referred to my mother by name (I always just said Mom), Eliana had heard everyone talk about "Gisele." She had taken it in as her own sound. Was she remembering? Was she in touch with something that I couldn't connect with? Could she sense my mom?

Oh, how I wish it could have been so—that it was my mom, somehow here with me, watching my child grow—that my child was taking care of her nanny, rabbit, Gazelle, making sure she was not cold.

"We adore you, Gisele Baroukel Miller."

Writing a eulogy for my mom seemed right for me, although no one of my generation in my family had done so. But I felt I had to do it. Frankly, I awoke one night, worried that the rabbi would not say what was necessary or right about her. As it turned out, I was wrong, so wrong. He wrote a beautiful piece, in which he alluded to Heinlein's book, *Stranger in a Strange Land*, and suggested that "Gisele Miller in her 53 years in Waterville conquered the hearts of its inhabitants."

I wrote about her elegant grace, something I felt I did not have. I also wrote because I needed to ask those gathered—to implore the whole community, from the temple, to the store, to the neighborhood, to the family, to those who shared the history of our lives—to help take care of Dad.

Although competent at many things, he was not good at taking care of himself, which he never had to do. Taking care of others was what he did. How would he be okay without Mom? He had gone all the way to Algeria to find her during World War II, marry her, and bring her here to this snow-laden small town in Maine.

"She came in the snow, and she left in the snow," he had mused out loud to me. He told me about driving her here for the first time, so, so many years ago in the month of October. It was snowing. She had never seen snow before. He recalled her face, the complexity of understanding revealed there, when she turned to him and said, "It is so beautiful, Howard, this white snow. How long will it last?"

"Oh, my darling, only until April," he lovingly responded, watching her eyes change from sheer pleasure to utter shock.

When I rose from my front row seat to go to the bimah to speak in the crowded synagogue, which had been beautified and decorated throughout the years by my mother, I felt my legs not particularly able to hold me for that distance. I moved slowly, still connected to my dad and sister. I leaned into my dad; he kissed me and said, "It doesn't matter, darling, whether you actually speak. It only matters that you wanted to." How perfect at that very moment to get the exact kind of support I associated with Mom!

I went ahead and read what I had written, slowly, through tears, as I stared out at all these people whose lives my mom had shared for two-thirds of hers, far from her homeland, her language, her exotic sounds and smells. North Africa was North America. Algeria was Maine. Oran was Waterville. As I read to the end, I knew in a stretched-out-instant that I had now been reduced to "white bread." Without my mother, I would be ordinary, plain, American, white. The exotic nature of our oneness seemed lost.

"We adore you, Gisele Baroukel Miller. May your soul rest gracefully in our hearts, and may your heart grace our restless souls."

"My mother had been stolen."

I was so angry. I couldn't possibly have realized how much anger would move through my system over the next five years. I hated to see women walk in the streets with their mothers. I hated to see women my mom's age on the plane, in the market, in the stores, anywhere at all. I couldn't relate to people anymore. I didn't like their innocence.

I couldn't make peace with the notion of her body in the ground, in the snow, frozen. My life itself felt frozen. I was numb. I was exhausted. I lived underneath the weight of the black blanket that comes in to surround and protect the grieving body—the auric body or whatever we want to call it.

I didn't care anymore. I was out of control, no reserve for anything that stretched my heart out of its cocoon. My reveries were like flashbacks, movies of our conversations and our presence together, sometimes so sad, sometimes so beautiful.

I wish I had held you longer that morning at the funeral home. It never would have been enough, nor would it be now. I wish I could have breathed in all that I would need forever to hold you unto me. Like a thief, I wanted to steal you just as death had done. It robbed us of you, robbed my daughter of you, took you from Dad, from life, from love, from the other end of the daily telephone line.

I remember the hospital, all of us together, each day a new awareness, the reality of the oncology floor. You were the recipient of all their probes. Becoming quieter, I held my black pen and my tiny sketchbook as if it were something I always did. I never expected these doodles to be the last, the only memory. They are the vague remnants of when our denial broke down, when the cancer's presence and your weakness were intertwined, threatening not only your body but our family's body. If anything, I expected to return to the hospital again and again, as if we were just beginning, not ending.

How you rallied! Now, it seems, it must have been for Dad. At Uncle Ludy's memorial service, as we gathered at the Levine cemetery stones, you walked and talked and held your own. There was little Eliana leaning up against your back, standing on a stone, her hand able to reach your hair. "I luff my nanny so," she whispered. I had no idea how her words would stay with me, resounding in their finality.

You were so open then, your words able to release themselves from the darkness that had quieted them. I heard you tell Aunt Glen: "You know, three weeks ago, I thought it would be me." Holding my heart, I thought to myself,

God forbid. After the service, at that restaurant we only go to when we leave the Jewish cemetery, I walked slowly with you to the ladies' room, your cane an affront to us. You were so proud, so assured. I heard you say to the mirror, "Now, that is not the face of a dying woman, do you think? I wouldn't have so much color. People have always told me that I have a beautiful face. I don't know what they are seeing; it is just my face. And I don't know if it is beautiful, but, now, do you think that is the face of a dying woman?"

Oh, my, you were so beautiful! Your face was so beautiful; it is hard to believe you didn't always know that, considering how well you recognized "not beautiful" in others!

"No, I don't think it is the face of a dying woman."

My mother had been stolen. A thief had come and stolen her. I knew, because she would never die on a holiday, the first night of Chanukah, the day her twin grandsons were born. I didn't know that it was her time, and she didn't know she was dying. I didn't get to be with her. Some people say that if you get a chance to be there for the dying process, do so, it is amazing. I wanted to dismiss them, tell them they did not understand. It seemed to me that she had died without anyone knowing, that she herself didn't know because she didn't die of her illness, as if her illness was her ticket to die, that she died of an infection, felt tired, got the shivers, lost her voice, took an aspirin Dad gave her, returned to sleep early, and didn't wake up. She didn't come back to show us the face of a dying woman. Instead, death stole her in the quiet hours of the night.

"Mom is always waiting for me."

How I needed a sign, some communication from my mother! But for months, nothing.

Then one day I was in a bookstore, aimlessly walking around, feeling unmoored from my own sense of who I was without my mother's unconditional love. After a while, a woman appeared from behind the stacks of books, a beautiful exotic-looking young woman. I have no memory of how we started talking, but in no time she perceived that I was deeply sad. Did I tell her that my mother had died? How did she know that I was existentially adrift? She sang to me, right there in the middle of the store. She sang a Sephardic song in Ladino. This was the very same song I used to hear my mom play on the piano. There she was, singing to me, as if she intimately knew me. At last, a sign—an Algerian-sounding voice that was familiar to my heart. I stood there, tears running down my face. I remember even asking for her phone number so that I could find her again, but she replied with a no, that she was only in town for a short while. Before she left this magnetic space that she had created between us with her voice-song, she told me that the music I needed to listen to was Flamenco, that no other music could capture the pas-

sion and intensity of where my grief was taking me. She recognized in me something I thought I had lost when my mother died. Maybe I am not all "white bread" after all. She sent me back to my mother's Spanish roots to find myself again. It was as if she had come out of nowhere and, after our exchange, went back to this same nowhere.

Many years have gone by already, and I still do not feel I could ever say goodbye to Mom for the <u>last</u> time. To do so would deny who I am,

In 2002 I made this installation art, "Prayerstones: Mother-Daughter-Mother," fired ceramic clay with fused glass inserts.

my Arabic, Algerian, Sephardic, Ladino roots. It would mean that when I say or feel or acknowledge "home," I would not think of her. I can't do that. Oh, yes, I have my own home. I have my own family. I say, "Let's go home," and I do mean my home that I have created. But, in my musings, in my dreams, in my mind, when I say home, it is the house, the community, the town, the childhood arrangement of pickup sticks that I grew up with. And Mom is always waiting for me, at home.

Wendy Miller, *sculptor, expressive arts therapist, and writer, works with individuals and families through mind-body medicine to restore creativity and health in the face of developmental, existential, and health challenges. She and her late husband Gene Cohen shared a deep commitment to family and community, which is carried on in their new book about their lives and careers,* Sky Above Clouds.

Helen Ricaby Stenstrom

Helen in 1948 with my brothers and me (in the stroller)

Helen and I in Washington, DC, in April 1969

Helen's Waltz*

by Ruth Stenstrom

Three years before the death of my mother, Helen, I was studying art in Venice. Late one afternoon I found myself alone in the art studio with a new student who was in emotional shambles. We hardly knew each other, but her tears flowed freely. "You see, I just lost my mother two months ago," she cried in deep agony, trusting that this heart-breaking statement would explain everything.

The experience woke me up. I had never thought how disabling the death of my own mother would be. Yet here it was right in front of me, a premonition of what was to come, an earth-shattering event.

Sometimes when my mother and I would travel together, sharing a room, I would listen for her breath in the middle of the night and sense that it might have stopped. I would wonder what I would do when she died. When it did happen, I realized that I had not been able to imagine the unimaginable.

My mother talked about death a lot. She did not want to get old and become "a vegetable." She talked about the logistics of death, her cremation, her burial site, her personal things and family heirlooms—who would get what. But she never asked me, "What will you do when I am no longer here?"

The reality is that you can never be prepared for this kind of loss. It was the most ravaging emotional pain that I have ever suffered. Losing her felt to me like life had no meaning; I was in an existential crisis. I wondered, why do anything, if in the end we die? I felt a black hole opening, a loss of faith in the future. A demarcation had been made in my time on earth—the time before and after my mother died.

I was lucky to have a family therapist who helped me acknowledge the significance of my loss. All she had to do was repeat, "You lost your mother," in her empathic way, and I would know that I was a part of a larger community of souls who were equally devastated.

It has been nearly thirty years since my mother died. It took over two years before the pain began to lessen and the wound to heal. During those first months, tears would emerge at the slightest cause. I vividly remember seeing a Mike Leigh film called *High Hopes* about a London family. In the story the elderly mother lost her purse and was totally defeated by the experience. I sat crying in the car afterwards, inconsolable at the film's expression of the helplessness of this little old lady, which seemed like the same hopelessness experienced by my mother and my inability to help her or to keep her from dying. I could not keep her from suffering those indignities that come from having to be dependent on people who ultimately fail you.

About the same time my mother was dying, I developed in my right shoulder chronic tendonitis that lasted for several years. I tried many physical therapies to heal it—massage, chiropractic, and regular medicine. Then a friend recommended John Preston, a serious student of traditional acupuncture techniques, and so I embarked on my first excursion into body-mind therapy, which turned into an inner emotional journey of about 18 months.

John said that my pain was in the metal (air) meridian. The color of metal is white, its time is winter, and its emotion is grief. Metal affects the lungs—breathing in—and the colon—letting go. In a very loud message my body was telling me what was in my heart, that my pain was related to the death of my mother.

This physical metaphor for what was happening to me was validating and made my experience of acupuncture more credible. My work with John was even more meaningful because he verbally processed our sessions to honor my need to understand everything that he was doing.

After describing what had happened to me the previous week, I would lie down and John would take my pulses, look into my face for colors to emerge, and based on his observations, insert a variety of needles. Some needles would be placed for a long time, some were just a short jab. Sometimes the pain would linger and fade, sometimes it was a big jolt. I often could not tell which needles were still inserted and which had been removed. I would relax for about 20 minutes, and he would return, recheck my pulses, get verbal feedback, and readjust the needles. I had a variety of unusual sensations. I felt the stagnant energy begin to move, often in a figure eight swirl through my body. I became more aware of my right and left sides.

In spite of this new self-awareness, the tendonitis remained a problem. Even though acupuncture ultimately did not heal my physical pain, it did help me process my mother's death. Just before our sessions ended, I had an experience with John that helped me understand the primal depth of my loss.

After the needles had been inserted for a while, John laid his hand on me, directing energy down my arm; unexpectedly tears began to drip down the sides of my cheeks. These were not tears of physical pain, but rather of grief. Imagine my surprise that when he removed his hand, the tears would stop. In our nonverbal communication, he continued the process, as I felt myself give in to the impulse to cry profusely.

As he continued to work in this manner, a vivid image appeared to me, unlike anything that I had previously experienced in my life. I saw myself as a naked, red, raging baby, lying on a white table, screaming at the top of my lungs. Although there were no words, the message was clear: "I want my Mommy." I was an infant with narcissistic needs and was suffering from classic separation anxiety. I wanted Mommy and only Mommy. Mommy was mine. Mine was underlined and no one else would do.

I had never had this kind of out-of-body event before. I experienced it without analysis, without trying to push it to be something that it was not. It was like a psychic catharsis; I felt how much I identified my own sense of survival with my mother. I felt a kind of closure. The shoulder pain remained, but there was the promise that I would finally begin to understand my grief.

My mother Helen lost both of her parents as a young teenager and so became a ward of the state. She moved in with a foster family, graduated from high school, moved out, and took an office job. Since it was the Depression, she could only afford two dresses for work. At age 20 she married my father, whom she knew in high school. She loved his family and had dreams of having a happy family of her own. Eight years later her first baby was born and died after three days. Because she didn't have a caesarian, she had serious complications. Then when my older brother was born, she was told that not only should she not have other children but that she was unable to conceive. My parents spent the next five years looking for a way to adopt a child. Along came the war and the subsequent baby boom. I was their "chosen baby" from the Cradle Society. Eight months later my mother gave birth to my younger brother. Posted on her refrigerator door was the John Lennon saying, "Life is What Happens When You Make Other Plans."

I knew as soon as I could talk that I was special because I was adopted. My younger brother and I were often mistaken for twins. However, I had all kinds of fantasies that I kept to myself about my birth heritage. I was told my mother had probably died in childbirth. The concept of an unwed mother was basically unknown to me. I think many adoptees don't question their birth heritage at the risk of hurting their adoptive parents.

I never felt illegitimate, but in some ways I felt like an outsider in my family. This was especially true when we talked about family history and who resembled or acted like another relative. I would look at people as I traveled and wonder if we were related. I waited for a time to search and ask the questions when it wouldn't hurt my family. Ironically, though the adopted child, I am the one who became the most interested in family roots.

When I was 30, my mother sent me a news article about an adoption registry that would list adoptees and birth parents who would like to be reunited. I mailed my information in, but my birth mother did not. The article mentioned a support group in my hometown of Evanston, Illinois, called Yesterday's Children. I immediately joined, got the newsletter, and was assigned a support person. She told me to get a copy of my adoption certificate, and from the court case number on it they would find out my birth name through one of their contacts. This was still an illegal endeavor in

1977, as adoption records from the 1940s through the 1970s in most states were sealed by the courts.

I had never thought about the fact that for the first six weeks of my life I had another name while I was cared for in the Cradle Society, a private adoption agency. It was Baby Girl Oist. I was lucky that it was an unusual name, as it could have been Johnson or Smith, and I would have had very little chance of finding my birth mother. From here, I was told to write to the hospital where I was born. I requested my birth records that would give me my mother's name in 1947. Armed with this information, I spent the next several weeks visiting the Library of Congress, looking up "Oist" in old phone books from many states and in something called the Polk City Directory. At the same time, I was mailing requests for birth and marriage certificates from different counties where she may have lived, coming up with nothing except one letter saying that they did not have time to do "these wild goose chases for family histories." All this time I was feeling that I was breaking the law and doing something I shouldn't. Without the support group, I would never have been able to start.

Two months after my search began, I got my birth mother's marriage license with her married name. Again, in another stroke of luck, she stayed married and never left her hometown. A month later I was in Evanston where my mother Helen and I attended a meeting of Yesterday's Children, and I was given a chance to role-play a script for calling my birth mother. It was important to have Helen there, to hear that I could be safe and protected in this process. As I had feared hurting her, she had feared that I might also be hurt in some way by the truth.

When I actually called my birth mother Betty, she answered all my script questions about the possibility of our being related, and then we began in our improvised ways to get to know each other. I told her of my plan to be in Minnesota, and she invited me to come stay with her. I was taking a shower when she called back, so serendipitously Betty and my mother had a chance to get acquainted. Helen thanked Betty for having me. Their connection helped to make me feel better about my search. Then Helen did a wonderful thing. She gathered together pictures of me growing up and sent the package to Betty. Later Betty said that it was the kind of childhood she wished she could have had for herself.

My support counselor had said, "You'll feel a lot less anxious now." I never realized that indeed I had felt anxious, nor did I realize that getting in touch with my roots would be such a grounding experience.

My adoption reunion story is a roundabout way of talking about heredity versus environment. Who is your real mother? The fact that Betty had also been adopted following the death of her mother made the conundrum even more complex. On the second night of my visit with Betty at her home, I was sitting with her family at the dinner table. Betty and her husband began to argue about politics, evidently a constant issue between them, and my half-brother interrupted to change the subject. I began to laugh; as an uninvolved observer I could see the humor in the situation of their disagreement. I could identify with my brother's desire to try to circumvent a potentially sticky situation, but I became aware that I was outside of it. This was not my family problem. If it had been, I would have been uncomfortable too, but I had been liberated from this entanglement.

My anxiety about being adopted abated, because at last I could put my identity and experiences into a new context in which I not only saw, but actually felt, that the family problems I grew up with were indeed mine, and I belonged to that family and no other.

Relationships with members of my birth family were still scary, because there was very little precedent for how we were supposed to be together. Each relationship is subject to invention. Betty and I still talk, write, and see each other. I've gotten to know siblings, cousins, aunts, and uncles. Each encounter is different but adds another piece to the puzzle of who I am. It was so important for me to find my birth family, but having done so, the information did not turn out to be as crucial as I thought it would be when I was deprived of the opportunity of knowing them.

But when Helen died, there was no doubt in my mind about the depth of my loss. I had lost my mother. When I had needed "my Mommy," Helen was the person I wanted.

I think I have always felt that people should be honored while they are alive rather than wait for the funeral. So I decided to give Helen a retirement party. I know it was a small attempt at telling her how much all of her lifetime of caring for her family was appreciated, but I imagined how this might change the paradigm, perhaps the start of a new Hallmark tradition in people's lives, a well-deserved honor, a new rite of passage for women. What if we all took time to notice and reward a homemaker's career? What if Mom could feel the joy of retiring and society's recognition of the value of her chosen work? What if she could really retire...?

Even into her seventies, Helen still took on the role of protecting and supporting her children. When my brothers came back home to live with her, it seemed as if her work was never done, and she received little recognition. Nobody says at the age of 65 that you stop caring for your family. Mother is always Mother, no matter how old.

On the day of my mother's retirement party, it was a lovely afternoon. I got a special mocha layer cake, decorations, and favors. I invited close friends and family. We dressed up, gave Mom a corsage and presents, regaled her with speeches. We took pictures.

A special event, but bogus, because at the end of the day, Mom had still not retired. Helen did not change her psychological view of herself, and perhaps neither did we. It had been a nice time, but Mom was still Mom, back on the job with only one day's break.

Funerals and memorials, on the other hand, are really for those who are left behind to share their grief, to journey through this terrible rite of passage with community support. But my mother's memorial service felt like a rushed ritual of doing the things we were supposed to do instead of grappling with the unfathomable.

We can only hope that we are able to portray a person accurately in sharing our collective memories at his or her funeral. But my mother died in the District of Columbia, transplanted from her dearly loved hometown of Evanston, Illinois. Nine years before she died, she had a minor heart attack and felt the need to come live near me. We found her an efficiency apartment a block away from my own. My friends reached out to her and extended our family. While she loved Washington on her visits, she was still afraid of big cities. She had moved to be near my older brother, my friends, and me but she was far away from the people that she had known for a lifetime and who truly knew her in all phases of her life. The people who attended her funeral came to support my immediate family in our grief, but the magic of remembering her or conjuring up her spirit was not there.

Because my mother led such a quietly suffered, painful life while sacrificing so much for her family, I sometimes courted her like a lover, to try to make amends for the things that no one could ever really fix—her mother's alcoholism, the loss of her parents when she was a teenager, the Depression, the loss of her first baby and a lifetime of physical problems that ensued, my father's unemployment at age 50 and the loss of her home, the loss of all of her teeth by age 50, the loss of her husband when she was 60, a mugging that left her bruised on the whole left side of her body, and emphysema, which drained her of energy and left her vulnerable to a heart condition.

Irrationally, after her death I identified only with her pain. I carried with me a dark emotional burden for months. I passionately wanted to rewrite her story with a better ending.

It seemed to me that she had no resilience to face life's catastrophes. After my father died, she fell apart and was not able to realize her strength. Yet she always adhered to her own moral code. She never questioned or shirked her responsibilities toward her family or the community. As much as I didn't like it, she always worried about me. Whenever I left her on one of our dinner visits, she would ask, "Will you be safe?"

I realize as I write this, that there was never a day when I doubted my mother's unconditional love for me or my love for her. I did not feel that she always understood me, as I traveled a different path from her conventionality. I did not marry and raise children. I was always aware that I deprived her of grandchildren, to validate her belief in family. I was trying to protect my identity from being defined by other's expectations. I had an irrational fear of immersing myself as my mother had done in rearing children, something I rejected as "suburban housewife syndrome."

We developed a truce, my mother and I, not to speak of the things that might tarnish our relationship. Within these limits we did not rock the boat. We kept it steady through all of our years together. But there were limits. And my mother obeyed the rules. She was needy after my father died. But she waited by the phone for others to call: she rarely initiated conversations. Whatever fell into her lap she accepted. She was afraid of expressing herself and taking risks.

Having since studied art therapy, I know a bit more about Adult Children of Alcoholics. They do everything they can to be seen as normal. They cover up and hide their pain. In this regard my mother was typical. My mother and father were both inordinately concerned with appearances. Therapy—asking for help, divulging secrets outside of the home—was not considered an option.

At a size six, my mother was worried about looking fat. Until the end of her life, she seemed to pick at her food. Now I see that she probably had an eating disorder, her metaphor for trying to control the only thing she could in an insecure, threatening world. A constant phrase used by my mother to remind me to control my tummy, "Hold it in," could easily be used to describe her mental state.

Mom was always worried about me; she wanted me to be secure. She expected me to fear the same things as she did—the big city, crime, travel, not getting married, and all of the risks of growing up and becoming independent. I have spent my life trying to deal with them, to set myself free from her constricting, irrational anxiety. Yet in spite of all of her fears, my mother could be as fierce as a lioness in her desire to protect her children. As long as she lived, she was the fulcrum of our relationships, and she tried her best to support us.

I was the adult child of an adult child of an alcoholic. When you grow up in a dysfunctional family, you may not even be aware of it, because this is the only "normal" you know. When I became an adolescent, I began to intuit the cracks and feel a kind of oppression that made me forever want to be independent, to leave the confines of my parent's inhibited lifestyle.

Dealing with these issues of alcoholism and how they have seeped down through the generations of my family has informed the rest of my life. In 1988, just before my mother's death, I met Harold Moss, an artist and activist for the homeless, who was recruiting donations of artwork for a newly renovated shelter in downtown Washington. Harold often said, "Art Saves Lives." As I looked at Harold's beautiful oil landscapes in his quarters at the shelter, I realized that I could write a grant to develop an arts workshop there. It was a serendipitous fluke that after I received the grant from the DC Commission on the Arts & Humanities, I was welcomed with open arms to work with the shelter's new residential drug and alcohol treatment program. I could be objective and helpful on a different playing field and perhaps turn a negative experience into a positive one. I couldn't solve my mother's problems, but now I had the chance to facilitate the healing of others in similar situations.

I am still trying to make peace with the things that I can't control. Working with the art program at Clean and Sober Streets has given me continuous joy and some remarkable encounters. I could not heal my mother. I can never heal my mother. Her story has been written. And I know that if she were still alive today, she would still worry about my path: "Are you safe?"

The only person I can really heal is myself.

Helen's Waltz refers to a lyrical, lamenting, musical interlude that I composed and dedicated to the memory of my mother.

Ruth Stenstrom *works in Washington, DC, as a multi-media artist, writer, and art therapist and has directed the CASSA Arts Workshop since 1989. She chaired the Art Department at School Without Walls, co-founded the Local 1734 Gallery, hosted "Critique" arts show on WGTB-FM, and collaborated internationally with installations/performance artists for the Terra Nova Project, Chaos, Rimbaud, and Café Noir.*

Helen Rowles Hansen

Photo taken around 1942 of Mary, Martha, Mother, and me

"You Better Get the Box Ready, Paul"

by Paul A. Hansen

When my mother spoke these cryptic words, I naively responded, "What box, Mother?"

She replied, "The box to take me home in."

Then I knew. It was time to say goodbye!

By November of 1979, at age 84 and 9 months, my mother had been living for many years with the effects of Type II Diabetes. She was partially (and legally) blind, with serious peripheral artery disease and claudication, and a steadily weakening heart. After Mother had been in the hospital for three weeks, my younger sister Martha called and said, "If you want to see Mother again, you'd better come." (For some reason, we usually called her "Mother" rather than the more informal "Mom.") I made hurried plans to fly from Denver and link up with my older sister, Mary, at the Kansas City airport, where we rented a car to drive to Sedalia, Missouri, where Martha lived. She had brought Mother there from the hospital in our hometown of Wamego, Kansas, 200 miles away, to make it easier for her to be with Mother.

Mother was asleep when we walked into her hospital room. I was shocked at how much older she looked. Her face appeared quite pale and thin instead of its former round shape. Her hair, now almost white, lay loose and brushed back on the pillow, rather than being up in a roll the way her beauty shop had always done it for her. That was one luxury she allowed herself, though I'm sure she considered it a necessity. I never in my entire lifetime saw Mother "do" her own hair. When I said, "Hello, Mother," she woke and seemed surprised that Mary and I had come.

We found Mother very frail, uninterested in food, and sleeping most of the time. During the next few days, we tried to encourage her to eat. She stubbornly, and I might add successfully, resisted most of our efforts. When I attempted to spoon-feed her, she would turn her head at the last moment, much as my children used to do in their high chair, with the food ending up on their cheeks or on the floor. I didn't know whether to laugh, cry, or just feel frustrated. Two or three days had passed when Mother made her cryptic statement about the "box." Now, nearly thirty years later, I don't remember exactly what I said next, but somehow I acknowledged her being ready and that I was okay with her letting go.

Now a man of 71, I am third of four children raised on a farm near the small town of Wamego, in eastern Kansas. Many memories of Mother return as I write. I see her in our old '41 Ford, driving us to 4-H meetings held in a one-room country schoolhouse lit with hanging Coleman gas lamps (not the camp-style ones, but the old ones with long glass chimneys) and to the county fair with our 4-H projects. Most of the year she did our laundry on our open back porch in an old Maytag wringer washer, with two tubs of water for rinsing. During World War II, she put up with four young kids clamoring to plant a victory garden, loudly insisting that the rows be laid out in the impractical shape of a "V," as we'd seen in a magazine. Funny how sixty years blur the painful memories and let the happy ones shine.

During that week at the hospital in 1979, I passed my own 43rd birthday. At the time I was self-employed as a management consultant based in Colorado, with three teenagers of my own. A previous 12-year career as a Methodist minister had brought me face to face with death. I had conducted almost 400 funerals in Wisconsin and Kansas and counseled as many families in their grief process. My father had died 18 years earlier of a heart attack, and now I needed to say goodbye to my mother. I knew I would miss her.

To continue the story, after nearly a week, with Mother getting neither much worse nor any better, Mary and I both decided we needed to return home to our jobs. Mother had already been in and out of V-Tac (Ventricular Tachycardia) several times, skirting the brink of death. Together, my sisters and I instructed the doctor to note on her chart, "No Code Blue," meaning no heroic attempts to resuscitate. The morning of the day we left, November 15th, Mother rallied enough to say, "Children, let me go!"

With tears in her eyes, Mary said, "I just can't let you go, Momma."

In the hall, outside her room, I said, "Mary, it's important to let her know that it is okay with you. She can't let go and die until you do." I seem to remember that Mary finally did get the words out shortly before we left for the Kansas City airport to fly back to our respective homes in Colorado and Atlanta. It was no surprise that neither of us had been home more than an hour when our younger sister called to say that Mother had died a peaceful death that evening. She told how Mother took four deep breaths, then just stopped breathing, and how she had remained sitting quietly with Mother for some time before pushing the nurse call button. When the nurse arrived and asked if there was a Code Blue, Martha said, "No."

At last the time had come for all four of us to convene in our hometown for Mother's funeral. At the funeral home, I remember being surprised at how pretty she looked in her casket. Though I helped plan the funeral service in the Methodist Church, I did not conduct it. After the service, we were warmed by greetings and comments from the many, many people whose lives she had touched.

Almost invariably I've noticed when families come together for a funeral, they share memories, both before and after the service. "Remember when..." is the prelude to launching into a story. I've watched those stories help families heal, with laughter as much a part of the scene as tears. But not all of our memories of our mothers are positive. For some, the memories may even be bitterly negative and painful. Mothers are not always paragons of virtue, love, and kindness. When that is the case, saying goodbye emotionally becomes all the more important, whether it is done before the actual death or after. Otherwise, that relationship can haunt us with leftover behaviors or cause continuing pain for years. I am no exception.

When we were children back on the farm, we cooked on a 4-chimney, New Perfection "coal-oil" (kerosene) stove, or on the old wood-burning black cast-iron cook stove, both more complex and yet at the same time simpler to manage. With those old habits firmly ingrained, in her later years, Mother frequently forgot to turn down or turn off her new-fangled electric stove and at those times burned food. My wife says that probably I still carry leftovers when I re-enact with her my old habit of checking to see if my mother had turned off the electric stove.

I feel fortunate to have had so many experiences in my life that give me a rich point of view about death, dying, and saying goodbye. Not only did I have those years as a pastor, but after my mother's death, I engaged in a long career as a psychotherapist-counselor, often assisting people with unfinished grief. As a meaningful part of my practice with some clients, I used Past Life Therapy, a mode of psychotherapy in which the client returns to one or more previous lives to help sort out current life issues or problems. Sometimes we bring baggage from previous lives, as well as from our childhoods in this current life. Many clients found it enormously helpful. Thus, I have had the opportunity as a therapist to "witness" literally thousands of deaths, some placid, like dying in sleep, and some traumatic, such as dying in battle as a Roman soldier, dying in the A-bomb blast at Nagasaki in 1945, or suffering and perishing at the Auschwitz death camp in World War II. No matter the circumstances, I always guided my clients through each lifetime's death, to bring completion and closure to whatever was occurring and, most important, to give them an opportunity to say goodbye to that life, to that body that was as dear to them then as ours are to us now. This process helped them to truly leave behind their "baggage" and freed them to live more fully in the here and now.

The soul experiences of my clients after their deaths inspired them and me as well. Almost without exception, when they lifted from their bodies, they expressed surprise at seeing "The Light." Some reported going through a tunnel on their way to the light. Most equated this light with God, and many said that it was so bright that, were they seeing it with their human eyes, they would be made instantly blind. In addition, on looking deeper into that light, most related seeing either a spiritual figure, such as Jesus or Buddha, or some loved one who had already passed, such as a parent, grandparent, or other family member. In this latter case, they usually found these figures reaching out to them. Their response was commonly a joyous, eager desire to go to those welcoming arms. They also recounted how, when they entered The Light, they felt the most intense love that they could ever imagine. Now they knew: God loved them, and they could love and accept themselves in a whole new way.

By the time of my mother's death, I already had made many explorations into my own past lives. That and going through such sessions with hundreds of clients profoundly altered my own outlook on death and dying. My faith and former work as a pastor was increasingly enriched by years of doing such therapy. Though I'd always believed in life after death, now I had a much richer context for that faith, grounded and informed by a large number of personal experiences.

My belief about life after death has continued to inform the process of my saying goodbye to my mother. It leaves me peacefully confident that our soul consciousness continues after the death of the body. Having observed how groups of souls tend to work together over many lifetimes, much like a resident theater group, with each soul taking many different roles and relationships, leads me to believe that I probably have lived with the soul of my mother before and likely will again, though our roles and even genders may be very different from those in this lifetime.

My mother knew she was dying when she told me to "get the box ready," yet I and my sisters were reluctant to talk with her about dying. How I wish now that I had taken time to share more memories and "remember whens" with my mother before she died. I also wish that I had shared with her my "I appreciates" and perhaps invited her to do the same. Any "I forgives" would surely have been heard and accepted, and perhaps I might have asked forgiveness for any of my own behaviors that were not always the best. Saying goodbye to Mother for the last time in this fuller way could have been an even greater gift—to her and to myself.

A retired psychotherapist and former Methodist minister, **Paul Hansen** *now writes novels full time. Raised on a farm near Wamego, Kansas, with a brother and two sisters, currently he lives near Longmont, Colorado, in a passive solar home he designed and built with his wife, Mimi. Paul enjoys creating video shows of their travels and flying his homebuilt GlaStar airplane.*

Isobel Goodall Henderson Roberts

Isobel and Debbie, summer 1960

Isobel

by Deborah Henderson Roberts

Even when my mother was still alive, I would sometimes close my eyes and envision my brother and me walking down the aisle of St. Mark's Episcopal Church for her funeral. I suppose I hoped that this practice would prepare me for losing the woman who had nurtured me for over 47 years. After my dad's death in 2001, I felt as if I knew what would happen next. I had a dress rehearsal, so to speak.

Perhaps it was her dedication to the task of nurturing me that made me feel obligated to my mother, whose life was now totally in my hands after she suffered stroke-induced dementia at the age of 74. Or maybe it was because I had been adopted by this strong Scottish woman and her husband when I was three months old. My younger brother and I knew that we were loved, even though we were not a demonstrative family; perhaps it was this love that motivated me. Regardless of the reason, I watched helplessly as she seemed to change overnight from the independent woman who had taken care of me to a vulnerable soul who herself now needed looking after. I dragged her from doctor to doctor trying to find a cure for her. Eventually, I came to realize that I feared if I could not restore her to health, I would be letting her and myself down. And I had already let my parents down by not meeting their expectations. I did not have the marriage and the children that would have seemed to signify the happy, normal life they had wished for me.

As the years passed, I had to face the fact that I was not able to interrupt my mother's decline. Although I had been warned that the hardest part of dealing with the loss of a parent was that I would have to face my own mortality, for me it was more the necessity of facing my own flawed humanity. Nevertheless, I had such a sense of duty and responsibility that I made taking care of my parents my life's work. Doing so contributed to the failure of an eight-year-long relationship and compromised my performance at work. But it also made me acknowledge that I could not go on without the help of others, an important realization for me. I simply could not do it all.

On Mother's Day in 2007, when Mom was 82, I began to notice a change in her. As she was trying to go upstairs to get ready to go out for lunch, she was extremely tired, and I could hear fluid as she breathed. I called the doctor the next day, and soon she was diagnosed with congestive heart failure. Over the next few months, I watched Mother's health decline and waited anxiously for the inevitable.

One Wednesday in August 2007, as I was going out the door on my way to work, my mother, who was sitting in the den, stopped me and said, "Remember, I love you very much, dear." I could only think, "This cannot be a good sign." Sure enough, two hours later I received a call from her caregiver. Mother had been in the shower and had what we believe to be a massive coronary. Her caregiver managed to get her downstairs and into the chair where she spent most of her time.

Knowing that Mother wanted to stay at home rather than go to the hospital, I notified the doctor who in turn contacted Hospice. Within hours, we had a Hospice intake worker, hospital bed, commode, and walker. The doctor explained that we would immediately start morphine, which would be monitored with the help of Hospice. The morphine would slow down her heart and eventually stop it. It would also lessen the pain and encourage her body to sleep the time away.

While Mother had caregivers with her during the day, I was alone with her at night. I used the time to prepare things we would need for the funeral. I was frightened that she would pass while I was the only one with her. I could feel her slipping away. It was so lonely. But I was expecting more from the Hospice staff than was realistic. I thought as Mother worsened that they would come in and take over. The social worker explained that it wouldn't be that way. They would be present and monitor the situation until the end, but basically the care and decision-making were up to me.

I asked Mother if she knew what was happening and how she wanted to proceed. She said that she was fine and very happy. When I explained her options, she stated that she did not want to go to the hospital. I assured her that Hospice would assist me in keeping her at home. She looked up at me with her broad smile, studied me as I hovered above her, swallowed hard, closed her eyes, and said, "Dolly, the only thing that I am worried about is you and leaving you alone." I reassured her that I would be fine, but I could not imagine life without her.

One day about a week later, while Mom was feeling better, I knew that I had to go and make funeral arrangements. I asked my friend David, an Episcopal priest and one of the clergy who would be officiating at Mom's service, to go with me to the funeral home. I had hoped that focusing on the task at hand would keep me from feeling like a grieving child, but I broke down as I tried to explain my mother's wishes to the mortician.

Perhaps embarrassed by my display of emotion, the funeral director embarked on small talk; he lamented how much churches had changed—even letting those gay people in. He went on to tell us that he had not moved his business out of the city when all those Latinos had moved into the urban environment where his home was located. Without knowing it, he was waving a red flag in front of me—I was a private, 48-year-old lesbian with a Latina partner. Why could I not simply be a grieving daughter without a distraction like this? Out of reverence and respect for my mother, I did not want to be sidetracked from my purpose, but within five minutes, this insensitive person had incited me.

Gathering my composure, I returned home to be a loving daughter to my mother, who greeted me with a tired smile as I approached her. She had insisted on remaining in her reclining chair in the family room, where she had spent the past five years sleeping or watching life go by. Between the osteoporosis and the loneliness she felt in the bedroom she had shared with my father for 53 years, she could not lie down again painlessly in this lifetime.

I decided to sleep in the hospital bed where I could be nearby if my mother needed me. One night, I awoke startled. Someone had pushed me. I felt a presence, and it felt okay. I woke up to Mom's coughing, so I adjusted her oxygen, and off she went to sleep again. I was puzzled by the push I had felt on my side closest to the fireplace. The next morning, I received my answer. My mother stated that she didn't know who all the people were over by the fireplace, but she liked them—a lot, she added. I assume to this day that it was family members already passed who had come to welcome her. I knew it was more than the medications talking. When I spoke to the nurse about it, she said, "That's a comment I hear a lot." I imagined all of these passed family members descending into our home, down the chimney like Santa Claus.

I puttered around the house, all the while staying within close proximity of my mother. The sound of the recliner rocking on the hard wood surface came to an abrupt stop. My mother looked at me with a dim smile but with a certain strength that I had known she possessed all of my life. "You are going to be fine, Dolly," she said. "I, too, am going to be fine. God is with us now." She went back to the labored rest that I was becoming accustomed to.

My new partner of two years, Nilda, who lived an hour and a half plane ride away, came in on weekends as she could. Mom would fade in and out, from sleep to wakefulness, for the next two weeks. One afternoon after the doctor had visited, my mother seemed particularly agitated, so much so that she screamed at me. She seemed delusional. She said that she was not going back to the hospital and to get away from her. In my head, I knew that this was not my mother's normal behavior. In my heart, I was saddened. All of her vitals had spiked. She was heading for a stroke.

The next morning as dawn was beginning to break, Mom tried to get up from the chair. It was at this point I realized that she had a stroke of major proportions. I sat her back into the chair and called for help. One of Mom's caregivers lived nearby. She quickly came to the house to help me get Mom into the hospital bed.

Isobel

We called Hospice and everyone else we could think of to notify them of Mom's impending death. I knew it was the end. I was glad that between the time she had the heart attack and the stroke, a period of two weeks, she had been able to go out to dinner and had seemingly done everything she had wanted to do.

Mom's caregivers arrived one by one to help. Mom would go in and out of sleep and had stopped eating. Hospice came in and inserted a catheter, while I waited outside. The women who had worked for our family for years came by to pay their respects, and my friend David gave her the last rites. I called for Nilda; she took an evening flight in. My job here with my mother was quickly drawing to an end.

For the past couple of years, I had been reliant on the baby monitor that I kept close to my bed; I took comfort in hearing her breathing, as a mother does an infant. Now I found it a handy tool for listening in whenever I left the room. As we were taking a break, organizing Mother's things for the funeral parlor, I could hear her caregivers, Dawn and Debbie, singing to her downstairs while they were attending to her. Mom all of a sudden blurted out to one of the caregivers, "I see you skating with that fellow and winning medals. Don't deny it." Dawn was dumbfounded. She had never told my mother that she had skated professionally.

Mother amazed me even more after Nilda arrived. She had remained stoic when Nilda had visited in the past. We had noticed Mother's unwillingness to embrace her and, by extension, my relationship with her. That Friday evening, even though she could not look at me, she asked for a hug. As each of us embraced her, she stretched for a hug from Nilda—and also gave her a kiss. At last she had accepted my partner into our family.

The hours and days had dragged on, and we were now past the weekend. Mom had not been coherent in a couple of days. We had basically kept a vigil around the clock but had found that Mom seemed to be lingering. The nurse suggested that perhaps she had a peace to make, that she was waiting for someone, or simply that she needed time alone. That night Nilda, Dawn, and I played a board game in the next room. Every once in a while, Dawn would listen for her breathing and noticed that it was getting quieter. She passed at midnight. The baby monitor that I had relied upon became silent.

Isobel died on September 11, 2007, at 12:00 a.m., nine days before my 48th birthday. She passed with the same dignity and love that she had been given and had given. The overgrown garden, which had once been my mother's pride and joy, tended by her loving hands, boasted a lone blooming rose this warm September's day—a worthy tribute to this kind, gentle, and strong Scottish woman, born the month of June some 82 years ago.

Unprepared was I for the loneliness that I would now experience. Having had the loving support and guidance of my parents for all these years, I now felt that my training wheels had been taken off my bicycle. Even though physically my mother is no longer on this plane, I know she is still guiding and loving me from an astral perspective. My mother is now part of my spiritual guide force, and if I listen closely enough, I can hear her and my father instructing, guiding, laughing, and praising me, just as they have always done.

Deborah Henderson Roberts *is a freelance writer and Reiki Master. She is the author of two stories in the* Chicken Soup for the Soul *series: "The Middle Rock" in* Think Positive for Kids *and "The Shoplifter" in* The Dog Did What? *She is married and resides in Florida.*

Isobelle Robertson Aitkenhead Beaujon

Mom with me and my brother Chuck, 1943

Mom and I on the Delta Queen celebrating her 80th birthday, 1994

Heron Rising

by Janet Beaujon Couch

When my mother died, I began to feel a deep sense of loneliness. In my youth and early adulthood, with different styles, ideas, opinions, and political views, we were often at odds with each other. Although I had unmet needs as a child, I know that my mother gave me all she had to give, that she did the best she could. And I knew that I was loved. Over time and with good therapy, I was able to accept her offerings and find a healing path that led both of us back toward each other. As I reflect on the end of her life, I feel blessed that our differences were really not as great as I had thought when I was younger. We spent our last years together sharing memories and comical stories of her youth in Scotland. We began to support each other through our own cancer diagnoses and treatments, and we were able to laugh and cry together and share the joy of the births of my own grandchildren.

My mother died after a long struggle with cancer and congestive heart failure. When her health deteriorated, she and I discussed her prognosis, funeral, and even what she wanted in her obituary. These conversations were difficult, so I fell into my comfortable clinical role as a Hospice therapist. While my mother grappled with leaving her apartment and giving away her possessions, my family looked to me to explain to them the dying process and to talk to Mom about their concerns, their needs, their grief. I found myself often slipping into my professional role and out of that of a daughter, sister, mother, grandmother. More often than not, I chose the therapist's role as a way of defending myself against my overwhelming grief as I watched her dramatic physical changes, and as a way to sooth Mom as her anxiety and loss of control devastated her.

Mom lived at a retirement home where I had once been on the staff. She was there for thirteen years and during that time made dear friends who became family to us all. Since many on the medical team were friends and former colleagues as well, I experienced a feeling of coming home when visiting Mom. Three months before she died, I received a call from one of my friends on the medical staff who knew how difficult it was for me to be far away as my mother's health deteriorated. She suggested that if my mother agreed, we could move her to my home; she estimated, however, that the move would have to be made within about two weeks, as Mom's strength was dwindling quickly. We discussed the pros and cons of this with Mom, and told her that we wanted her to be with us, not to die alone. When she decided to move, my husband Dick and I raced around buying flannel sheets, arranging for medical services, and re-organizing our dining room into a bedroom. A week later I received a call from Mom saying she had decided to stay where she was. It was too cold in Michigan and she really did not want to leave her friends or change her medical staff. She knew we could not visit often but still wanted to stay in Virginia. I was shocked, angry, relieved, and sad, and I wanted to strangle her friends who had influenced her decision to stay put. Finally, in this mixture of conflicting emotions, sadness won out.

To be separated from my mother by a thousand miles was the hardest part of dealing with the end of her life. I accepted her decision to stay where she was, but the choice affected our time together, and I resented having to schedule trips when I could have been with her every day in my home. I also felt guilty that I wasn't with her more often. My son Andrew accepted the responsibility of helping the most because he lived the closest. It relieved all of us when Hospice was brought in. Then our whole family planned our visits to provide a continuous flow of company.

I remember in the movie *Shall We Dance?* a character saying, "We need a witness to our lives—so we won't go unnoticed." This line stayed in my mind as we, her children and grandchildren, took turns traveling to Virginia, staying as long as we could, to be witnesses to my mother's remaining life so that she would be accompanied, feel valued and noticed, until she was ready to leave, close the door, and move on into my father's arms. Perhaps we only give this attention to our family when time is running out, but it became an important part of all of our grieving, this honoring of her, giving her the time she had often craved when we were busy living our lives so far away from her.

One of the most difficult things I had to deal with was my mother's changed appearance. She was withering before my eyes. But when I saw her take out her teeth for the first time, I was shocked. She did not even look like my mother! I made an excuse to leave for a bit and called my brother Dave who had been her last visitor. He too had seen this alteration when Mom's teeth came out and had the same reaction. We both found this transformation harder to accept than all the others. I began to ponder this issue of appearance and how tied that is to our perceptions of people's personae. I thought of how my mother looked as my young Mom, her clothes, hair styles, shoes, as well as her love of and training in fashion design at the Pratt Institute. And here she was with no teeth. These changes had begun years before, of course, when her vision dimmed, when her hands, that once modeled lotions and jewelry in New York advertisements in the 1930s, became disfigured with arthritis, and when her feet became unable to wear her vast collection of shoes. Throughout my life, she had seemed to offer continual critiques of my dress and hairstyle, which ended only when her eyesight failed!

Mom had many dreams and then visions of my Dad being in the room with her. She spoke about being together again and chuckled as she told me they would have their first dance in a long time. She awoke one day and spoke about dancing to the Native drums all night. I have worked with Native Americans for years, and although she was fascinated by the Teachings I shared with her, her dreams of dancing and later of stringing beads interested her still more, and she insisted the experiences were real.

Mom spoke about how she and Dad loved bird-watching and how one of their favorites was the great blue heron. As she became more fragile, unable to move at all, Mom would speak of watching herons and of how she envied their grace and ease of movement. Then she would return to reminiscing about dancing and how much she missed the flow and movement of her once-supple body.

When Mom began to move resolutely toward her death, she drifted in and out of dreaming, waking, smiling at me, and attempting to tell me about what she had seen, but words often failed her. And then all of a sudden she would become alert, almost as if she had returned for a minute, to relate a vivid dream, and then rest again. She would talk to Dad, to her old friend Annie, or to others whom I couldn't see, and drift off, looking peaceful. Once she asked who had come in, and I said that I didn't know, did she? She replied, "Santa Claus," and we laughed together. One dream was particularly striking, as she described herself in a shop, trying on a pink suit. It was too tight, and she struggled to get out of it. When she called me to help her, the shopkeeper told her that she didn't need the suit anymore. As we discussed this dream, I found myself uncomfortable with the idea that the pink suit represented her skin that was now too tight to wear much longer. She did, nonetheless, seem to shrink inside her skin every day.

As I watched her sleep, I was struck at the role reversal. I thought about how often she had watched me sleep and wondered if she was flooded with as much love as I felt when I watched my own children sleep and as I felt now for my mother as she approached her long sleep. She would wake and call to me, asking me to stay. I reassured her, settled back in the chair to watch, and continued with my quilting to calm my soul and shaking heart.

I had made this quilt for my mother, pieced with cardinals, the state bird of Virginia, her adopted home. When her health changed dramatically in June, my son Andrew was with her. He called, and I rushed to her bedside along with my brothers Chuck and Dave. I brought the quilt to work on as we waited for her life to ebb. We shared a day and night of sitting by her bed, reminiscing, watching with love and fear for her journey to be over. Mom would wake for a bit and then drift off again, and we simply waited and watched. Perhaps our presence helped, since she began to improve for a while. I continued to bring the quilt with me and worked on it whenever I was with her. It helped me to stay connected, grounded, and present, as I sat witnessing the fading of her energy. Although I had often been with dying patients and had witnessed many deaths, I felt afraid of this one. I struggled with the fear and parting and was not ready to let my mother go. It was strange to be caught in this way, and it threw me firmly into the daughter role for good. Every tiny stitch represented a memory, an hour, a minute more that I had a mother.

The quilt became a bridge that helped me to reach across the chasm between her waning life and impending death. Humor has been my family's main defense, and before Mom was close to death, she would occasionally joke with me about the quilt, saying, "Well, I'm lucking out with that one." She would not say that she would never receive it, that she was dying, and I was unable to say those words either. That's when we could have used a different therapist with us! She was always cold and I covered her with other quilts I had made for her, thinking that the last flannel one was really a shroud. I quilted as we talked, visited with her friends, helped shift her to a more comfortable position. I gave her Reiki, as touch had become painful for her, ran errands, listened to her halting words, and wrote in my journal. My son Ben visited her not long after and spent his watching time drawing his Nani. These contour drawings are poignant, beautiful, and incredibly difficult to see, as he almost caught her spirit in flight, leaving the shell of her life behind.

During my last visit I continued to quilt, to help Mom in any way she needed, but she was already distant, moving away too quickly. There was little talking, but she knew that I was there, and when she woke, she seemed comforted by my presence. The center of the quilt was done, a circular shape formed as I stitched and watched her transition; I was full of memories, sadness, joys, laughter filled with tears, as the circle of her life ended. The day I left she rallied briefly, and talked about coming to visit us in Michigan, saying, "I think we [she, Dick, and I] make a nice circle together." I agreed, and as we chatted, relishing this unexpected return of her energy, the nurse came in to help take her to the beauty parlor! I was dumbstruck and protested that the time before my flight was short, but Mom went gaily off, smiling and oblivious to my confused emotions. I knew that she would feel better with clean hair, but I railed at the interruption. I waited until she was done and watched as she returned looking happy, but extremely fragile, saying how well she felt. It seemed so incongruous that these precious last moments I had planned she spent in the beauty parlor. She was quite alert, though her energy began to fade as we talked for a while about her plan to visit us; then we said goodbye, kissed, expressed love for each other, and I turned and left. It felt unreal, like a dream. I was numb and tired and didn't cry. I returned my rental car, got on the airport shuttle, and sat there struggling with my emotions when a man got on, swung his bag onto the rack, and hit me in the head! He apologized, and I could not respond. Somehow I held on until I got off and ran to the bathroom, called my husband, and cried.

The night before Mom's death, I called her Hospice nurse Cindy, as I did each morning and evening. She told me that the end was near. Mom had stopped eating and her skin, that tight pink suit, was breaking down. I hadn't spoken to my mother in over a week, talking only to one of my friends, the Hospice Nurse who sat by her side, and I longed to hear Mom's voice again. I hung up, walked out to the herb garden, and stood in the center of the Sun Wheel. I lay down tobacco as an offering and thanksgiving for her life and then burned white sage in the center. I spoke to Mom's tired Spirit, letting her know that I was with her and that she could leave, follow the smoke, let go, and move on....

I slept fitfully as I waited for THE call, and the next morning Cindy phoned to tell me that the time was near. Mom wore her death mask and was wrapped in the flannel quilt I had made her. Visualizing her in the quilt, I began to cry as Cindy told me that my Mom was wrapped in my love and knew that I was there with her. I was comforted to know that she was not alone but was racked with sadness, anger, and guilt that I wasn't there. I had helped so many others die, had made this same call to several families, and wasn't there for my own mother. I didn't know what to do, so I called my brothers and children, and went to work. I cancelled my clients and was filling out a leave slip when the call came just after 11:00 a.m. She was gone, just short of her 90th birthday. I fell apart, gathered my things, left, and went home to make the calls.

It was fitting then, that two days later as promised, Mom came to visit us as a heron. Dick and I were driving along a road on Sugar Island, where we have a cabin. A heron stood in the middle of the road and did not move. We stopped the car, and we three sat and looked at one another for at least five minutes. She walked toward us, kept eye contact, then moved slowly to the side of the road and rose into the sky. It was 11:00 a.m. Dick and I looked at each other and knew that Mom had come to say goodbye. I thought of Mary Oliver's poem, "Heron Rises from the Dark, Summer Pond." We watched the heron rise into the air, and I was struck by the presence of this bird and how its move toward flight reflected the journey my mother had just made, as she shed her frail frame and moved gracefully, rising slowly from the months of pain. We watched the heron rise further and further until she was almost out of sight; I was reminded of Mary Oliver's words: "into a new life...toward the wind; see how the clasp of nothing/ takes her in."

As I planned the funeral, I chose Scottish hymns and songs, hired a piper and a dear friend to sing Scottish Aires. My grandfather had played the bagpipes, and those haunting sounds reminded her of home and her father. Mom had chosen to be cremated so the funeral was held two weeks after her death to allow family and friends to arrive. I spent time gathering photographs, covered large boards with tartan fabric, and made a collage of her life. These were displayed at the reception after the funeral. This process became a balm for my sadness and grief as I sorted and chose pictures, seeing her life's transitions and changes.

The morning of the funeral, I arranged my mother's favorite Asian lilies and heather for the altar. Mom's grandsons and granddaughter read the scriptures and Mary Oliver's poem. I had illustrated the poem with a heron and inserted a copy into each memorial bulletin. I knew that Mom would have been pleased with the service when all of her children, grandchildren, nephews, and four (and a half) of her great-grandchildren entered as the pipes played. I walked in, holding my granddaughter Isabelle's hand, and when we sat down, I felt comforted by her presence on my lap as it linked me to both four-year-old Isabelle and my mother Isobelle.

We chose to follow the Native American tradition of a ceremony to honor her life again one year later. We gathered in our hometown of Canaan, Connecticut, to lay Mom's ashes by the headstone for her and my father. We read poems, reminisced, and sang, "I'll Fly Away." We dug a small area, deposited the ashes, and burned sage to honor Mom's journey. Tobacco was passed for each of us to send prayers and say goodbye, and each placed our tobacco onto the burning sage. My brothers and I covered it up and laid down wild flowers.

I finished the quilt and it comforts us on snowy nights. About a year after my mother died, I made a companion wall piece with some of my favorite photographs of Mom (her engagement photo, two from her young motherhood, and finally one taken two years before she died). I printed them on cotton cloth and pieced them to fabrics from her quilt. I added lace from Mom's sewing box, embroidered starbursts all around, and added tiny French knots reminiscent of her wedding veil. The process was quiet and introspective; every stitch became another goodbye, a final tribute to the years we traveled together. Both were displayed in a quilt show. The other quilts I made were passed to family, but I kept the flannel one that circled Mom's shoulders as she died. I wrap it around myself when I miss her the most.

I look down as I type and see my mother's hands. It has taken me time to accept my own changes in dexterity, these awkward arthritic joints. I remember comforting my mother when she was unable to button or snap her clothes, telling her that who she was was more important than what she could not do anymore. My daughter Keri always accepted her Nani's hands, loving them as part of her. And the circle of life revolves, as Keri accepts, consoles, and soothes my own self-consciousness. So my mother's and my own hands continue to move toward each other in shape and memory, as I reflect upon those last months.

The heron continues to visit. I feel blessed when this happens and know it is my mother. She appears in my dreams, and when she comes into my thoughts, I am grateful for her presence. I don't run to the phone to tell her something as often anymore, but when that occurs, waves of grief wash over me again. Last summer I sat outside at the cabin and painted a heron on a piece of driftwood. As I painted, a bald eagle flew ten feet in front of me, and I felt both the image and experience were blessed by my own Spirit helper. The heron painting now greets us as we drive into our cabin on Sugar Island, where my mother made her first visit to us, to let us know that she had shed her heavy body and moved into the light.

"In Memory of Mom, 1914–2004," mixed media, 13 x 15½ inches

Janet Beaujon Couch *is an artist and art therapist. Her love of the arts was nurtured by her mother who created marionettes and performed classic ballets and fairy tales. Janet's painting, hand spinning, and rug hooking are inspired by her home in Michigan's Upper Peninsula, where she lives with her husband, dog, and angora rabbits.*

Juanita Smith Price

My Family in 1951

Nita at Orkney Springs, Virginia, in July 1998

Nita's Last Week on Earth

by Paula Rose

How remarkable that I asked Mom to go to Orkney Springs with me! The year before, I didn't ask her to go, and she was not happy. She had never been there. Orkney Springs, in the mountains of Virginia, is where I go for my annual painting retreat, a graduate-level art course offered by James Madison University. It's my time that I have every year.

I knew I had to start preparing her for my trip. When I asked her if she had thought about what she'd like to do when I went to Orkney Springs, she said she was thinking of visiting her sister, the one with Alzheimer's. She looked so sad. I thought, "You know, she really needs to have a vacation." I decided to ask her if she wanted to come with me. And then, as soon as I asked her, she was so happy. She started planning what she was going to wear, wondering whether she needed to buy new clothes, packing her suitcase, calling people to tell them that she was going. And I, of course, thought, "What have I done? Will she be sick up there? There's no air conditioning; will she be able to breathe? Will it be this huge drain on my creativity? Will I be able to paint?"

Then I thought, "Well, I'm just not going to worry about it." The plan was for Mom to drive with our friend Joan Limbrick. Mom liked Joan a lot. I was to take the art supplies in my van. We left on that Monday, July 6th, I think it was. And we made this little caravan. I was in the lead, then Joan and Mom, and Helen Butler in the rear. We stopped at Knakal's Bakery in Culpeper to get doughnuts and coffee for breakfast. Mom chose three pastries. I said to her, "Are you getting THREE?" She said, "I might want something later."

When we got to Orkney Springs, the weather was a bit warm, but it wasn't real humid. Right away Mom settled into things. When I went to find out where her room was, I discovered that she was in 101. No one in our group was ever in that room except for Roberta, who didn't come to Orkney that particular year. "Mom, this is great, this is Roberta's room." And she loved Roberta. "Also, it is at the heart of the facility. Everybody walks by here ten times a day. You're going to love this room." She would enjoy looking out over the geraniums planted symmetrically (my life, at times, too lopsided for her comfort). "Rest," I said. "The bell will ring for dinner."

As our week got started, I had my usual routine of spending my days painting in the ballroom where there would be nude models, usually female students from James Madison University. Ordinarily the models do their work and then go drink beer in their rooms; you never see them except when they are modeling. Well, this year these two young women were not like that. Their names were Cara and Mia, and they learned all of our names. They were just darling girls. They would get movies from Harrisonburg and then invite us to watch them in the parlor. On Wednesday they got "Good Will Hunting." Since I had seen that movie, I encouraged Mom to go. She was unsure. I told her, "You know, if you don't want to watch it, you can always leave. Everything is really relaxed." When my friend Cathy arrived after the movie started, she saw Mom sitting right up in the front row with Cara on one side and Mia on the other. She said it was so cute; it was like a little group. Mom really bonded with these two models, and she spent most of her time with them on their off-hours, talking and laughing and enjoying life.

On Thursday night, Phyllis, the wife of Jerry Coulter, the professor who runs the Orkney summer art program, came up from Harrisonburg to spend the weekend. I mentioned to Mom, "You should talk to Phyllis, because she used to be the reading coordinator in Rockingham County, and I think you know the same people."

Phyllis got there in the afternoon, and Jerry introduced Mom to her as "Juanita Price, Paula's mother." They got to talking. My mother was good friends with a woman named Helen who was on the faculty of James Madison University and had died about a month before. Mom had gotten a letter from her, and it was a real shock when Helen died so suddenly. It turned out that Phyllis knew Helen and told Mom the details of Helen's death, which Mom was very curious about. Mom said that she knew Helen through an organization she belonged to called Delta Kappa Gamma. Phyllis remarked, "I belong to that organization, too." It seemed they knew all of the same people. Phyllis looked at Mom, and asked, "What did you say your name was again?" After Mom repeated her name, Phyllis exclaimed, "You mean, THE Juanita Price?" She explained that Mom had been the state president and then the executive secretary of this organization. "You're the one who started the scholarship program for members of Delta Kappa Gamma who were getting advanced degrees, and I was the first person who got one. You helped me when I needed help; it changed my whole life. You're MUCH MORE than Paula's mother!" Mom just beamed.

After Dad died, Mom moved to Fredericksburg to live with me (in a separate level of my townhouse). Because she had been born within 30 miles of Cumberland and then had lived there for over 20 years, the move to Fredericksburg was much harder than she expected it to be, and certainly much harder than I thought it would be. What bothered Mom the most was that she felt she had lost her identity as a person. No matter how much I told her that my friends were friends with her, not just because she was my mother but also because they liked her, she was never quite convinced. She did make some friends, though, and there were enough of them to keep her from feeling lonely. But she missed her home and her community.

I tried to take Mom to places where she might make some friends on her own, such as the elder study program at the Presbyterian Church. She claimed the classes were boring to begin with. Mom was always so lively in her ideas and interests. There were some classes she liked, but she could never go out and bond with a group of people her own age.

That week in Orkney, however, she made new friends—with young people. After all, she'd spent her entire life as a teacher, and there she was, bonding with these two young women. During the week, Cara, who was studying philosophy and religion, gave her a book of Buddhist poetry. Mia is Korean; I'm not sure if she is a Buddhist or not. But the three of them spent hours talking about religion and the afterlife. The only other person I ever knew her to discuss these kinds of topics with was Joan. Once she brought Mom a huge healing crystal, which came from some monk in Mount Shasta. She brought it to her the first time Mom was in the hospital after she moved to Fredericksburg. Joan told her, "Just tuck it under your pillow or hold it." And so Mom did—she kept it in her bed most of the time, and she took it with her to Orkney Springs; I later found it in her suitcase. She and Joan had been talking about a lot of things like that.

Joan wanted to get a book for Nita to have while in Orkney. She was looking for one about Taylor Caldwell, but she couldn't find it. So she chose another one called *A Soul's Journey*. I haven't read it yet, but it's about teaching after death, and it describes different levels of the astral plane. The first afternoon that we got there, while some of us were painting, Mom walked over and asked, "Well, Joan, did you bring me something to read?" Joan went and got her that book. She read it right away, and she told Joan she was excited about what she read: "I didn't know that I could teach after death! I'm really sort of looking forward to it!"

"You don't have to die, Nita, in order to have that experience," Joan replied. "You can stay here and do the same thing." Later, I found in Mom's pocketbook a little notepad where she had written her thoughts about that book. She was able to talk with Cara and Mia about her ideas. She was really inspired.

There were many unusual experiences that week at Orkney. Mom had forgotten her hat; she always wore a hat outdoors. My friend Elsie gave her a straw hat to wear. You know the hats in those paintings Gauguin did in Brittany? That was the shape. And she was so cute in it; everyone was taking photos of her or drawing pictures of her wearing that hat.

Don Crow, my favorite teacher in the world, was there. Mom came to his critiques. In the past, she rarely mentioned my paintings, but all during that week she would say things to me like, "Paula, everybody that walks by here tells me that you are doing the most colorful paintings, and they say you are the most confident painter here." And her eyes would just sparkle! She was proud but did not want to seem too proud.

During that same week my son Matthew, who lived in Harrisonburg at the time, came up to Orkney to visit. I had told him earlier, "If you have Sunday off, come up and eat fried chicken." Because he had injured his knee the weekend before, he wasn't thinking about us. It turned out that Mia knew Matthew. On one of her trips to Harrisonburg, she went to where Matthew was working and said, "Matthew, your grandmother is at Orkney Springs, and I know her. You better come up there and see her."

"I forgot she was there," he replied, "and I do want to see her." Despite his difficulties, he caught a ride up on Tuesday night. He got there about 9:30 that evening and stayed until 11:00, sitting on the porch with Mom. She bought him Coke and gave him snacks. They sat and talked; it was wonderful.

Later, I looked back and remembered that the week before we left for Orkney, Jack, my other son, and his girlfriend Laurie, out of the blue, called and said they wanted to come spend the night in Fredericksburg. Mom got to see both of them and took us all out to dinner. It was such a nice evening. Mom actually saw a lot of people who were important to her the few weeks before we left for Orkney: my cousins, her sisters, her friends. I remember her calling a friend of hers the week before we left and talking to her for a long time. She was doing things like that.

On the final Wednesday night when we were to have the reception to show all the art that was produced in the week we were there, Mom told me that Cara and Mia had come by to help her choose an outfit to wear. I remember hearing Mom say to Cara as she left the dining hall that evening, "Cara, after you get dressed, will you come zip me up?" And I thought, well, that is so sweet! It was like they were girlfriends. As I was walking across the lawn later, I saw the three of them coming out of Mom's room. Cara was dressed in a black tube dress with a big split up the side, and I looked at Mom, and she had on a print dress that was split on both sides. It was her dress, but I had never seen it before. She wore a pink t-shirt underneath and had white earrings and big white beads like a choker. Her cheeks were rosy, and she had on gold sandals. Mom came over to the reception; she was a little tired, a little out of breath. When it got too hot, I took her out to the porch to sit. Thirty-five years of September beginnings as a teacher, she knew all the names by the end of the week. Everyone gathered around her, eager to hear her opinions on the art.

After the reception, Cara and Mia had to leave. They left a gift of black-eyed Susans and tiger lilies for Mom with a darling note about how much they enjoyed her company, how they loved that she was filled with ideas, and how wonderful it was that she was ready for "a new journey." They actually used the word *journey*.

I sat with Mom at the reception, but after it was over, I was really tired. In fact, I went to bed early. Mom had packed Amaretto for this trip, and she was inviting folks to come by her porch for a drink. Everybody wanted to come and have a little sip with her. Mom told Joan in the car on the way back that Don Crow had come by and sat with her, just the two of them on her porch, at midnight, and they had a little Amaretto, and they talked for over an hour. But she didn't tell Joan what they talked about. I imagine that these two great teachers recognized in each other how much they cared about their work.

The next morning we were getting packed up for our trip home. I went by Mom's room to see if she had left for breakfast. Every morning she'd been out before 8:00 a.m. She had three full meals a day, which was unusual. Plus, she never complained: "I wish I could taste this, I can't smell this, I don't want to eat this." That's what I heard all the time at home. Not one word. She cleaned her plate and enjoyed her meals. But when I saw her that morning, she said, "I just don't feel good today." So I went over to get her some breakfast.

The weather had gotten warm. Since it had been cool with no humidity, she really did not have much trouble breathing. But this day it was humid again, and it was affecting her. She said, "My stomach is upset and it aches, and my lower back hurts." Joan came in and mentioned that she had an upset stomach, too.

After taking Mom her breakfast, I came back and got mine. I was one of the last to leave the dining hall that morning. When I saw that Don Crow was still there, I went over and said, "Don, this has been the most wonderful ten days to be up here with you." And I felt teary-eyed. After I told him goodbye and came downstairs, we pulled our caravan of vehicles together to load our stuff in them. Jack Darling, who never missed being at these classes, was there, and I gave him a hug goodbye. I got in my car and I thought, "This is probably the last time these three people will be here." I figured that Don probably wouldn't teach here again. And Jack will be gone; he's very frail. I thought that this time at Orkney was unique and wonderful. There together were the teacher I love, my mother, and Jack, who has meant so much to me.

On our way home, for some reason, when I got to where Route 42 comes in, I decided to turn. Route 42 goes down through the valleys, through Timberville and Broadway, and gets to Harrisonburg the back way. We had lived on Route 42 twice when I was a kid, once at Buffalo Gap and once at Craigsville. When I turned onto the old road, Joan told me later that my mother started reminiscing with her about the old familiar places where we had lived. Joan thought it took Mom's mind off of her discomfort.

We got home at around 1:00 p.m., and I gave her some oxygen. After about ten minutes at the most, she said, "I want to lie down." I went upstairs with her, and she undressed, her thin arms and legs burning, too warm for a sheet or blanket. I started to unpack her suitcase, and all of these books popped out. We had gone to the book fair in Harrisonburg one day that week, and she had bought some books. I picked up one. She asked, "Have you read that?" I hadn't. "Well, I'm giving it to you for your birthday." But my birthday wasn't until November. And then there were books for Jack, Matthew, and Jack's girlfriend. There was a book for her sister Hazel. She had gifts. She must have known.

She asked if I would rub some Aspercreme on her back. "Do you feel like you're in pain, or do you feel sick?" I inquired. She said that she just felt sick. I knew that she had this insidious aneurysm that was discovered four years earlier. The surgeon had called the respiratory doctor, who was adamant that under no circumstances was it a good idea to operate; it would be dangerous and she might not make it through the surgery. He had told her, if she ever had a really bad pain, she should go to the emergency room.

I wondered out loud, "Do you think it could be the aneurysm?"

"I don't think so," she answered. "I wish I hadn't eaten that apple stuff last night. I think Joan and I have a bug, but maybe we should call Dr. Ameen."

I called him, and miracle of miracles, was connected with the nurse. While I was on the phone, Mom had a convulsion. She simply drew up, and then I've never seen anyone look so flat, but I knew she wasn't dead. I can't really describe how it looked. It wasn't like losing consciousness. Her eyes were open, and she was breathing, but I knew she was dying. I hung up and called 911. The person on the phone was telling me what to do. I shouted, "Where are you? When are you going to get here? She's dying!"

"I know it seems like we've been on the phone a long time," he replied, "but it's only been a minute. They're on their way. Say something to her. See if she can answer you."

"Mom, can you hear me, can you hear me?" She didn't say anything, but since I was holding her hand, I suggested, "If you can hear me, squeeze my hand." She did, but faintly. Then she came out of it and wanted to get up. I was still on the phone with 911. Mom yelled, "Paula, stop talking, stop talking!"

"I have to talk, Mom. The rescue squad is coming. Please don't get up. You've got to lie down." And I got her to lie back down. She wasn't confused; she was in distress. I think of the term *fighting for your life*. It was like that. Then the rescue squad came in, and it was wild. There was one young guy who was trying to get her history from me and a man and a woman working on her. I couldn't see what they were doing. They asked her if she knew who I was. She said, "My daughter." They asked her what day it was, and she said, "Thursday"—she was conscious and knew where she was. The woman told the man, "Don't be so rough with her." They were having a hard time with her IV. Someone inquired, "How are we going to get her out of here?" It's really hard to pass through that stairwell. They called the fire department, and then Mom was put in a little swing. I called down to Amy, who was working in the shop that day, "Clear out the hallway and call Joan and tell her what's happened." We came downstairs, and they put Mom in the ambulance.

The guy directed me to go straight to the emergency room. I knew the situation was desperate. He said, "Don't try to follow us. Are you able to drive?" I replied that I could. I don't know how I got there. I was probably a danger to every other person on the highway. The ambulance had just pulled up, and she was whisked right through.

I went to Mom's room and walked over and kissed her. They had put restraints on her, and she was struggling. When they loosened her restraints, she looked at me and uttered, "I think this is bad." I told her to hold on. With the possibility of an aneurysm, she would have to have a CAT scan. Then the doctor asked, "What are your mother's wishes about medical care?" I suggested he call Dr. Ameen, who confirmed what I knew she had stated, that if she could be "fixed," she wanted to be fixed, but she didn't want to linger on. Joan was with me at this point, out in the hallway, and I looked at her and blurted, "I don't want to make these decisions about my mother." Joan asked what I wanted for Nita. I answered, "I want her not to have a lot of pain."

"You won't have to make any more decisions," she declared. I believed her and felt relieved.

Mom made it through the CAT scan. The doctor announced, "Dr. Ameen's surgeon is on call, and he's coming over; his name is Dr. Thompson." Joan recognized that it would be Dick Thompson. When he showed up, he seemed shocked to see us there, and asked, "What are you all doing here? Who are you here with?" He knew Mom. In fact, his wife Anita had become somewhat close to Mom. After Dick checked her chart, he reported, "She has a ruptured aorta. If we don't operate, she'll die. I'm going to operate." So he made the decision; I didn't have to make it. He wheeled her out and suggested, "You can say something to her if you want; she can hear you." I bent down and kissed her, stroked her hair, told her that I loved her. She opened her eyes and looked at me. And I said, "Mom, this is Dick Thompson, you know, Anita's husband? Dick is going to take care of you." He took her to the surgery, which lasted about two and a half hours. He repaired the aorta, but she hemorrhaged and had a heart attack while she was on the table.

I did get to say goodbye to her. I don't think she was ever really in any pain. Of course, I was devastated, but I couldn't help but feel that it was a perfect death. I mean, if we hadn't gone to Orkney Springs, she wouldn't have had that wonderful last week of her life. There were any number of things that could have been different, but as it was, many people played their part, and they did it exactly right.

I wanted to have Mom cremated and needed to find a container for her ashes that was personal. She loved our local potter, Dan Finnegan. When I went to Dan's, he came right over and gave me a big hug. He reminisced about the first time he had met my mother. "I want to get a pot to put Nita's ashes in," I said. "She really loved you." We looked over the pots in his shop.

"I think these are too small. Can you wait?" he asked. He came back from his house with two beautiful pots and told me, "I kept these for myself because I thought they were special, and I didn't want to sell them. Take your pick." I decided on one. When I reached to get my checkbook, Dan stopped me. "There's no money in this transaction. I feel honored that my pot will hold Nita's ashes."

Into that pot, along with her ashes, I put in her wedding and engagement rings, because she never had them off in 55 years. And I put in two pieces of Werther's Original hard candy. Practically every night she asked me to pass her a piece. I was going to bury the ashes in the cemetery next to my father.

The obituary I had written for the funeral home was not accurate, it didn't say enough, and I didn't like it. I went upstairs to Mom's apartment looking for some personal things to put into her urn vault. In her desk drawer I found a typed manuscript, an autobiography of my mother. It had everything about her, not only what she had done, but what she believed in, too. She had written it for the Delta Kappa Gamma newsletter before she became state president. I was reading it, and suddenly the phone rang. It was a reporter from the *Richmond Times-Dispatch*, and she was doing a news obituary about my mother. I had this autobiography in my hand, and it was ideal. At the funeral my aunt asked about the article, "Did that girl know Nita?" It was that accurate. That was the first psychic experience I had after Mom's death. I couldn't believe it. I had been worried about her obituary. And there it was. I had a second chance to get it right.

I had already decided when I was doing the obituary that I wanted donations sent to the Cumberland County Public Library. Mom had helped to start that library, and they adored her there. On Friday I was reading Mom's mail that had come while we were at Orkney. First thing I opened was a letter from the library: "Dear Juanita, Thank you for your $25 donation. If I'm not mistaken, yours was the very first we received. Wouldn't it be wonderful if your donation sparked a ground-swell of such responses?" I looked at that and thought, "Now how about that?" This was my second psychic experience.

Then there was the issue of filling Mom's vault with the things I thought she would like to have around her. I began to think of it as her psychic vault. I chose photographs to put in it: of her parents, several of my Dad, of her and Jack hugging each other, of Matthew and my Dad next to one another, of her dog, of each house she lived in. I put in the book that Cara had given her. I pulled the cover off of A Soul's Journey and put that in. I wanted her gold shoes included, because she was famous for those, and a scarf from Delta Kappa Gamma that had the little insignia on it. I added maps, one of Cumberland County, and one of Athens and one of Florence, places I have been. I thought, "Well, she can go there now."

Jack put in a tape of him playing the guitar when he was 14. But Matthew hadn't chosen anything, and I was beginning to get a little irritated with him. I asked, "Have you thought about what you want to put in Nita's suitcase?" He wasn't ready. But, when I came downstairs on Tuesday morning, the day of the funeral, lying on the kitchen table next to Nita's urn was a letter in an envelope. Matthew had written on the front of it: "Juanita Price, Care of: God in Heaven." He had written her a letter. He told me, "I didn't want to put something in there that was a gift I'd already given her." I had felt that he had been holding back, but he really wasn't; he just wanted to give the right thing in his own way.

The service was perfect. People were there from every single phase of her life. I found a beautiful poem that Mom wrote, "Ice in July," that was read, along with some poems by e. e. cummings, her favorite poet. I stood up and said what I wanted to say. I didn't blubber. Greg, who was a young black divinity student who used to mow Mom's lawn, read part of a letter she had sent him. She had signed it, "Your Adopted Mother." He was eloquent, and what he had to say was heartfelt.

Then John Robbins got up. My mother had bought his book, Strings. It's about his liver transplant and also about his Buddhist philosophy. When he left Thailand to come here because he was ill, one of his Buddhist friends tied little strings around his arm. They are symbolic of attachment, but I've forgotten the exact meaning. He made very clear when he had his liver transplant that those strings were not to be removed. Mom had read his book two months before she died and had given it to everybody she knew. John spoke and quoted Thoreau. He said that to him, my mother's greatest legacy was the thousands of young people she had taught and influenced. There were other family members and friends who shared lovely memories about Mom.

Coming home in the car, I thought, "You know, I kept some of Mom's ashes, I could take them places." I was going to put her travel book in her urn but decided not to. The only trip that she ever took to Europe was to England, and she loved it. I made a plan to go there and take her ashes with me. I figured that the book would tell me where to leave them. In the meantime, I decided to put some of her ashes in Smith Mountain Lake near the cottage Mom and Dad built and owned for many years. They both loved it there.

The week after Mom's funeral my son Jack had told me his lower back hurt him on Thursday. He said he had never had a backache like that. That was the day Mom had died. It went away when he woke up Friday morning. He must have been experiencing Mom's pain. I also realized that when I left to go to Orkney Springs, my neck was stiff and hurt so bad that when I was doing a yield at that intersection in Culpeper, I could not turn my head far enough to look back. And I got practically no sleep the entire time

I was at Orkney. In retrospect, I realized that the two things my mother complained about were her neck and her insomnia. But when we were at Orkney Springs, she slept from the time she went to bed until 7:00 in the morning, and she never had her neck brace on. It occurred to me that I took on all of that pain. The thing that amazes me almost as much is that I was the most creative I've ever been, and I did the most wonderful paintings I have ever done, the most beautiful paintings, the most meaningful paintings, and I could not stop doing them.

On the Thursday before we left for Orkney, Mom's respiratory doctor put her through a lot of tests. He told her, "Mrs. Price, you're going to have to go on oxygen full-time." And she did not want to. There were so many coincidences that I have to believe somehow, on some level, she knew.

I think the message that I've gotten is that there is a plan in the universe. Everybody told me how wonderful Mom's funeral service was. But I didn't select the poems, and I didn't choose the music. I just asked people for help. And at every stage, whenever I asked, I got the right thing. I was trusting and willing to receive it. Each person loved her and wanted to honor her. There's a lesson here. I don't understand a lot of it, but I think that if you can be open to it, that's the best way to be. And our trip to Orkney Springs, her last week on earth, was amazing. Everyone who was there felt it was the best time we ever had.

Paula Rose *owned a frame shop and art gallery for 32 years. She has maintained an active art career, winning many awards for her paintings. Paula is the author/illustrator of* Mme. Matisse and Her Cat in France, *a book for children and adults who love art and cats. She is proud of passing along a love of creativity to her two sons.*

Laurie Brown Johnston

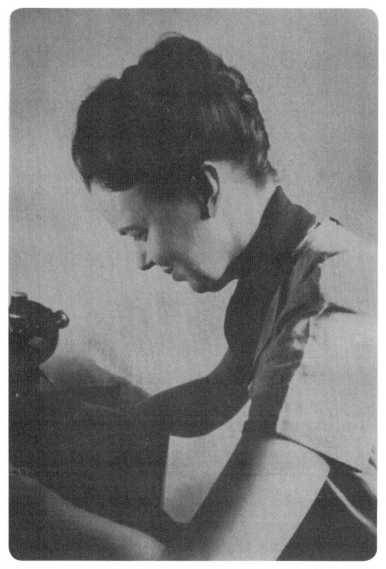

My mother at her sewing machine

Reserve the Perfect Fruit

by Katherine J. Williams

Slicing the Orange

Legs dangling from the table, I watch the swift
arc of my mother's wrist as she slices
an orange, juice dripping into the waiting
bowl, ribbon of peel sliding to the table,
golden sections slipping onto the growing
mound of fruit. She drops a sliver into my mouth
and reaches for another orange. As the bright
flavor shines across my tongue, I don't
imagine the knife that will slip the silent
tumor from her spine a few days from now.
I don't yet know that lumpy packages
will arrive from Haverstraw, a name so foreign
it translates as banishment. I haven't seen
the stamped leather purses or the awkward
clay cups for my dolls – fruits of the will to master
her hands once more. And on this day
I have not yet watched her wheel
back to this table, prop her elbows for leverage,
take up the knife, and the orange, and slowly
release the flesh from the membrane
as the winding sheet of skin
drops away.

It was almost always goodbye with my mother. It was goodbye that morning she woke up and couldn't walk and left the house on a gurney when I was four. It was goodbye when she went off to the rehab center at Haverstraw later that year. My life was breathing little goodbyes, since once she had returned to live with us, I repeatedly left her—on to another room, off to school, up the stairs to bed at night. But there were also hellos: She was always where I had left her, a reliable fact of my life, and something I marvel about as I am now at the stage of my life in which few things are where I think I left them. But the experience of her leaving so suddenly has rendered me able to say, "It's gone" and "I'll just have to get used to it," whether it is the book I was reading last night, a friend who seems to have grown distant or who moves away, or someone who dies. My life with and without my mother has also engendered in me a fierce determination to hold on to and to celebrate friends, old pictures, experiences, moments that are here and may be all I have.

I have been speaking of the "goodbye" in the title of this book—I should also speak of "saying" or not saying. My mother was a woman who was as careful with words as she was with a French seam. She chose the fabric of her discourse carefully, stitching the rough edges inside. When she returned from rehab, having learned to manage her compromised body and relearned how to write and sew, she had also mastered the skill of sealing off question and complaint. It was as though she willed her life to be reborn for us as she rolled across the threshold of our lives, and I didn't notice that there were things she was not saying. She and I communicated in actions. There were early mornings, the household grey with sleep, when I crept downstairs to perch near her feet, leaning against the hard, cool footrest of the bed so I could face her. Together, in companionable silence, we would welcome first light as it seeped across the awakening room. Or she would wheel herself to the sewing table, somehow propping her unwieldy torso sufficiently to sew me a white cotton dress sprinkled with flowers and finished with periwinkle scallops. She guided my hand as I leveled flour across the cup with a single stroke of a blunt knife, taught me to arrange the slivers of pie apples in concentric crescent moons. By the time I was old enough to wonder about her experience—the missing rage, helplessness, and fear—it seemed as though it would be a disservice to her discipline to ask her to share the feelings she had so carefully tailored.

One might call the last few years of her life the "goodbye years," since there were numerous premature goodbyes, as she languished in the thrall of the respirators. When this happened, I would somehow place my life as wife, mother, professor on hold in Washington, and, driving through the night, would emerge as daughter in the chilly morning light of the Mohawk Valley. My father and I became accustomed to time being measured by the regimen of the ICU—for 15 minutes each hour, he and I took turns leaving the tiny waiting room outside the unit, and serially completed the troika of mother and machine in her room. On my turns, I did not speak of her death, nor even much of my life, since I had written countless letters trying to introduce her to the house she would never see, or my children's friends, whom she would never meet. Rather, I often brushed her long hair, her head being one of the few sensate parts of her body. The slow strokes became another kind of breathing, back and forth, back and forth, and I could see her shoulders relax into themselves with pleasure. Her unwashed hair smelled strong, animal, a reminder of her physical presence otherwise obscured by tubes, antiseptic gauze, stiff hospital sheets.

Route 81N unfurled like a ribbon in my dreams as my trips between Washington and New York became more frequent. As the weeks passed, my mother's assisted breaths seemed to suck the breath from my father and me and began to strip us of the will to keep her in this state so little resembling life. We decided to bring up with her doctor the possibility of effecting a final goodbye. He was, no doubt, a busy man, but every time we inquired after him, he had "just been there" or was "on his way." We found ourselves getting up earlier and earlier, driving through the upstate New York dark, to beat him in his morning rounds, or deciding we could manage to skip dinner if we heard a rumor he would stop by in the evening. When we finally ambushed him, he responded laconically, "Not yet, she may come around." And, astoundingly, she did—after the first terrifying moments of the first trial without the respirator, after the fear dissipated and she was temporarily back on the machine and breathing again, she motioned for paper and pencil and wrote, "This will set the Karen Quinlan case back!" My mother was again saying hello.

Several years later, on what would become her final respirator, she lay on the bed, unmoving, as our own breath gradually paced the artificial rhythm of her labored breathing. Each night we drove home, feeling as though the respirator had become the patient in room 24B and Mother had already departed. But there is nothing like death to illuminate the distance between near death and the real thing. When they finally called us in the grey dawn to say we should come, we arrived just after she had died. My father cried, "Goodbye, my darling, goodbye," but I only stood beside her, holding her hand in silence, aware of a seismic shift in my existence that seemed, strangely, not a goodbye. I walked through the next months, trying to live myself into goodbye, saying to myself, "I am a person without a mother" over and over again. I looked at the natural world and felt somehow less impervious to the rain, and at the peopled world, more vulnerable to loneliness and loss. Yet I still rocked between goodbye and remembering, a kind of hello. I wrote poems like this one harkening back to her life as Miss Laurie Brown, Home Economics teacher:

Miss Brown's Illustrative Materials

Awakening into the early dark, head pillowed
in the crook of my arm, I smell my mother,
the musty, sweet scent of the tissue of skin
on the inside of her waiting arm. I'm small,
tearing down the hall, picking up speed
as I leap on to the bed where she lies,
monolithic and welcoming. Her skin smells
old, like the soft paper shrouding
the contents of boxes stored on the shelf
above the garage of my parents' home.
In the watery morning light of a later day, lifting

160

the lid of a box labeled "Illustrative Materials,"
I smell overlapping years in the deteriorating
tissue. Permutations of velvet emerge –
gowns draped on the bias, folded
softly along the grain, ruched and cascading
at the shoulder, remnants of my mother's
life as a teacher, herself the model, before
I entered her world. I call my daughter,
just lengthening into the woman
she will be, ask her to shed her sweats, toss
her a dress. She slips it over her head,
her silhouette an amphora. The gown slides
in sibilance over her waiting body
as though sewn precisely for her. I remember
my mother, bending over her little black Singer
scrolled in gold, guiding the fabric with one hand
and pressing the foot pedal with the other,
the way she learned after the tumor, after
the rehabilitation, when she and her heavy
body came home. I look at Rachel, in that moment
after the dress slips into place, and I see
Laurie Brown, in a body I never knew,
rising up out of velvet, hands reaching for the sun.

As a psychologist, I know that the process of mourning involves working through layers of rich and often paradoxical memories, eventually incorporating the essence of the person who has died into one's current sense of oneself. Fashioning the rush and refulgence of memories into poems is part of this mourning. But I have lost my father, my husband, my good friends—and all those losses were palpably different from the experience of losing my mother.

Saying goodbye for the last time didn't happen when my mother died, because goodbye was so woven into the ongoing fabric of our discourse that I was always saying goodbye as a prelude to saying hello. This might come as an impulse to call her to ask about the proportions of apple crumble pudding or to tell her a wise thing one of my daughters had said. Only later, as an ongoing sense of her, did I understand that her detailed recipe for cranberry sauce, which included the words *reserve the perfect fruit*, was really a recipe for the way she chose to live her life.

Saying goodbye to my mother for the last time will happen like making love for the last time or ironing a shirt for the last time or getting on the train for the last time before a loved one dies—these only become the last times after someone has died and the living look back. Saying goodbye was so much a part of the way I knew my mother that while I am alive, I will always be saying goodbye.

Katherine J. Williams *is an art therapist and clinical psychologist. She is Assistant Professor Emerita at George Washington University where she was Director of the Art Therapy Program. Her poems, one of which was nominated for the Pushcart Prize, are in journals and books such as* The Widow's Handbook *and* The Poet's Cookbook. *She can be heard on the Library of Congress's* The Poet and the Poem.

Lillian Straschun Cohen

My mother and I with my older brother in 1946

My mother and I playing the game together; she is holding a
Memory Card of the picture of her great-granddaughter Ruby.

When My Mother's Inner Light Began to Flicker

by Gene D. Cohen

When my mother's inner light began to flicker, I knew as an expert in geriatrics and as her son that this change in her life force was likely foreshadowing her departure. I began to think how I should spend the time left with her, what I would do, what I would convey, how I would approach saying goodbye.

My mother, Lillian Cohen, did very well until she was approaching 90. Then, a series of small strokes had a devastating effect on her cognitive capacity, leaving her with major memory impairment. Her pre-existing cardiovascular problems became worse, dangerously so, as she developed cardiac arrhythmias with very rapid heartbeat rates and rising blood pressure, resulting in a life-threatening health status. Many individuals, with the magnitude of dementia my mother developed from the strokes, also suffer from personality, mood, and behavioral changes. Despite her greatly diminished reservoir of words, memories, general knowledge, and recall of people's faces and names, my mother fortunately maintained her good spirited, gracious, and kind disposition. This was a great asset for her and endeared her even more to the staff at the nursing home where she resided.

When members of the staff would approach her, she would brighten up and with a smile on her face ask, "How are you?" even if she did not know who they were. And when they would start to leave, after giving her medicine or carrying out another nursing task, my mother would say, "Thank you" and "Have a nice day." She made it easy for staff to help her, and she made them feel good. If only all residents as mentally challenged as my mother could muster a smile and utter those few seemingly simple but effectively engaging one-syllable words, they would become their own best advocate.

Celebration and Biography

I wanted my mother to experience a combination of celebration and biography—stories of her family—in the final part of her life cycle. She brought me into life telling me stories; I wanted to help her re-experience that joy through story-sharing in the final chapter of her life. At the same time, this plan would allow me to celebrate and review her biography with her, since I would need to assume a key role in making both processes happen, given my mother's impairment. It would be like anticipating the end of the play, but being prepared for an unknown number of encores until the final curtain fell, focused on living life as best we could along the way. Life went on three years this way, until just before Lillian Cohen reached her 93rd birthday.

Developmentally, when people reach my mother's age they are in what I describe as the Summing Up Phase in life. During this phase there is the desire to tell their stories and give back from what they have experienced in life by sharing what they have learned in the process. Many people in this phase get involved in organizing scrapbooks or photo albums, creating an oral history, participating in a reminiscence group, writing a memoir, or even creating an autobiography.

With disorders that cause dementia like Alzheimer's Disease (AD) and Multi-Infarct Dementia (MID), the period of time to say goodbye is shortened, and the ability to say goodbye is compromised by growing cognitive, comprehension, and communication problems. I faced this problem with the patients and their families I treated trying to cope with AD, and then with my father who died with AD, and again with my mother challenged by MID. When it hit home, I was motivated to draw upon my night job as a game inventor and developed the first game, Making Memories Together, patented for AD. It was evaluated on a grant from the National Institutes of Health, and along with a companion project I also developed, using video biographies for persons with AD, the two projects were awarded

First Place in the International Healing Arts Competition administered by the Society for the Arts in Healthcare.

Making Memories Together is a non-competitive game in which everybody is on the same team, collaborating as necessary on moves. The game consists of a colorful playing board with four different categories of squares: People, Animals, Places & Special Events, and Favorite Objects. Players draw a Playing Card or roll an oversized die, whichever is easier; the playing cards correspond in color and category to the squares on the board, while the die has actual numbers on it instead of dots. One moves to the square indicated by the playing card or the die. Since everybody is on the same team, there is only one marker, a small beanbag, further reducing the likelihood of confusion.

Each square is associated with Memory Cards with borders of the same color as the squares on the board. Hence, if you land on a blue People square, you pick up a Memory Card with a blue border—a Memory Card about some family member or friend of the person with dementia, who is referred to as the host of the game. Once you select a Memory Card, you discuss it with the host and any other players in the game. The Memory Cards have a personal picture on one side and text on the other telling about the picture. The Memory Cards would have been previously made by family and friends or often through the assistance of young volunteers (such as college students) using templates that are provided with the game. The memory cards function like flash cards, facilitating discussion. Hence, even a volunteer who never knew the person with dementia would be guided through the interaction because of the text on the cards that tells who or what is on it. The team decides on the number of moves to be made before a game is won, at which point the host gets a reward (for example, being taken for a walk or a ride in the car, a special treat in the form of food or drink, or some other personally meaningful prize that would bring a feeling of satisfaction).

On a typical visit to my mother at this point, if the conversation were not structured, she might say the same thing that was on her mind several times over a period of 10 to 15 minutes. But playing the game with the images on the Memory Cards helped her to tap into pockets of memories that structured our visit and allowed her to focus on the story of her life as contained in the Memory Cards. She still had some capacity to read at this point, and the large font and simple sentences on the Memory Cards would allow her to read part of her story to me.

Even though I am a geriatric psychiatrist and an expert on Alzheimer's Disease and Multi-Infarct Dementia, this fact did not diminish the sadness and sense of loss I felt in witnessing my mother's serious decline. Her memory had been so sharp not that long before. In fact, she became the oldest person to have a Bat Mitzvah in the history of the town where she lived—at the age of 75. She had to learn Hebrew and study with dedication for more than two years, but she persisted and prevailed with great pride. The contrast now was deeply painful for me, but for all involved the game helped restore the image of her as a person instead of merely a patient dying with dementia. It provided some continuity with what her life as a whole had been, enabling us to say goodbye, thus adding grace to her own endgame.

A particularly poignant incident around the game occurred during one of my visits at the nursing home when the new social worker introduced herself to my mother, who happened to be looking at the Memory Card of her brother Bud as a young man. The social worker asked if she could see the card, and my mother held it up so she could see the picture side of the card with Bud's photo on it. The social worker exclaimed what a handsome young man he was, which brought a big smile to my mother's face. Then the social worker asked about him. The smile gradually changed to a stressed frown, as words would not come. My eyes were watering as I could feel my mother's despair and dismay. Then my mother realized that she was looking at the text side of the card, in the way that leading political figures read from an electronic monitor in front of them at the podium. Her expression then eased to one of comfort and she began to very slowly read from the card: "This is my younger brother Bud. Bud was a very talented food chemist. He consulted to developing countries on food preservation." She then looked up at the social worker with an expression of satisfaction, and the social worker enthusiastically remarked on how talented he was, at which point my mother beamed.

One of the phenomena I discovered while using the Memory Card is that persons with dementia often have an easier time reading than speaking. This is analogous to people learning a foreign language—for example, French. If you ask them if they can speak French, they will often say that they can read it easier than speak it. To speak, they have to form the words and sentence in their minds, integrating conjugation, tense, and syntax. With the written material, this is all done for them.

The Challenge Increases

We had a system in place that seemed to be working. My mother was in a very good nursing home outside Boston where we all grew up. Her sister lived nearby, calling her and visiting often. My oldest brother lived very close to the nursing home and visited our mother almost daily, which was a great comfort to her. Living in the Washington, DC area, I flew up often and called every day, when a staff person was available to help my mother hold the phone. Meanwhile, her memory continued to deteriorate, though her spirits remained unusually well intact.

But then my oldest brother unexpectedly died. His loss was enormous but painfully exacerbated by the fact that my mother could not recall being at his funeral to say her goodbyes—even though the funeral service was held at the nursing home. This scenario repeated itself an anguishing number of times. She became distraught whenever she would think of how terrible it was that she had not attended her firstborn's funeral. Fortunately, my wife Wendy Miller, an art therapist, had us take photographs of the burial and funeral services to literally show my mother she was there. Wendy also arranged for the register at the funeral service to be left with the nursing home staff. Everyone, including my mother, had signed it. Whenever she would go again and again through this scenario, the staff would show her the state's evidence proving she was there. Lillian would intensely study the images and her signature, and gradually a sense of relief and comfort came to her. Here, too, as with the game, the role of imagery was orienting and comforting.

My Worst Fear

My worst fear was that something would happen whereby my mother would be sent to the hospital for emergency intervention. The problem apart from what might precipitate such an event was that hospitals do not excel in providing care—their specialty is acute treatment. Consequently, the presence of staff not trained to provide the level of personal care that is delivered in a good nursing home often results in worsening disorientation and emotional discomfort. I had carefully instructed the nursing home that no matter what happened, I did not want my mother to go to a hospital. She had not long to live, and her functioning was compromised in so many ways that I saw no benefit to a hospitalization that would likely only add misery. I did not anticipate what followed.

I received a call from the nursing home staff that my mother had lost all circulation in one of her legs. She had vascular problems, which had elevated to this critical condition. Her physician advised them that medical treatment with drugs would not work, given her state, and would only add to her discomfort. The physician consulted with a surgeon, who agreed and said that she would need to go into the hospital and have her leg removed. I spoke to the surgeon, and he advised me that he would prefer not to do the surgery, but if he did nothing (and there was no other alternative), her leg would slowly become gangrenous, generating intense pain, compounded by my mother's smelling her own flesh rotting. My worst fear was that she would have added unnecessary discomfort. What a dreadful situation, what an awful choice. It became clear, though, that it would have been a worse scenario not to have the surgery than to have it. The only consolation was that my mother had for several months been wheelchair-bound, no longer able to walk. Hence, she would not miss the leg in a functional sense, but I needed to see how she felt about it in emotional terms.

My mother was admitted to the hospital, and by her bed I sat down to try to discuss the situation with her. I was not sure how much she would understand, because she now had very severe cognitive impairment and limited ability to express herself. Using careful, simple language, I described to her the problem with her leg and her doctor's conviction that it was in her best interest to have it removed. She nodded in silent acquiescence. I was not sure that she had really understood what we were talking about, so I repeated everything calmly in paraphrased language. This time my mother stoically responded, "You do what you have to do." Trying to hold back my tears, I hugged her, regained my composure, and then asked her if she had any questions—was she afraid of anything? She shook her head no. I asked her again, "Don't you have any questions about what needs to be done?"

Then, with a response of someone in the cohort group who had lived through the Great Depression, my mother asked me, "How much will it cost?" This was classic Lillian Cohen, whom I loved. The surgery was a success, the wound healed completely, and because of her wheelchair-bound and cognitively impaired state, my mother did not seem to be aware of or notice the loss of her leg. She never mentioned it.

Our Last Supper: My Mother's Final Seder

Not long after her recovery from the surgery, it was Passover, and my family and I flew up to visit and have the Seder with her at a special event arranged by the staff at the nursing home. That afternoon, I was not sure my mother would be able to tolerate the Seder. The staff took her to her room for a nap to refresh her for the evening event. They guided her chariot (her wheelchair) carefully up to the side of her bed. My mother, already asleep and immobile, was looking very frail, pale, and sallow, as if she were in a coma. The nursing assistant ever so gently and caringly lifted Lillian to place her on her bed. A deep sadness swept over me seeing my mother that way. If ever there was picture of death warmed over, this was it.

But just before Lillian Cohen landed on her bed with a perfect touchdown, she suddenly opened her eyes wide, saw me, and a broad smile spread across her face, as she commented with an upbeat spirit, "Good service, huh!" The nursing assistant and I also broke into broad smiles ourselves as my mother's indomitable spirit filled the room with warmth in the face of death. It was a classic moment that illustrated how I have described aging as "the whole being greater than the sum of its parts."

That night she was able to join us for a sit-down dinner at the Seder. She spoke a few Hebrew words she had learned for her Bat Mitzvah and was totally delighted with the whole event, despite her marked weakness and very limited ability to eat. Death was passing over that evening, but I knew the end was imminent. What an extraordinary opportunity it was for me to share her last Seder with her, our last supper together. I felt in retrospect it was an ennobled goodbye.

A few days later my mother, Lillian Cohen, died peacefully in her sleep while taking a nap.

After her funeral, I went back to retrieve the biographical game about her life. Unable to tell her story by herself, she had enabled me to tell it for her, and so left me with a poignant exit gift. I looked through the Memory Cards with loving tears, making memories in my heart.

"To live in the hearts we leave behind is not to die."

—Thomas Campbell (19th Century Scottish poet)

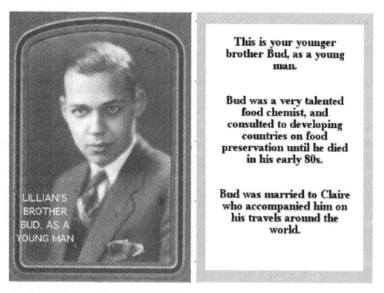

The front/picture and back/text sides of the card of Lillian's brother, Bud

*The late **Gene Cohen**, geriatric psychiatrist, expert on Alzheimer's Disease, researcher, game inventor, and author of many articles and books, received numerous awards in the field of creativity and aging. His intergenerational board games encourage mental exercise and social engagement. Gene's contributions shifted the emphasis in geriatrics from a problem-focus to one of potential for growth. He continues to touch countless lives.*

Louise Mary Jones Capps

From the left, in the front: Paul (my father), me (Paula), and Louise
(my mother); my sisters Joan and Evelyn in the back

The Little Glories

by Paula Engelhorn

In a far-off land, a long time ago, I am a young woman. I am still living at home finishing my last year of study for a teaching credential. I will finish the year and marry, all within thirteen days. It is the night before the countdown begins. I am ready to go to bed and start walking down the hallway to my bedroom. My mother calls out to me, "What time do you want up in the morning?" I feel irritated. Why does she always have to ask me the same question every night? She knows what time I want up. I barely glance over my shoulder and say, "seven," as I keep on walking toward my bedroom.

In my mind I used to repeat over and over what happened next, until it became an unforgettable mantra. I went over every detail of the next three days; I repeated every painful memory until the days were branded like a permanent scar into the very fabric of my being. I wonder if other people do the same thing with horrendous, difficult times in their lives. Is everybody left wounded, scarred, changed through searing, painful times?

I am young, and once I am in the safety of my room I sleep well. I have no inkling of impending disaster. It seems like an ordinary night, like many other nights. I am asleep and know nothing of what is going on in my parents' bedroom. Around five that morning, my father calls out to me. I do not remember what he said; I just remember standing by the side of my mother's bed. As I look down at her, she keeps moving her head from side to side and saying "my head, my head." I touch her; she is warm and seems frail. My father leaves the room to call an ambulance. We both know this is very serious. At one point she seems to stop breathing; I reach down and touch her chest, pressing downward to help her breathe. I do not know what else to do. The ambulance arrives; my father and I follow it to the hospital in his car. The night has not left. I am shaking and cannot stop crying.

I am in the waiting room at the hospital; I do not know where my father has gone—I suppose to call my sisters. I am still shaking and crying, I guess pretty loudly because a nurse comes over and tells me I cannot see my mother unless I stop crying. Somehow I sit quietly after that and just let the tears roll down. My sisters arrive, white-faced. But they do not understand what I understand. My mother, our mother is dying. How could they know? They were not there. They understand stroke; they do not understand as of yet that this is not a small, can-be-overcome kind of stroke. My brother-in-law is jovial, saying he wished he and my sister had planned a wedding like the one I was soon to have. He wished they had not run off together. I look at him, smile weakly, and already know there will not be a wedding in less than two weeks.

The pretenses continue. No one seems to realize Mother is dying. I see her for a minute before we all go back home to wait, to wonder, to not understand. At some point my in-laws-to-be show up. I do not know what to do with them. We are not close; we are not friends. Our house is small; yesterday's newspapers are scattered about. Mother's stroke must have happened on a Monday morning, because the Sunday funnies were lying on the table with the rest of the newspapers. The house looks disheveled. I feel embarrassed and wish I knew what to do. I now realize they had come to try and help, to try and express their sympathy. I just sit there, wondering what is the proper thing to do at such a time. They leave and family members come. I am not alone, but I feel so very much alone. I am on my own grief island, and my sisters and father are on their own islands. Somehow the morning passes. At some point John arrives, my husband-to-be, but I cannot feel his presence either. He tries to comfort me, but we are both out of our element. We are young—what does sickness, possible death, have to do with us? At three in the afternoon the hospital calls and says Mother has stopped breathing. I run outside and, holding onto a small tree, I scream over and over again, "No!" My father chooses to put Mother on a breathing machine. I know this is wrong; I know she is gone.

My mother had said to one of my two sisters that she would rather die than lose me. She kept saying to me, "Why do you want to get married?" It was not that she did not like my fiancé; she just did not want me to marry and move away from her. Funny how the mind blocks things, funny how I cannot remember which of my sisters told me what she had said. Nor do I remember exactly when this was told to me. Today I really cannot imagine why one of my older sisters would say such a thing—"Mother said she would rather die than have you marry." We were so dysfunctional. My sisters were ten and seven years older than I. To them I had everything—clothes, plus my own car. I was pampered and they were jealous. I had everything except my freedom from Mother. I could not go away to college, because Mother was perpetually sick and needed me. I lived in a smothering, mothering kind of love—of course not all bad, she really loved me. Today I do not blame anyone for what happened. It simply happened. Life happens to mothers and fathers and children and sisters and brothers. We are all just a human imperfect sorry lot, bound together by love, and those shimmering moments of happiness coming by in the least expected circumstances.

My grandmother and aunt come to the hospital. Grandmother is confused, my aunt stunned; their daughter, their sister lies in a hospital bed on a breathing machine. How could this be? I try to comfort my grandmother, but I do not know how. My favorite aunt stands beside my mother's bed in disbelief. The day rolls on; everyday, ordinary tasks seem strangely bizarre. We eat lunch and it seems odd to be eating when Mother cannot. I stand beside her bed and look at her and know she is gone. In her place lies a facsimile of her, an empty husk. The breath of life is reduced to a breathing machine making her dead chest go up and down at mechanical regular intervals. I cannot say to my father, "turn off the machine, she is gone." But in my mind I beg him to do just that. I cannot seem to speak to anyone about my feelings.

Somehow I make it through the first night without my mother, and the dawn comes on the second day of Mother's deathwatch. I still feel alone, people are around, but I am stunned into isolation through my grief. I am cast in a drama I do not completely understand. I do not know the rituals of death. I stumble through the day. The faces of family, our home, every-thing seems washed in gray shadows. My family members begin to say to me how strong I am and how much faith I have. I do have a lot of faith, but they do not realize my supposed strength is nothing more than a frozen facade of grief.

My family decides to go pick out a coffin and a gravesite. It seems wrong to me, premature somehow. I know Mother is gone, but still she lies in a hospital bed, with a white sheet tucked up to her face and the terrible breathing machine going up and down. The whole experience of selecting her gravesite and coffin is crazy to me. Why are we picking out a coffin when my father has not turned off the breathing machine? We go to the mortuary, sit around a table in a cold room, and talk to a stranger about how to bury my mother. Quietly and in hushed tones, we discuss plans and choose a moderately priced, nice pale blue coffin and a burial site near a fountain. The whole morning seems macabre and not real. How is this possible? What kind of death ritual is this? After we leave the mortuary, my father goes to the hospital and consents to having Mother's breathing machine turned off. That afternoon the mortuary calls and asks for a pic-ture of Mother. I wonder why they need a picture of her. As of yet I do not understand the distortion death brings about.

Many, many more times I will sit in a cold hushed room, discuss-ing funeral arrangements with strangers, having to pick out coffins for far too many relatives, including my beloved sisters. It never gets easier; it always seems crazy, wrong, morbid, and awful. Especially the money part—it never occurred to me that coffins are priced just like any oth-er commodity. Every kind of coffin is available, from the plain pine box hidden in the corner to the fancy walnut coffin featured near the front of the display room. I have never grown used to this whole bizarre process. I do not want strangers making my beloved ones look worse in death paint and then stuffing them into fancy boxes lined in satin. I prefer to have my loved ones touched as little as possible in their state of death. I want them left alone, and I want to remember them as living, breathing, won-derful human beings.

Mother will be in her coffin, painted up, and ready for us to go and see her tonight. How can everything be happening so very fast? Stroke on Monday morning, now Tuesday night she will be all laid out, and tomorrow is the funeral. One of my sisters has made chili and brought it over for all of us to share before we go to the mortuary. My father decides not to go; he wants to remember my mother as she was. I feel it might help me if I go and see her. The chili sits in my stomach like a hot lump of coal. I did not eat chili for many years after that night; the memories connected with it are just too painful. I am scared. What will she look like? I walk into the small cubicle where she is laid out, and I am stunned. Death is so still, so completely without any movement, so empty of life, and so opposite of life. She is wearing the beautiful pink satin dress she was going to wear to my wedding. She looks terrible, and I wish I had stayed home with my father. How could a living, breathing, lovely human being be reduced to such complete and utter stillness?

I had seen her in the dress only once before. She was trying on many dresses for my upcoming wedding. When she put on the pink satin one, she seemed shy when I told her how pretty she looked. On that bright, full-of-hope morning, she really did look pretty and alive and excited. When we arrive back at the house, my father asks, "What did you bury your mother in?" We reply, "The dress she was to wear to my wedding." It is such an infinitely final answer. The dress she was going to wear to my wedding is such a far cry from the dress she is wearing to her funeral. That dress was a particular shade of pink I retired from my personal color code. I never bought another pink item for myself, not a dress or towel or accessory. The color simply stopped existing for me.

After going to the mortuary I feel sick. I do not want to go to my bedroom by myself; I want company. I do not want the dark night's shadows of death lurking around me. I cannot comprehend what I have just seen— Mother in a blue box wearing her pretty pink dress. I sleep very poorly, playing over and over the scene of my ever-so-still Mother in her coffin. The house is quiet, and even though my father is there, it feels empty. The morning of Mother's funeral dawns gloomy. In Southern California this kind of weather is called June Gloom. The sky is gray; high cool fog is everywhere. The day of the funeral is also John's graduation from college. He must race to his graduation, and after the graduation take off his robe and race to the funeral. His parents must feel very disappointed, cheated somehow from what should have been a day of celebration.

My father and I arrive at the church. It will be a closed coffin service. I am grateful. The church begins to fill up with family and friends of my father, my sisters, and me. Mother did not have friends outside of her family. She was a very shy, retiring person. I think today she would be diagnosed as clinically depressed. I tried to help her, to bring her cheer and happiness, but I never was very successful. She was happiest when surrounded by her family. When my sister had her first baby girl, Mother was overjoyed. For a while my sister and her husband and their new baby lived close to us. When I look back, it seems to be the happiest period I can remember Mother experiencing. She loved her granddaughter, and so did I, because for a while at least Mother's intense focus on me was directed toward my little niece. But like other couples who want a better life for themselves, my sister and her family moved to the suburbs. Mother's happiness dwindled away into a never-ending, deeper and deeper depression.

Tears start to fall down my face as the church fills with friends and family. I cannot control the tears or the pain. The organ is playing a Bach prelude, one that is well known. Even today whenever I hear it played on an organ, I remember Mother's funeral; even now on the verge of old age, that music brings me right back into the church where Mother's coffin stood in the aisle. Only a few months ago, I stood in a small chapel surrounded by people I did not know very well, and when the Bach piece began, tears ran down my face. Not just a few tears but a flood of tears. I could not hide them, and it was hard to be in front of strangers and cry as I did on the day of Mother's funeral. I was surprised, embarrassed, and somehow also deeply moved by the experience.

I do not remember the rest of the funeral day. I suppose people went back to the house with our family. I suppose we ate lunch and possibly dinner together, and then everyone went home. I do not know where John went after the funeral, probably to be with his family on the day of his graduation. The next day a new era in my life began. The house is quiet; my father owned a small business and always worked long and hard hours. He had gone to work early, as he always did. Mother is not there. I am alone. This same alone experience must happen to many who lose a mother, father, husband, sibling, or child. There has to be a day when everyone simply leaves, and the house is extraordinarily empty, quiet, and completely different.

I can hear the clock ticking in the kitchen. My big poodle Bessie is with me, but of little comfort. Somehow I eat, shower, get dressed, and go off to the college I attend to let my professors know what has happened. I need to know what I can do about my grades. I just feel I cannot attend class right now. There is only a week to go. I walk into my jewelry class wearing dark glasses. One young man looks up and says, "What happened to you? You look like your Mother died!" I answer, "She did." His face registers complete shock and horror. How awful for him. The moment is like some sort of huge black comedy routine. I feel sorry for him, and there isn't anything I can do.

I get through the day, the next, and the next. Life is settling into a pattern of sorts. John is spending a lot of time with me. He is a great comfort and help. We change the date of our wedding. I wonder whether I should wear my beautiful wedding dress. Should I still have five bridesmaids in lovely yellow and white dresses? How about my little nephew? Should he be the ring bearer? Should John wear a morning coat? We start cutting pieces out of the wedding. I will wear my dress, John a plain suit; there will be only one maid of honor, no other bridesmaids. In what must be an infinitely petty reaction, I am disappointed. My Mother just died, and I still want all the bells and whistles at our wedding. I can grieve over losing Mother and at the very same time grieve over the loss of the Big Wedding. I feel creepy.

I cook dinner every night for my father. Because Mother was perpetually ill, I had been doing most of the cooking since I was fourteen, but to be painfully honest, not very much else around the house. My father and I are still on our separate islands. He comes home late; we eat a quiet dinner together and then watch TV. I begin to sit where Mother always used to sit. It is less distressing than to look over at her empty seat. I think because I have always lived at home, in many respects I am young for my age. I am not very aware of how certain things operate in the real world. Because I need money to buy groceries, I start signing my father's name to checks. He does not seem to care or notice. I think my representation of his signature is pretty good. But eventually the store calls and tells my father about the checks. I am actually surprised there is a problem with my signing my father's name. I am not stealing, just trying to buy groceries so we can eat. After the store calls, he starts signing blank checks for me.

Sooner than I would have liked, my father wants Mother's clothes taken out of the closet and given away. On the day the closet is to be cleaned out, one of my sisters comes over to help me. I hate doing this, taking down all of her clothes, putting them in boxes, taking away everything that is left of her essence. I bury my nose in one of her dresses and can still smell the special smell that meant Mother. I had a similar experience recently when I was lying on the bed with my little granddaughter as she cuddled up to me; she buried her head in my side and said, "You smell just like Grandma." How lovely to smell just like Grandma.

The day of my wedding is here. I wake up, walk into the kitchen, and my father says, "I'm going to work. I'll be home in time." It is then I realize there is no one to be with me on the morning of my wedding. I wish I had asked one of my sisters to come over, or my aunt. I think brides are supposed to have help on the morning of their wedding, at the very least someone to help them with their dress, to put their veil on in just the right way, someone to ooh and ah, or something anyway! I get dressed, my father arrives in time, he changes from his work clothes into a suit, and we drive to the church, or really the parish hall. The change in dates has made a difference in our wedding plans. The old beautiful church we were to be married in is closed for renovations. Our priest is on vacation so we have the curate. There is no big organ, fancy stained glass windows, or altar. I still feel guilty complaining about not having the wedding I wanted. My mother had just died two months ago. Where in the world were my priorities? Was I nothing more than a rotten, spoiled young woman? Maybe my sisters were right all along. They always said I was spoiled and pampered. After the ceremony I say to John, "This is the happiest day of my life" and immediately feel guilty. I am singing the same song in my head, "How can I be happy if my mother just died?" Perhaps this is what life is: guilt and happiness rolled up into one tangled ball.

It is a year after my mother's death; much has changed, too much. In one short year, my mother, grandmother, and one of my twin aunts die. About a month after Mother's death, one of my sisters tries to commit suicide. John and I rush her to the hospital, the same one where Mother had died. A nurse who had been on duty during Mother's death was on duty that day. She looks at both of us with recognition and sympathy. They pump out my sister's stomach. Later my brother-in-law says we should not have bothered; apparently she is always trying to commit suicide. He is so unconcerned and acts so superior to our feeble efforts to rescue my sister. I guess he thought she would just get better, and I did not know enough about psychology at that time to suggest she needed therapy.

We move into our first small condominium; my father has sold our home and is living with us. John and I do not realize what it is like to live on our own, so his presence is simply part of our new life together. I start teaching at a high school. I feel overwhelmed—too many deaths, too many changes, too much newness, and no oldness to go back to visit: no Mother, no home, no connecting point. I sort of realize I might benefit from some therapy, but I do not know how to even go about finding a therapist. I begin a long journey to find a strong center within myself, a new home where I can always return. This is not an easy task, and it takes many years.

I was twenty-three when Mother died, and she was only fifty-one. For many years after her death, I would talk to her and explain the new gadgets coming into the world. I used to look around a room and realize how many new things Mother would not even recognize, like ever-smaller cell phones, microwave ovens, compact discs, high-speed internet, and words like Google, text messaging, and Wii games. It is a different world, in many ways better, and in some ways not so good, but probably the same world she knew except for all the fancy gadgets. I realize I have finally stopped talking to Mother about all the new things in the world. I guess I did that inner talking because

I kept thinking she should still be alive. She should know my children and her great-grandchildren. But somehow I have finally let her go.

Time to return from the faraway land of a long time ago: the years have passed and the hurt has softened. Now I remember the best of Mother, what she taught me, her legacy. I could dwell on the smothering person who was part of my mother. But all of us are only human, wrapped up in ourselves, limited by our deep hurts, our wounds, our pains. My mother's hurts, pains, and disappointments deeply limited her potential for growth and a fulfilling life. I wish she could have found joy through a great passion for anything—her husband, a career, something to carry her through the tough times. But she did not. She lived the life she had and died too young, too unknowing of what might have been.

These are some of the gifts my Mother gave me. I am twelve coming home from a friend's house. I tell Mother I want to buy a pie mix and make a pie just like my friend had done that morning. She looks at me and says, "If you want to learn how to make a pie, you will learn how to make it right." My grandmother and grandfather had owned a Tea Room in Maine, and Grandmother taught Mother to make delicious pies and cakes. It was a matter of personal pride for Mother. If I wanted to make pies, they would be the best pies she could teach me how to make. So that day I began to learn the secrets of pie-making, how to touch the pie crust with a light hand and roll it out delicately. Over the next months, she taught me all the wonderful fillings that could go into a good pie crust: banana cream, apple, coconut cream, chocolate were some of her favorites. I once said, "I don't like chocolate pie." She simply said, "Then you don't have to eat it." After that day I found chocolate pie really, really delicious. She went on to teach me how to make cakes; one we made so often we simply called "the old dog white cake." In my family anything that was beat up, or had been around a long time, was called "old dog," as in "old dog sweater."

I have a great love of the beauty in small things; I call them the little glories—the modest miracles of everyday life coming my way when least expected. I think this love of beauty in the least things among us is a gift from my Mother.

I saved the best for last—Mother's love of Christmas. I thought we always had the most beautiful Christmas tree of any of my friends and the most glorious Christmas mornings, which usually began at 3:00 a.m. We just could not wait for daylight to arrive. The gifts were there and it was time to get up and start that wonderful come-and-get-it day. When I was little, Mother made me beautiful doll clothes, fit for any child or baby to have worn. The clothes were hand-embroidered, smocked, and hemmed with a perfection brought about through love. My favorite little dress was made of a coral crepe material; it had been my sister's dress, made over for me, and finally turned into a doll's dress. It was embroidered with small blue flowers, including a matching coat and hat. I still have in my closet a small trunk filled with some of the doll clothes Mother made for me.

This is a small portrait of my mother's death, limited because it is seen through the clouded glass of my memories and experiences. How would she have described herself and her death? I am sure my sisters would have written a very different account. They knew her longer than I had, when she was younger and not so continuously ill. Memory can distort and change all that really happened. It is as if I describe her as a flat, still, black and white photo, and in reality she was three-dimensional and in living, moving color—a complex individual, just as we all are.

*The **Rev. Paula Engelhorn** is an Episcopal priest serving in the town of Macomb, Illinois. She is also a retired art therapist and is devoted to the Earth, all sentient life, and the reality of the circular changing patterns in our lives. She focuses on finding bridges between Christianity and Native American traditions that are ingrained in her philosophy.*

Mabel Elizabeth Jeffery (nee Vaughan)

Left: Red-headed Mabel Vaughan at age 16. She said she hated the bow.
Right: 1945—Mother wearing my Air Force Bombardier Silver Wings.

Conversation with
My Comatose Mother

by William W. Jeffery

A hot August day in 1956 found my mother driving her little blue
Ford over one hundred miles to have her eyes examined by a doctor who
was a childhood friend. While in his examination chair, something in her
brain ruptured. What our family feared had happened. Our mother had suffered a massive cerebral hemorrhage. She was clinically alive, but comatose.
She could live in that nowhere condition indefinitely or die at any moment.

That day was over 50 years ago. Mabel Elizabeth Jeffery (nee Vaughan)
was 62 years old. I was 33 then and am 85 at this writing.

The news of our mother's dreaded condition was a shock to the family,
but it was not a surprise. "The other shoe had finally fallen." Mother's life
had teetered on a knife-edge for some time. Her blood pressure had hovered
around 200 for months. Frequently she said she was "tired to exhaustion
and ready to go." In quiet gestures she gave family gifts to each of her five
children, knowing we would recognize them as remembrances of her love.
I don't suppose she really wanted to go, but I feel sure that she expected it
and was preparing for it.

Memory of how I learned of my mother's condition, or how I got to
where she was, is now lost in time. I do remember entering a room, where
in my mind the scene seemed a vignette, that is, everything in shadow
except for where my mother lay. When I saw her lying there in a coma,
"clinically alive," tears came. These tears I unashamedly recognized as
being for both of us: for my mother, whose death would deny her the full
measure of many future happy years, and for me, the irreversible loss of a

187

presence and the love of a mainstay in my life, FOREVER. It was the absolute finality of death, the harsh fact that my mother would never again be part of the happenings in the life of my family, FOREVER. The finality was and is the hardest thing to deal with.

My mother's brother, a doctor, was the only other person in the room when I entered. He greeted me and quietly said, "If you're praying for anything, pray that she goes. She will never be anything you recognize…a vegetable." Then he left me alone with my mother. His words were crude and cruel like a glass of ice water in my face, but they delivered a jolt of reality. Still in that message, there was just a glint of hope that my mother was still alive. I hoped she might hear me from the dark, inside her deep coma.

Mother lay on her back, her arms along her sides. Her face was serene, not as the word "massive" had me imagine. I took her hand and spoke of things she knew. I told her that her children would soon be here but have sent messages of love, of appreciation for her dedication to us and for how strong she had to be to raise five of us, especially in the hard Depression times.

I tried to suppress my emotion and to speak facts to my mother. I thanked her for my life and all the things she had done for me. I told her I loved her and promised to work on those things I knew she wanted done. For a brief moment there was a barely distinguishable movement of a finger of the hand I held. Was it just a nerve relaxing in death? Could it possibly be a response to my words? Had she actually heard me? I like to think so.

My mother died a few hours later.

At the cemetery, in a sentimental moment, the last words I thought of saying to my mother were the last words I remembered she always said to me as she tucked me in for the night—words that promised safety and peaceful sleep…"Night-night."

William Wallace Jeffery *is appreciative of the good fortune to have had forbears who passed on to him a variety of talents. This has allowed him to enjoy a lifetime of fulfilling pursuits in art, music, and writing. However, his primary love and interest is in his family of four children and Dorothea, his beloved late wife of 65 years.*

Mabel Elizabeth Vaughan Jeffery

Early 1940s—Barbara (me), my sister Jane, Mom, Daddy, my brothers
Kenneth and Bill (Waddie)

Do We Ever Say Goodbye?

by Barbara Jeffery Stimson

My mother was an important influence on my life for 30-odd years, and it was a great shock when her life was snuffed out so quickly when she was only 62.

Mom was vivacious, energetic, full of life, a person who would tackle anything, whether it was sewing dresses for her two daughters, making pants for her three boys, or chairing committees to raise funds for her offspring's activities. It was said that, when she heard the whistle of the train, she would finish the hem on a dress, pack the suitcases, grab the children, and be waiting on the platform at the station to meet my dad, an engineer on the B & M line, by the time the train pulled in. Sometimes, she would take the five of us all the way up to New Brunswick, Canada, where my father hailed from, and we would spend school vacations visiting our relatives in the small town of Bagdad, where everyone seemed to be related to us. Our ancestors built the church there in 1895, and many of the tombstones in the graveyard behind All Saints Anglican Church bear the last name of Jeffery or Jeffrey.

Mom took the five of us to plays and museums and, on Sunday afternoons, played the piano at our home in Keene, New Hampshire, while our friends joined us around the piano, singing. She took care of my grandmother, who stayed in a bed in our dining room, while she was also looking after my dad, who had a stroke. She even learned to drive at age 55.

Mom enjoyed entertaining her grandchildren and was returning two of her granddaughters to their mother in Lisbon, New Hampshire, after a week of staying with a good friend in Maine. The purpose of her trip to

Lisbon was two-fold: to visit my sister and me (we lived only four miles apart) and to see an eye specialist for a second opinion, as her doctor had told her that she was going blind.

My husband Paul and I stopped at my sister Jane's to chat with my mother awhile before she took off for her eye appointment and we for a cattle auction. While Paul did some errands, Mom and I talked about her daughters and her young grandchildren, for each of whom she was planning to crochet an afghan. Among other things, she said, "Treat your children fairly. James and Jane were my favorites, Wad was your dad's golden-haired boy, and that meant you and Ken were out in left field. Treat your children equally."

I pondered her words, but I realized that I had had music lessons like James and Jane, that Mom had supported my outside activities, that she had given me the first afghan she had made, and that she had even made my favorite—blueberry pie—for my surprise 16th birthday party. We had picked the berries the summer before, and Mom had canned them, as freezers weren't available in those days.

Although Mom was staying at my sister Jane's, for some reason I got the call from her eye specialist. "Your mother had a cerebral hemorrhage in my office and is in the St. Johnsbury hospital."

I was thunderstruck. How bad could that be? What would I do? I should go over, but not alone. Jane could not go—she was tending our four young children, all under seven years of age. Paul was working. I called Mom's brother, who was a doctor, and my oldest brother Jimmy, who went with me. There lay Mom, ghastly white, in a coma, hooked up to so many tubes. My uncle told us that, if she survived, she would "be a vegetable." No, not my mother! She was too alive and active!

Shortly after I arrived at home, the call came that Mom was sinking fast. "Will you be over?" I froze. "No," I said. Seeing her "tubed up" was enough. I was afraid of death and could not face it. A few minutes later, the call came that she was gone.

That was 50-odd years ago, and I still feel badly that I did not go to be with my mother in her last moments.

The next thing I remember, we were in Keene at Fletcher's Funeral Parlor. As I observed my mother in her casket, I thought of how pretty she was with her beautiful white hair and glasses and how serene and peaceful she looked. I also thought that she was too young and full of life to be there. The large room in the funeral parlor was assigned to a Keene official who had died, but hardly anyone was there. Mr. Fletcher, a family friend, apologized for having put Mom in a small room as he had not realized she was so popular, with so many friends. I felt a sense of pride; there were others who knew her worth.

Mom was a music lover and particularly liked Perry Como. As we entered the beautiful stone chapel in the cemetery overlooking our family's gravesite, Perry was singing, the chapel was full, and Mom had gone quickly, as she would have wished. She was now at peace.

Maybe one never says goodbye. Years later, I was in an automobile accident in which I was severely hurt, bleeding from an artery in my head. I felt myself becoming very calm and peaceful because, I thought, I was on my way to see Mom and Pop and many others.

I continue to think of Mom often. On Mother's Day, memories come of a piano-playing mother who had community sing-alongs in our living room. This past Thanksgiving Day, we had two reasons to celebrate, as it fell on her birthday. On my December birthday, I smile as I think of the blueberry pie that Mom surprised me with on my 16th birthday. I write thank-you notes because Mom taught us to do so. I can sit comfortably at a table because Mom taught us manners. Over the years, I have thought of Mom's final words to me and believe that they made me a better mother.

Today, I am alone for Christmas, but Mom is here in memory. She always had a special Christmas tree—one year with blue balls, one year with angel hair all over it. Her trees also included the Christmas decorations that the five of us had made at school.

Last spring, I got a call that my sister Jane had been rushed to the hospital. I had just spoken with her that morning, when I had called to sputter about the charity duns that we were receiving so frequently. She had just gone upstairs to take a nap after finishing breakfast, but we talked for almost half an hour, with a laugh now and again, and Jane was pleasantly humorous and responsive. So, it was a great shock when her son-in-law Ken called a couple of hours later to say that Jane was in the hospital, with her daughter Audrey on her way.

I went to the hospital to find Jane in a coma, all tubed up, struggling to stay alive. It was so upsetting to me that I almost wished I had not gone.

I went home and when my niece Carol Linda arrived the next day, suggesting that I accompany her to the hospital to see her Aunt Jane, I said, "No, I don't want to." I finally did decide to go, and we joined Audrey and Ken in Jane's hospital room. As I held my sister's hand, I remember saying, "I think she's waiting for Gail [her deceased daughter] to come to take her hand and show her the way."

At that moment, Jane breathed her last and lay there, free of pain and care. It was an awesome experience, even beautiful. It left a much different feeling than when my mother passed away.

I think that, at that moment, my fear of death evaporated.

At 89, I wonder if I have ever said goodbye to my mother. I frequently think of my mom, cherish my many memories of her, and look forward to meeting her again, someday.

Barbara J. Stimson *taught elementary school, participated in many civic affairs, soloed in the church choir, raised two sons, and cared for her husband with Alzheimer's disease. One day, a pupil whom she taught over 35 years ago in sixth grade recognized her while shopping and gave her a hug. It made her proud that to some she had made a difference.*

Margaret Walton Elliott

Passport photo taken in May 1966—Margaret W. and Keith C. Elliott

Feminine Connection

by Keith Elliott

*Emotion is the chief source of all becoming-conscious.**

Both my outer and inner worlds changed drastically in my 50th year. Just a few months before my birthday, I gave only random thought to my relationships. I had a long, stable marriage, closeness with my daughter, almost daily contact with my parents, and many ongoing in-depth friendships. However, my connections with these people became noticeable only in times of trouble, such as a family illness, an emotional conflict, or an unexpected death. In some respects I was naïve regarding my personal relations and took them for granted. Maybe my attitude was a defense to shield me from my own vulnerability. Who wants to acknowledge that a relationship or a life can cease to be at any moment or that we have no control over our destiny?

My life changed profoundly over the course of a few months. My mother suddenly became ill in August 2007 while my wife, daughter, and I were away on vacation. I returned to witness an emergency operation and a grueling few months of hospital care that finally resulted in her death from a Methicillin-resistant Staphylococcus aureus (MRSA) infection. It felt surreal at the time and still does upon reflection. Before we left for Montréal that summer, my mom was a seemingly healthy 83-year-old woman. My parents lived independently in their house with a dog and three cats. She walked her dog daily, though with age, her pace was slower and required more effort. She drove to the store, paid her bills, and seemed above the norm in regard to health. My father said that one evening she felt sick, threw up, and told him to call an ambulance. My mom had never been in an ambulance before. Emergency room records revealed that she suffered a massive heart attack and had various underlying chronic health issues, all of which was rather hard to fathom, considering that she had regular check-ups with her primary care physician and that her only ongoing condition was seasonal allergies!

Without going into numerous medical details, I found my mother's hospitalization a suffering experience for all of us. I am a medical professional and have worked in hospital settings, but this was harder than anything I had been prepared for. The number of doctors in and out of her room, the scarcity of nurses when needed, the seeming lack of overall coordination of care, and the absence of meaningful communication between doctors and family were all truly shocking. My father came to the hospital daily in the morning and went home in the evening, while I visited after work, called the current attending physician, and even went through patient advocacy on a few occasions. We were not passive or overbearing, just trying to navigate in uncharted waters. In the end, we learned the extent of what transpired only after purchasing the complete medical record of her admission and treatment.

Because of that emotionally wrenching episode, my family relationships were forever affected. Watching my mom's suffering and death was traumatic for both my father and me. My father's generation trusted doctors and the medical establishment to provide exemplary care for their loved ones. Unfortunately, neither of us believes that anymore. We encountered many caring medical professionals, but our experience convinced us that the system has major problems. Despite our best efforts and the prayers of many friends, we could not save her from her suffering. Maybe I was deluded in believing that our collective positive intentions would have a healing influence. If they did, it has been hidden from my understanding.

Our talks before Mom entered her final coma still haunt me. Her mind was clear and sharp, while her body rapidly continued to fail. Mentally she wanted to live, but physically all systems were shutting down. Any nourishment she took in was immediately expelled, so eventually she had no energy or interest in trying. The infection starved her body. Even after she lapsed into a coma, I continued to talk to her, letting her know of my love, gratitude, regrets, and promise to care for my father. It's so difficult for the life force to let go. Beyond the biological imperative, we hold on to life for so many other reasons as well, and fear of the unknown is a big one. I offered to her what I understood might happen when we die and pass into the next chapter of existence. But only those who have crossed over really know.

My mom died at home on November 1, 2007, at around 2:00 p.m. as the Hospice nurse was cleaning her; I wasn't there but arrived soon after. Her lifeless form appeared so tiny, though finally evident in her high cheekbones was that hint of Native American blood. We decided she should be at peace in her own home until the next day.

My father has rarely left this house since then, except to take his two dogs and two cats to the vet and to reluctantly take himself to doctors for his increasing medical problems. Now I am his primary bridge to the outside world. He has always been an isolative type, and my introverted mom was his only connector to others. As I write this, it has been three years since her death, and he continues on with cancer at his heels. His animals give him focus and a reason to live. My role in my family changed during this period, too. It has been a challenge for me to juggle work with caring for my father in addition to finding time to be with my wife and daughter. We have each had conflicts in our priorities. It became an ongoing necessity to determine who needed what and when.

In the beginning of my mom's ordeal, Nancy, a friend and mentor, suffered a brain aneurism and unexpectedly died. She had been there in the beginning of my Jungian quest. We worked together on the boards of two Jungian organizations, co-led dream groups, and were associates in a number of dream institutes. Nancy was an inspiring force for psychological and spiritual growth. She made things happen. My wife and I also have a close relationship to Nancy's artistic husband. Like many men, he came to the inner work through his wife. They complemented each other's creative efforts. The sudden loss of Nancy spread deepening shocks through all of us. Our lives together, after all, are temporary, regardless of our wishes.

During this same time period, my spiritual teacher of over 20 years was diagnosed with pancreatic cancer, and she died at home a few weeks following my mom's death. Rose was my second mother who emotionally supported me through the adult part of my life. She made the spiritual life real and necessary. It is because of her that I became a therapist and a father. Our relationship enabled me to feel the depth of life, gains and losses. In the space of barely two months, three major female figures passed out of my life. And their male companions suddenly occupied more prominent relational positions to me. I felt a great void of feminine energy, and these men remarked that they each felt this loss as well.

About six months later, I lost the remaining substantial elder woman in my life, my father's sister, Betty, who lived in Australia. They grew up in Liverpool, England, without a father during the bleak bombings of World War II, and she lost her husband suddenly to lung cancer over 30 years ago. Somehow she managed to believe that life was a cheerful enterprise and a good adventure overall. My family visited her in Australia the year before she died, and though ill and crippled, she maintained a positive attitude.

I search for the meaning of such a huge loss of the feminine in a short span of time. Each of these women was uniquely powerful in her own way, and I did depend upon them to fulfill significant roles in my life. Although "nature abhors a vacuum," and something must fill the vacancy quickly, it is not apparent to me yet what this will be. Even as a youth, I often felt lonely and apart. It has been my lifelong task to seek, from person to person, my tribe, to locate those who would explore life with me in an open and adventurous way.

Now I depend on my female friends for more support and demand a bit more expression of feeling from my male friends and myself. Rather than project onto women for my salvation, maybe the feminine I need is embodied in all relationships—internal and external. I used my mom's inheritance to buy about ten acres in Mother Nature's wilderness, and being there has enabled a closer bond with my Self. That is the connection, I discovered, I most greatly neglected.

My mom was caregiver to her mother and six older siblings as well as my dad and me. She put her dreams for self aside until they were forgotten or no longer mattered. I took on her caregiving and added a Boy Scout attitude of doing "the right thing." To paraphrase Carl Jung, children may be burdened to live out the unfulfilled lives of their parents. Both my parents passed on a wealth of unlived dreams. The difficulty for me is to determine what is theirs and what is mine.

The deaths of my mom, Nancy, Rose, and Betty awoke a spirit in me. They were catalysts. As Mary Oliver asks, what am I doing with this "one… precious life"? No longer do I passively wait for that day when my bliss will come. I try to be an active participant in life rather than a witness, to experience the full spectrum of being present. It feels as if a God-energy broke me open so that a new appreciation of living could be born. Jung supposedly designated God "as that which crosses my willful path dangerously and recklessly, upsetting all my plans and changing a course of my life for good or ill." I have no clue how long this birth process will take or even what will be born, but I feel a new something moving and growing inside me. I'm neither saint nor devil but experience the whole continuum within me. As the Aboriginal shaman repeats in the film The Last Wave, "Who are you?"

*Jung, C. (1938). Psychological Aspects of the Modern Archetype.

Keith Elliott, *a social worker, has a challenging job in corporate healthcare. For soul relief, he has facilitated a weekly men's Jungian dream group for 25 years. He supported his father through four years of multiple cancers until his death. Keith finds renewal at an isolated cabin in the mountains of Virginia. He lives with his wife, daughter, and dog in Richmond.*

Martha Florence Strong MacKenzie

My mother's yearbook picture, 1912

From left to right: Me, Father (Kenneth), my brother Kenneth,
Mother (Martha), my brothers Donald and Robert

Death in Early Spring

by John MacKenzie

On March 13, 1959, on the Durham Road down the hill from the campus of the University of North Carolina at Chapel Hill, I was dining at Brady's, a comfortable place most notable for its Brunswick stew that was often a magical cure for hangovers, or so it seemed. I don't know whom I was with—someone who had a car—perhaps Bill Orndorff, a kindly man with a scintillating wit.

Midway through dinner about 6:00 p.m., I was told that my mother was sick. The message was somber, but indefinite. I was taken back to town, where I walked the streets in uncertainty, sometimes on the verge of weeping, but quickly covering up an expression that might have seemed eccentric. I decided to look on the bright side, that I would soon receive better news. I went to a college entertainment, musical and satiric, that included a brief sketch illustrating "The mind of President Eisenhower" with a clash of cymbals. The anarchic sixties were being announced several months ahead of time by all-knowing youth. I soon left the entertainment, suddenly realizing that if so much effort had gone into reaching me, the problem must be serious. Satire would have to wait.

By 11:00 p.m. I was sure the problem was severe. Her death was a possibility. I got on a Greyhound bus around midnight. Sitting or lying in the back, I was sure she was near death, and I said to myself, or God, that I wished I could die in her stead, that I was willing to make this sacrifice if God would have me. I arrived in Asheville on a chilly morning, where even the taxi I had to take was delayed in starting due to the cold.

When I got to the hospital, I walked down the hall to her room. There, I contemplated her body, mouth open in agony just after death, with Robert wailing terribly while kneeling at her bedside and my other two brothers standing, much more composed. It was a bleak, arid March in the mountains, with a cold, mean wind forever denying serenity.

I learned later that my mother had died of a stroke. She lived about two days longer in extreme pain. After her death, my father mentioned that she might have had angina, but no matter of ill health was spoken of during her lifetime. However, when I was a child while vacationing in Maine, my mother, clad in a swimming suit, noticed a heavy vein on her leg and remarked, "I'll die of this some day."

Back at the house after her death, during the days before the funeral, I spent many hours in a closed-off room silently weeping. In the evenings I would go to the funeral parlor, where I would commune for several hours at a time with her body lying in the coffin. She would be buried in a beautiful, finely and richly brocaded red-toned dress, which I remember her buying at a street rummage sale for 75 cents. This was presumably her best dress, discarded by one of the more affluent women of the town.

Her face still had the fine-boned beauty of her youth, with the molded cheekbones and the deep-set eyes. It did me good, strangely, to sit for hours in the nearby chair and gaze at her earthly countenance for the last time. At the church service, we sang the missionary hymn that starts with the line, "From Greenland's icy mountains, from India's coral strands"—appropriate, since my father, from Scotland, and my mother, from the Midwest, came to India separately but met, married, and became each other's destiny, both driven by the benevolent idealism of Christian service. (As far as coral strands go, my cupboard of memory is here rather than India, but moral strands were much in evidence.)

Many mourned at her funeral at Mountain View Memorial Cemetery, ringed by mountains. She had lots of friends, since she was helpful and very accepting of people. Several remarked on my resemblance to her, as, sixteen years later after my father died, people remarked on how much I looked like him.

I had last seen my mother when she had driven to Chapel Hill and back in the same day to give me money to complete the term. She had been dressed in a powder-blue wool suit, and she was, as usual, keen-witted, practical, and kind, with a depth of meaning in her hazel eyes.

After her death when I was back at school, the term was hard to complete. I would go through the day attempting to look normal, except in the library, where the fantasy and reality that all would die dominated my thoughts. As each young undergraduate face would appear suddenly through a doorway or in casual mirth with friends, I would in my mind's eye, not in hallucinatory fashion, imprint a skull and a skeleton.

At least once I had the archetypal dream in which all sorrow is erased, and she was, indeed, alive. And the waking to reality on these occasions was more terrible than ever.

I never did complete the degree—the Ph.D. for which she had given me the money. I had no heart for further study after I completed my final paper that was due, a study of the varieties of dialect in Robert Burns' poetry. But I did finish the term and credits sufficient for me to earn a variety of jobs before my final post at Germanna Community College.

We had many links. She was born in Paxton, Illinois, very near the town of Hoopeston, where I was born. She finally got to name one of her children and gave me her family name Strong as my middle name.

She helped me with my homework in Geometry, other math, and Latin through much of high school and into college, her knowledge just as keen as that of my teachers. In later years we both would often get up early and talk about the books she had been reading and other matters while the household was asleep. Then she would set about her work-filled day, which never in my memory included a day in bed until the end.

My mother was an undemonstrative Christian, used to bearing many burdens and disappointments. She was almost in tears when she returned from the trip that ended up with the purchase of the house in Black Mountain, North Carolina, bought with money she inherited from her father. She had hoped to retire in a college town, take courses, and perhaps rent out a room or two for income and for company.

My father dealt nobly with his grief, aided by his profound religious faith. And he did, during that bleak March time of bereavement—like the king in "The King and I"—do something wonderful. He wrote in his formal Victorian but clear handwriting the following verses from "The Song of Solomon," which he pinned up for all to see on the wall of the living room:

> *For, lo, the winter is past, the rain is over and gone;*
> *the Flowers appear on the earth; the time of the singing*
> *of birds is come, and the voice of the turtle is heard*
> *in our land;*

> *The fig tree putteth forth her green figs, and the vines*
> *with the tender grape give a good smell. Arise, my*
> *love, my fair one, and come away.*

Mother's death was unexpected. Two months before, she had driven to Chapel Hill and back—an eight- or ten-hour round trip in those days—to give me money to finish the term. The death was a much more profound shock than my father's, since he was almost 93 when he died.

I have a friend who has been asking me to pray with her (the 23rd psalm, the Lord's Prayer, and others) for those who have passed on, among her family and friends and among mine. These prayers do not belong to my religious background, but I do believe the very least we can do for the dead is to keep them in remembrance. I write brief reminiscences about members of my family on memorial occasions.

What more could I do? Since my retirement in a college town, the many audit courses I have been enjoying are mainly pastime events, which do not require any great commitment, achievement, or finality. It has occurred to me that I might try to accomplish some degree program at Chapel Hill, not the same one since the credits have long expired, but some other one that might demand continuous effort of the sort my mother exhibited.

A way of living is partly what my mother left for me. I specifically think of her whenever grit, courage, or endurance of adversity needs to be called up. She embodied all of these qualities, in addition to intelligence and grace.

206

She endured a hostile stepmother in her youth. As an adult my mother adapted to a different culture and way of life, trying to do good for humanity in India, necessitating seven years of study of a new language. She accepted, with good grace, mainly utilitarian presents on special occasions, performing housekeeping duties in New York in a house with five levels, and tolerating retirement in a community she had not chosen.

And yet she adjusted to each of these circumstances without bitterness, finding both respect and love wherever her influence was felt. Samuel Eliot Morison remarks in his essay on Anne Bradstreet that she embodied a key virtue of Puritanism, the impulse to find good in difficult or evil circumstances. In my mother's embodiment of duty and responsibility, she was a representative of that strain of American life. But she was never censorious or overly critical. She looked always for the best outcome from any circumstance. Mother retained her intellectual curiosity all her life. Before the day started for most people, she immersed herself, through reading, in the beautiful, the good, and the true.

That constant desire to learn kept my mother, a Muskingum graduate of 1912, eager for the next day all her life. In the yearbook, citing Shakespeare's *Twelfth Night*, her classmates called her "the wittiest piece of Eve's flesh that e'er lived."

If I were to choose for myself from all the various examples of how to live that were evident in my mother's life, it would be the pattern of grace in adversity and the determination, while life lasts, to keep on taking interior and sometimes external journeys. Like my mother, I want to understand myself, other people, and the world a little better, and comprehend this journey on which I have embarked and its relation to the infinite universe of stars and spirit.

John Strong MacKenzie *loved teaching English for 46 years. He received a commendation for his thesis on William Blake from George Mills Harper, a major Blake-Yeats scholar. His greatest experience was receiving the Air Medal with Gold Star in World War II. John has traveled extensively. In retirement, he enjoys writing, painting, exercising, auditing college courses, and studying the Great Books.*

Jane Stadtmiller Harrison

My mother and I in the summer of 1943

Mother standing in front of her house in 1999

Dear Mom

by William A. Harrison, III

My mother died on Wednesday, January 24, 2001. She was in a convalescent center, where she had been for about a month after her last, long, vain stay in Riverside Hospital in Newport News, Virginia. She was 84 years old.

Although I was her first-born, in another sense I was her middle child. My brother Jim stayed in Newport News after he grew up, and when a toilet wouldn't stop running in Mom's house, or anything of the sort occurred, particularly after Dad died in 1980, he was the person she called on for help. I lived two hours away, talked to her by phone every week, and visited once a month or more. My sister Mary had moved to California, so she and I were both too far away to be of much use with the kind of practical help Mom increasingly needed as she got older.

Mother's life had been contracting for several years. After a lifetime of smoking, she suffered from Chronic Obstructive Pulmonary Disease (COPD), for which she took several medications, including Prednisone and oxygen. She had lived alone in the house in which she brought up her children, but one day she blacked out while struggling to take the trash to the curb. Soon after she returned to consciousness, lying on her back in the driveway and wondering what had happened, she realized that this event marked still another transition in what could only be characterized as a downward spiral during her last few years. After more blackouts and failing eyesight that resulted in close calls in her car, we helped her close up and sell the house, get rid of her beloved Honda, and move to an assisted living facility. But she was there for only a month before another blackout, fall, and injury sent her to the hospital.

The months that followed entailed a dizzying string of transfers from assisted living to hospital to convalescent center and back. Her stays in the hospital were complicated by infections she contracted there and what she regarded as misdiagnoses and mistakes in medication. Over the Christmas season, I had visited with her twice in the hospital. During the first of these visits, on December 22, she told me that she was ready to give up. The medicines and medical care just never seemed enough to bring her back to a level of health that would make it worthwhile to continue living. While I tried to be positive and suggested that things could improve, I had to acknowledge that nobody else's judgment about it mattered but hers. The next day I visited her again, this time with two of my three daughters, her beloved grandchildren, Katie and Maggie, and Katie's husband Marc. This was a cheerier visit. I remember that we sang to her. Katie had majored in music at William and Mary; Marc was a talented pianist and singer; and Maggie was in several choral groups at St. Catherine's. But after we had left, I brooded about what it was like for her to be alone in a hospital room at this time of year.

A week later, on December 28, she was moved by ambulance to the convalescent facility. Jim and I were both there to help her get settled. She was not in the new place more than ten minutes before I had the feeling that the staff was neglecting her; there was no one available to take care of something that needed to be taken care of. Jim and I went out and ran errands, bought supplies she would need, and talked over the situation. I went back and stayed with her through dinner. I helped her get her dentures cleaned and tried to see that she was settled for the night, but I could not help thinking that, optimistic as we had all tried to be, things were not going well. Even with Jim or his wife Linda coming by daily, and my doing so every couple of weeks, the convalescent center was intended as an interim facility and was not suitable for long-term care.

I visited her again four days later, on January first, when she was doing better. Jim and I toured a couple of nursing homes in his vicinity, one of which seemed particularly appealing, but it had a yearlong waiting list, and we both knew that something really needed to be done long before that. Again, I spent the evening with Mom and tried to reassure her that her sojourn in the convalescent center would be as brief as possible. But actually we were all unable to think of any immediate, workable solution to the problem of providing care for her. Neither Jim and Linda nor Beth and I had homes or lives that would accommodate moving her in with us. All four of us had full-time jobs; our houses were not set up for the needs of an invalid, and with children at home in Jim's case and three in colleges and private boarding school in mine, he did not have the space and I did not have the financial resources to take her in.

Honesty about it requires me to add another element to the equation. Back in 1996, after Mom had been in the hospital—again—and when she needed nursing care at home in order to recover sufficiently to live alone in her house, I took three weeks of summer vacation and went to Newport News to take care of her. The regimen was difficult. Mom required five or more little meals every day; her difficulty breathing meant that she was exhausted after a few bites and then hungry again a couple of hours later. There hardly seemed time in the day for anything else, like grocery shopping or doing laundry. In addition, we were getting up several times during the night for visits to the potty-chair and snacks. But the worst part of it was Mom's attitude. She was a demanding, whining, complaining patient. A setback like constipation would send her into a tizzy of panic and infantile behavior. This should have been a time of intimacy and solidarity for us, but instead, in just about every way, it was an ordeal that seemed to stretch on much longer than the three weeks I was actually there. I realized during the course of it that I could handle Mom with patience and concern for short durations but that having her live with me for the rest of her life was like a punishment I was just not willing to pronounce upon my family and myself.

I returned to see her in the convalescent facility with my wife Beth on Saturday, January 13, when she seemed to be doing all right. The following Saturday I called her on the phone. It was our regular time for a talk, but the staff was bringing around breakfast, and Mom, no good at multi-tasking, was distracted and unable to carry on a conversation.

On Tuesday she was sick with another respiratory infection, always dangerous for her. When I called her Wednesday morning, she was desperately ill, so much so that she could not or would not talk. There was an unspoken plea in her voice for me to DO SOMETHING. I called Jim, who said that he had been by to see her. He said that she was in a bad way, but that Dr. Robinson had also been in to see her, that she was getting medication, and it seemed to him that all that could be done was being done. I went about a long day of professional and personal business, and when I got home after ten o'clock I had a message to call Jim no matter how late. Mom had died.

Why hadn't I dropped everything and rushed to Newport News to do whatever I could for her or, if nothing could be done, at least to be with her? Why had we left her to languish in the convalescent facility instead of taking her into one or the other of our homes? When I look back over my life and my relationship with my mother, I see glaring at me several instances of failure, abandonment, and neglect, the more painful to think about as her dependence on others—me—became greater.

But the next four days, Thursday through Sunday, which were given over to Mom's funeral, I remember as one of the richest and most satisfying weekends of my life.

Beth and I arrived at Jim and Linda's just after noon on Thursday. Jim and I went to the Peninsula Funeral Home to finalize arrangements. Mom wanted to be cremated and to have her ashes scattered at some appropriate place and above all to have nothing expensive in the way of exit arrangements. No ten-thousand-dollar coffins. The cost of cremation and use of the facility for a service was under two thousand dollars, which would have pleased her. Now we could concentrate on the service and on reminiscing about her and Dad for their grandchildren.

Before we left, the mortician asked me if I wanted some time to say goodbye, which of course I did. I went through a doorway to an adjoining room where Mom or, rather, her body was laid out on a stretcher or gurney under a sheet. Her pretty gray hair was clean and brushed, and there was no sign of the struggle for breath that had brought her life to an end. She was not there, however, and after a few moments I knew that whatever "good-bye" was going to entail, this was not it. I re-joined Jim in the other room, signed the papers, and returned to his house to work on the homily I was to read at the funeral on Saturday afternoon.

Friday was given over to planning the ceremony. Beth, who has a seminary education and a wealth of experience in liturgical matters, put together a beautiful service. We engaged the organist at Mom and Dad's church, St. Andrew's Episcopal, to play hymns. I got a haircut.

By Saturday, my sister Mary had arrived from California. All six of Mom's East Coast grandchildren were present, along with my son Allen's very-pregnant wife Maura and Katie's husband Marc. We stood around in Jim and Linda's kitchen and told stories about what it was like to grow up as children of Jane and Bill Harrison. Some of them were funny, all revealing.

Jim suggested that Mom, who loved board games and cards, cheated when she played with her bridge group. She was a smart, cagy player, how-ever, so maybe her winnings were honest. She read the daily bridge column in the paper and crossed out the cards from each hand as they were played in the account of how declarer won or lost. She was no great sports fan, but she followed the Pittsburgh Pirates and always watched the World Series on television, whoever was playing. She did not like dogs, and although I was permitted to have one when I was a boy, he never set foot in her neatly kept house. She did allow Dad to have a parakeet, and when Mary moved back in for a time, she allowed her to bring her cat, which they ended up adopting, though unwillingly.

When Jim reminded us that Mom had died the day before Medicare stopped covering the cost of her stay in the health care facility, Beth sug-gested that there might have been an element of intention in her dying when she did. Now that I think of it, Mom was frugal to a fault. Like my father, a child of the Depression, she paid every bill as soon as she received it. As I look back on it now, I think that the respiratory infection that killed her was accompanied, in her mind, with some determination that her estate was not to be eaten into by end-of-life expenses—well, that and awareness of the fact that her grown children were not going to undertake caring for her themselves.

That evening we all gathered around Jim and Linda's dining room table where Linda served us dishes from my mother's recipes. There were Pepperidge Farm dinner rolls and her delicious crab casserole, broccoli with Ranch dressing, and lemon meringue pie for dessert.

The funeral service the next day was just perfect. Beth's ceremony combined beautifully appropriate readings with familiar, touching hymns; it gave everyone who wanted a chance to take part. Mary played her flute. The grandchildren and I sang "The Lord Bless You and Keep You" with its sevenfold "amen" *a cappella*.

Present that afternoon among a gratifyingly large crowd in the funeral home were Mom and Dad's oldest and dearest friends, Ella Walker Mitchell and Bo Peep Hundley among them; my second-grade teacher Mary Charlotte Corson and her husband Maynard, whom I hadn't seen in many years; and some representatives of families with whom Mom had feuded and only lately become reconciled. What a surprise it was to see Butch Lambiotte there.

Then we went out to dinner, all 14 of us. It gave me a chance in a toast to acknowledge the debt of gratitude we all owed to Jim for being the progeny-in-residence and the one who responded immediately to so many of Mom's needs and demands.

On Sunday, a clear, cold winter's day, Jim, Mary, and I took the box with Mom's ashes to Buckroe Beach, where she had taken us as children on so many hot summer days to play in the sand and swim in the Chesapeake Bay. We found a place where there was access to the beach not too far from where we had swum fifty years before. Jim walked out onto a jetty and scattered Mom's ashes over the water while Mary played "Amazing Grace" on her flute. We rode back in the sun-warmed air of Jim's cozy little car feeling a sense of solidarity the three of us had never experienced before—and never have since.

It was only after the funeral and "burial at sea," which I naively thought would take care of my grieving, that I began to understand that losing one's mother was going to take some getting used to.

Dear Mom

When she was alive, I did not much appreciate my mother's occa-sional letters. They seemed taken up with such petty, mundane, superficial things and expressed so ploddingly. Now that she was gone, how I would have enjoyed receiving one!

Then there were our Saturday morning telephone conversations. As time went on, her part in these was taken up more and more with recita-tions of doctor's appointments and medications, symptoms and treatments, and while I really did want to know how she was doing, I found it depress-ing to think that this was what her life was reduced to. It was only after she was gone that I realized how much my end of the conversation had meant to her. It was not just that I cared enough to listen to her. She was paying rapt attention to what I was saying, too, and every bit of news about my life, the good and bad that I shared with her, my worries and delights, she was attending to with a focus that I did not appreciate at the time. Only later, after there were no more of these Saturday morning calls, did I realized that gone from my life was one person who understood and empathized, as no other living soul did, with the meaning of the things I had shared with her.

I had confessed, for example, to feeling bereft when we sent our baby Maggie to a boarding school in Richmond, an hour away, starting in the ninth grade. So our nest was empty four years before I had expected. I felt at the time that nobody but Mom understood the grief I was experiencing.

But every relationship with a mother is complicated, and if I felt at times that I had lost the first most important person in my life, as I had, there were also times when I was troubled by regrets, accusations, unan-swered questions, and a host of feelings I had no words to name. After sev-eral months, I started writing letters to my mother in a notebook. I did not put them on stationery or attach postage to envelopes, of course, though perhaps I should have. They would have gone to a "dead letter" file, which would have been appropriate. That process would have emphasized that they were to her, after all, not to me. Nevertheless, they helped me bring some final peace to our relationship.

I expressed my regret for some of my failures and asked her forgiveness. I also brought up longstanding complaints, things about her and what she did that I resented. I suppose what I wanted initially was a response of the same kind from her, some expression of regret and a request for forgiveness, which, of course, under the circumstances, I was not going to receive. Instead, I got something quite unexpected and much better. As I went through my litany of complaints, my list of the ways in which she had let me down, failed to give me encouragement, affected me with the narrowness of her outlook or the occasional pettiness of her actions, I came to realize that she, too, was the child of parents who in many, many ways, more than I could know, had failed her, that she was doing the best she could, given who she was and what she knew. Aren't we all.

She was my mother, Martha Jane Stadtmiller Harrison. I realized after she was gone that I loved her when she was alive, as she had loved me, not because we were perfect or always did what we were supposed to do, but because we were mother and child, that nobody else could ever be what we were to each other, that, for better or worse, our lives were inseparably bound together and that, with her death, a part of me had died as well. Here I was at 58 years of age feeling like an orphan. I still do.

Bill Harrison, *now retired, taught English at a large community college in the Virginia suburbs of Washington, D.C. He lives in Ashland, Virginia, with his wife Beth. He has four grown children. In retirement, he enjoys painting, studying works related to Jungian psychology, and reading literary classics and biographies. In 2013, he surprised himself by writing a novel.*

Mary Catharine Ritchie Farrelly

Mummy and I, Christmas 1949

Mummy in her garden in Mendham, New Jersey, 1952

A Gentle Ending

by Mimi Farrelly-Hansen

My mother died quietly at home in Mendham, New Jersey, at the age of 86. Her passing came at the end of a steady decline lasting some five years, culminating in a series of strokes caused by worsening arterial sclerosis. My father had passed on in 1970. By June 28, 1991, it seemed that Mummy and we, her surviving six children (at 45 I was the youngest), were ready to let go.

Like many a daughter I had worked hard to sort through the tangled connections between my mother and me. By the time she began her final journey, allowing old age, a distaste for exercise and healthy eating, and the absence of any compelling goal to slow her down, I had long since moved to Colorado, begun my art therapy career, married, and acquired a family. Thus, unlike my three siblings who lived within minutes of our family home, I charted Mummy's progress via Sunday afternoon phone calls and twice-yearly visits.

As always, my most honest feelings about this time came through in my art. "Letting Go," a poem I wrote after a New Jersey visit in August, 1990, ten months before my mother died, describes my struggle to come to terms with this increasingly dependent and frequently dissociated parent.

I

My mother's back is dry and freckled;
loose flesh hangs from her arms.
On her right shoulder rises one small mole,
talcum powder white in an eerie, lunar way.

Visiting for two weeks, I learn to navigate that spot.
Rubbing my mother's back becomes
important to us both.
Often at my approach
she unzips her dressing gown,
offering stooped shoulders trustingly.
I knead and stroke, glad to be invited.
My fingers are strong like my father's, she says.

The air at the beach is limpido.
Soft susurrant tide and traffic moan
encase this rented lodge.
Light brown sugar sand, decking of faded grey,
windows propped wide with the odd chair rung;
even the seagulls wear weather-beaten.

II
Mother, I cannot hold you in the hammock of my heart.
Daily, hourly
your presence slips
through the web of my attention.
Next to you my daughter cavorts, 81 years away.
For her it's a time of butterballs and waves,
horseshoe crabs of all dimensions
and sugarless sweets hitherto unknown.
My arms pain to keep you both in touch.

At times I snap, though never at you.
Like moths to a candle,
anger bubbles to my throat,
little beads of want and need
pressing at my mouth, my neck, my chest,
pressing for expression,

even as you turn to me, unseeing,
and with practiced, after-dinner grace:
"Won't you have some coffee before you go?"
Better you should nag about my hair
than leave me in this land of non-identity.
Mother, I am your daughter...still!

III
The day we left, Jori and I bought flowers,
deep purples and pinks,
and a heart-shaped, helium balloon.
Only the flowers made it to your table.
The balloon had other plans.
And standing in the busy parking lot of King's
we watched, dismayed,
as that boisterously vital form
propelled itself heavenward
and faded
beyond even a speck
into the great blue blue grey.
Four eyes filled.
Letting go was here.

Six months later I began "Comfort Ye," a small ceramic sculpture prompted by tearful reflections on a recent visit to an even more remote mother. Like other spontaneous expressions from the unconscious, the sculpture's strong, graceful bird-woman nestling a smaller human figure carried me beyond my initial sorrow. Once the central forms and rhythms had been established, I spent several hours over the next two months refining them. Finally I allowed the piece to dry and began to sand it smooth. Holding this pale creation in my lap, caressing it with the finest of sandpaper, I appreciated anew the wisdom of avoiding color and fluid media when emotions are chaotic. The grey clay and slow refining soothed me, allowing me to express tenderness not only towards my mother but towards myself as well. Time and again I was reminded that I am both the comforter and the one who needs comforting.

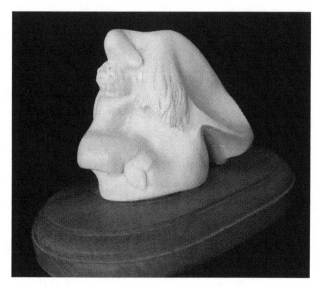

My ceramic sculpture, "Comfort Ye"

In late May my family flew east to help celebrate Mummy's 86th birthday. By now she was sleeping until noon or later every day. Since getting her bathed and dressed took her housekeeper almost an hour, Mums was only downstairs and awake, though largely silent, from about 2:00 to 7:00 p.m. Nonetheless, it felt important to gather with siblings and honor her with a cake whose army of candles several great grandchildren were happy to help extinguish.

That Sunday night I sat on my mother's bed, held her hand, and told her goodbye. "Will you be back soon?" she asked.

I gulped. Maybe now was the time to risk a truly honest response. "I'll buy plane tickets for next month," I replied, "but it may be that you'll be on a different journey by then."

"Oh?" Her tired blue eyes seemed suddenly more alert.

I plunged ahead. "Maybe it's time for you to go be with Daddy. Your body's not working so well these days. It's really okay to leave us now." Awkwardly I went on; ours was not a family who easily discussed feelings, especially with parents, nor was my mother one given to introspection. Still I continued, describing how happy and fulfilled I felt in various aspects of my life. I thanked my mother for being my mother and for all she had given me. I forgave her, out loud, for not being perfect. I apologized for the times when I, too, had acted less than perfectly. Then I tucked her in and kissed her goodnight. Did she hear me? Had she understood what I'd said? I like to think so. By the time I stepped back from that tender farewell, her eyes were shut and the hint of a smile played across her lips.

Mummy had a stroke the day after we left. Partially paralyzed on one side and barely able to swallow or speak, she was moved to a hospital bed right in her own room, where she could remain in the care of her loyal housekeeper and my two sisters, under the supervision of our family doctor and a visiting nurse. Hearing the news, I was more perplexed than sad. I had said my goodbyes and felt at peace with letting go. Still there came the niggling question: did more need to be communicated? And if so, by whom?

The following night I awoke spontaneously at 3:00 a.m. and went to my studio. In a familiar ritual I asked my deepest Self, "What is it I most need to understand about this situation?" Working quickly with colored pencil, I drew a jovial blue-winged, red-haired, green-eyed angel and a brilliant butterfly hovering over a pale woman in an open casket. The setting was a favorite New Jersey cemetery with its renowned 600-year-old live oak tree. The vitality of that outrageously Irish cherub was infectious. There she was, Mary Catharine Richie Farrelly...airborne! I laughed aloud and went to bed.

In the days that followed I prayed frequently to know whether or when to return east. Mummy's condition had improved slightly. She could swallow several tablespoons of baby food a day. Since it was a particularly busy month for me workwise, I bought a beautiful embroidered blouse to wear to her funeral, and I waited. It was an interesting few weeks, a time in which, despite geographic distance, I experienced a new closeness with my mother. Remembering how she loved my piano playing, I got out the music for Strauss waltzes and showtunes to serenade her. On more than one occasion,

I felt certain she could hear me. Often, carrying out simple domestic chores, I would speak to her out loud, assuring her of my love and giving her permission to let go. Physical work and exercise helped me through the less tranquil times, as did the permission to pound out my part on the baritone marimba in a class I had recently begun.

My poem "Go In Peace" celebrates the final event, not my mother's last breath but the week she spent in a coma without life support, in her own bed at home, attended around the clock by her children and familiar live-in caregiver. Having returned to New Jersey immediately following word of a second stroke, I cared for Mummy in the most intimate ways: helping shift her position, changing her diaper, brushing her hair, gently freshening her face with a damp cloth. Between times, we siblings talked, reminisced, laughed, and cried. Unlike my father's sudden death sixteen years before, here our family had the leisure to adjust to a parent's departure and to plan a funeral celebration of the finest order. Each morning we organized ourselves to accomplish the various tasks: obituary writing, meeting with clergy, notifying far-flung friends, answering the phone, meal planning, and so forth. I happily accepted the assignment to visit the county library to procure opera librettos and Broadway scores for a personalized musical medley to precede the funeral service. Towards evening we just naturally congregated at the dining room table; among other things we argued over favorite hymns and prayers, then gathered 'round the piano trying them out with a dear friend and musician who would play for the service, and ended each day with prayer and singing at our mother's bedside.

> And we sang round her bed
> as we sang in the church
> as we sang to rehearse
> in the days that she died.
> Round her bed
> we sang rounds,
> round her bed
> glory-be's,

round her bed
Kyries and Ave's
and, always,
Alleluias.

And the priest and the doctor:
"So at peace," they proclaimed.
Came the friends with their comfort,
came to sit or to stand,
came to stroke her cool arm,
came to cradle her hand.
By her bed
said goodbye
in their own special ways,
by her bed
in her home
all seven long days.
And we sang round her bed
as we sang in the church
as we sang to
rehearse
in the days that she
died.

That week Mummy's bedroom became a veritable sanctuary. Once it was stripped of habitual clutter, its pale blue carpet, fresh flowers, and billowing organdy curtains welcomed family and friends alike. People who had known and loved this woman came to sit beside her for as long as they liked, speaking silently or aloud their memories, joys, and regrets, talking to their friend "M.C." (Mary Catharine) who had lived in the same community, in the same home, for more than sixty years. For me, being there without my husband and daughter was a special blessing. Sleeping in my old room, I could tiptoe down the hall to visit Mums at odd hours. Initially I sat and sketched her, trying to reconcile her angular, emaciated form with the round-figured lover of sweets I had known most of my life. Later I brought colored pencils and paper to her maple desk overlooking the garden. What emerged in my sketchpad over many hours was an elaborate Nordic Christ figure reaching out to five underwater, open coffins, each containing an image of Mummy at a different life stage. All kinds of details of my own life crept onto that page as well, much to the amazement of those siblings who watched its evolution. At other times I simply held Mum's hand and talked to her. Often I did yoga on her soft carpet. It was as if I could finally let her and the rest of my family see who I had become—an artist. No apologies needed.

After a week of no food or water, Mummy slipped away. It was perfect, really. A gentle, uneventful parting with only my sister Patsy there to keep her company. Patsy, who over the years had been her most attentive companion and confidante. Patsy, who helped Mums organize her household, from wardrobe to social calendar to her twenty-four grandchildren's birthdays. Patsy, who maintained her equanimity in the midst of Mummy's tirades. Gracious, warm, practical Patsy, who accompanied Mums to many of her friends' funerals and took notes on what types of services, prayers, and hymns Mummy liked, who made a notebook of favorite psalms for Mummy to read at her leisure. Patsy, who assembled a basket of old picture postcards from family members and friends on various worldwide trips for Mummy to browse through or for a visitor to use as a conversation starter. Patsy, who made sure Mums always had her favorite rosary near at hand. Thus, by the time I returned from the Newark airport with my husband and five-year-old daughter, the doctor had already stopped by and verified Mummy's death, someone had closed her eyes and tied a soft tea towel around her jaw to keep it shut, and two men from the mortuary had arrived to take my mother's body to be embalmed.

What happened over the next few days were the formalities: the gathering of the clan; the return home of my mother's embalmed body in an open casket to be on view in Daddy's den; neighbors, parishioners, and parish priest gathered in the living room to pray the rosary for her soul's swift journey to heaven; the family wake when three generations of Farrellys recounted all kinds of stories, often surprising one another with descriptions of events previously known only to a few; a beautiful funeral mass and, following it, a festive meal with friends; and the burial. Clearly it was a time for those who hadn't been present during Mum's last week to begin coming to terms with their loss. But for me, who had so appreciated the opportunity to fully and intimately engage with Mummy's gradual dying, those few days before her funeral began to feel endless. I remember longing for the comfort and quiet of our house in Colorado. Still there were precious moments whose memory consistently makes me smile. First, our young daughter, Jori, and her almost-same-age cousin, Catherine, cautiously approaching the open casket, poking "Granny's" arm, then debating earnestly whether it was "really Gran" or not. Or me, contentedly in the kitchen making four enormous lasagnas, while an older nephew fed snacks to a bunch of enthusiastic great-grandchildren just back from hunting frogs at the same pond he himself had frequented during many a summer's visit. Then the thoughtfulness of my oldest niece Lisa and her husband creating a video of our family home that featured Lisa and me walking up the driveway, passing through the front door, and visiting each room upstairs and down while sharing memories and conducting impromptu interviews with whomever we met. Once edited by its makers, that video was generously distributed to all the closest kin—a precious souvenir.

Reflections

As I look back on the ease of my mother's passing, several things stand out. For one, we were graced by the support of longtime caregivers. Imagine a doctor who still did home visits! Imagine a housekeeper and her husband who both had previously worked in nursing homes! And don't forget the close family friends, people whose relationships with my parents (and especially with Mums during her sixteen years of widowhood) spanned decades. Another key player on the support team was my older brother, Louis. Living just three minutes away from Mums, both he and his wife were called on frequently. Added to Louis's patient, caring nature and his tact in resolving domestic disputes was his long-term diligence about managing Mummy's finances and ensuring that her legal documents were in order and a notarized living will in place. Finally, there was within the family the spiritual support of a shared Christian (in most cases, Catholic) faith with its rich heritage of oral prayer and its firm belief in an afterlife where souls were reunited with God and particular loved ones.

That said, the years before Mummy's final six months were far from smooth, especially for my siblings who lived close by. My mother hated being out of control. Often she railed against her failing mental abilities, lashing out at and accusing of thievery those nearest to her when she'd misplaced, for example, a favorite necklace or notepad. The growing forgetfulness of early dementia enraged her, as did needing help with dressing, bathing, and navigating stairs. A confirmed night owl, she resented being told when to go to bed, and often sent the housekeeper away so she could sit up and fall asleep at her dining room table "when she damned well pleased!"

In that last year, conversation with Mums became difficult. On the telephone with me she frequently asked where I was, and once I told her, repeatedly quizzed me about why I was living in Colorado. When I did visit her in person, she often confused present with past in ways that were both amusing and poignant. On one memorable afternoon at the New Jersey shore, Mummy and I were sitting drinking tea near the ocean. She was all smiles, clearly loving the environment with its familiar sounds of gulls and waves, and children racing along the beach. Then she looked me squarely in the eye and stated that this restaurant was the place where she could work to earn some extra pocket money. She thought starting as a dishwasher would be okay, then moving up to a hostess and finally a waitress position. Wanting to enter into her fantasy, which seemed, the more she talked, to belong to her teenage summers at a town nearby, I replied encouragingly, then wondered aloud whether her parents needed to be consulted. "Don't be stupid," she retorted. "They're dead." Right!

My mother died twenty-five years ago. But have I really said goodbye to her for the last time? I think not. For better and for worse, she shows up on a regular basis. Just looking around our home I see pieces of furniture from my childhood. In my closet is a faded cashmere sweater loved by my mother and by me, moth holes notwithstanding! When I work in my garden, arrange fresh flowers, insist that there's always room for one more at our dining table, organize a theater outing, or sit down for a quiet game of "Pounce" (an old fashioned Solitaire variation), I am my mother's daughter. But I am also my mother's daughter when I get over-committed and strung out, when I stop listening to others and try to force my own way, when I become upset at things not looking perfect, when I get stuck in the giving role and fail to ask for help, when I reach for an extra helping of food instead of being willing to experience whatever sensation or feeling has just paid me a visit.

Happily for me, my mother died at what most would call a "ripe old age," having accomplished many of her life ambitions. She also died when I had gained a certain measure of maturity. In my twenties I blamed Mummy for much of my unhappiness. "If only she had been more..." I had a long list of resentments and judgments that fueled my anger for several years. Eventually I came to see how self-defeating that was. With the help of a 12-step program and several good therapists, I was able to forgive my mother's perceived inadequacies and begin assuming responsibility for mothering myself. By my mid-forties, when Mummy passed, I had a solid marriage, wonderful friends, meaningful work, and fulfilling hobbies. Then, as now, I was and am truly blessed. And I feel grateful to have participated so intimately in my mother's final passage.

Mimi Farrelly-Hansen *replaced the wooded farmland of her northern New Jersey childhood with expansive views of the Rocky Mountains that she and her husband Paul enjoy from a passive solar home they designed. An art therapist for 30 years and founder of Naropa University's graduate art therapy program, Mimi continues to display her paintings and cherishes unfolding relationships with family and friends.*

Myrtle Elizabeth White Alexander

1952 family photo: from left to right, Quincy, me, Mom, Bill, Dad, and Steve

Mom and I in her house taking a break from going through her things
prior to moving to an independent living facility

Walking Through the Valley of the Shadows

by Beth Harrison

My mother was orphaned at a young age—she was under two. Her mother, her mother's sister, and her grandmother died when she was a toddler. When her mother died, her father left for California, taking her older siblings. She never saw him again. She was raised by her beloved Great-Uncle Henry, who was an invalid, and her cherished Great-Aunt Mandy, who died when my mother was in her teens. My mother finished school at Pineland School for Girls and stayed there during vacations and holidays when other children went home to their families. Everyone my mother loved, in those early days, either died too soon or left when someone else did. Nevertheless, she always thought of her childhood as happy.

Perhaps because the mothering in her life came from a Victorian grandmotherly figure, she never seemed to be a child of her own time and place. She was always a bit formal and old-fashioned, attentive to the details and customs of life—she monitored our syntax, our grammar, our table manners, and our appearance. If her children have somehow failed in adulthood to meet her high expectations, I guarantee that it was not her fault.

She expected to die young. I remember one conversation at the dinner table when she suggested to my father whom he might marry, when (not if) something happened to her. My father laughed at her preoccupation with who might be acceptable to marry him after she died and raise her four rambunctious children. He believed, but she did not, that they would live out their lives together, as indeed they did. She wasn't particularly fearful about it, as I remember, but that's who she was. In retrospect, I think it created a need in her for every meal, every holiday, the details of life itself, to be memorable.

My mother always had a garden, and flowers were on the table and in the house, fresh if it were possible, dried weeds beautifully arranged if it were not. When we were in the car going somewhere, she would spy something and we would stop to pick roadside cattails, to gather pretty rocks or shells. She played the piano, and our lives were full of music from the time we could say, "Play it again, Momma." As we got older, we had records and tapes of popular music. But the real music in our house was always created at that piano. We all learned to play musical instruments, though not particularly well. What I really learned was that I couldn't live without music in my life.

For my mother, her home was a metaphor for her inner life. She filled her house with things she loved and tangible reminders of the people that she cared about. She had antique furniture, and she knew the story behind each piece. She loved flowers, books, music. Meals were occasions, and most of them had someone extra at the table. Hospitality was for her a sacred obligation and a joy. You were always welcome in her house.

My mother was a genius at making something beautiful out of the ordinary. She could take a bunch of weeds and turn it into high art. When my husband and I were helping her move back to North Carolina from Virginia, I remember our carrying a box of rocks, which she insisted we take because they were interesting and beautiful, part of the natural world she loved. I think she loved her children in the same manner. We believed we were beautiful and handsome, smart and talented, unique and valued—because she believed it to be so. And so we were.

Few people outside our family recognized my mother's innate intelligence, in part because she wanted it that way. She was an introvert pushed by the circumstances of my father's vocation (he was in the state legislature, then in the U.S. Congress) into the public domain. In that other world before speechwriters, televised campaigns, and big money, she helped my father write his speeches. She had profound insights into political matters, and she was a voracious reader. She read four papers daily for most of her life. No matter how old or how well educated her children got, we all were the recipients of articles she had clipped out that she thought we needed to read.

She was deeply in love with my father, and I think my brothers and I have measured our own marriages and relationships against their marriage. I believe we all feel we have fallen short. When my father died, almost twenty years before my mother did, she had to recreate herself. She had never really imagined that she would be the one left behind. She had to learn to pay bills, to invest money, to take care of the mechanics of the house and car. She did, of course.

After she died, I read through her journals of those days, which she wrote as letters to my father. I realized, as I had not when she was alive, how much of her life in her later years was tied to what she thought were his expectations of how she should live. She believed that she would eventually see him again and be accountable to him for her choices. My mother was a religious person, and her traditional Christian beliefs were a part of all this, but the most palpable reality for her was about my father, his love for her, and hers for him. She had begun their marriage writing letters to her husband in the Navy for the duration of the war; and the last twenty years of her life were spent writing letters to that same man, pouring out her anxieties, fears, and affection, no stamps necessary.

Her expectations about her own death changed after my father died. She said repeatedly that she "didn't want to be a burden to her children," and she made sure the insurance premiums were paid and that she had the financial means to pay for her care. But underneath this concern to take care of herself was an unspoken assumption that her children would be there holding her hand and she would be kindly and compassionately cared for, as Great-Uncle Henry had been. She would be surrounded by loving family. That was what was supposed to happen. That's what families do.

I wish it had been that simple.

My oldest daughter Katie moved to North Carolina after she graduated from college and moved in with my mother. She lived with her for nearly three years. That allowed Mom to stay in her own house, surrounded by her garden and her beautiful belongings. It also gave her someone to do things for (that's another story, one for Katie to write), as it became more and more difficult for her to climb the stairs to her bedroom and work in her beloved yard. After Katie got married, my mother decided it was time to look at assisted living facilities, while she could still walk into one. I drove down some six hours, on successive weekends, and we looked together at several continuing care retirement communities. She decided on the least elaborate of the three we visited, put her name on the list, and waited to be called.

Meanwhile, over the next year and a half, I went home nearly every weekend. Mom and I would go through her treasures as she decided what to take with her, what should be given away and to whom, and what ought to be tossed. It was painful for her, not much less so for me. The first weekend I went down to begin this sorting process, she was sitting on the floor in the guest bedroom with a pile of used Christmas wrapping paper. When I asked her what she was doing, she said that she was deciding which wrapping paper to take with her. I just stood there, stunned, and realized that I was going to have to do this with her, not just get her started. Every antique, every knickknack, every Mason jar, every rock, every piece of paper had a story. I heard them all. We sorted through the stories, sorted through each piece of her life, separating it all out, and gave it away.

She scaled back her life and moved into Trinity Oaks, where she spent many years. She had hospitalizations and scares, but good medical care. Her doctor had known her all his life; his mother was my mom's best friend. For most of that period, she was still able to drive in the daytime; she had friends who visited, and she could still read three newspapers a day and books from the library. There was never anything wrong with her brain, but her eyes were failing, and her erratic blood pressure, diabetes, and other issues were taking their toll. She moved from independent living into assisted living and back several times—then, finally, into the nursing home. We moved her, at that point, into another nursing home in Raleigh, where my youngest brother and his recently retired wife lived. In the last year of her life, glaucoma took her eyesight. She could no longer watch television because the glare hurt her eyes, and she couldn't read. Her

Charcot-Marie-Tooth neuropathy syndrome made her bedridden for that last year and in considerable pain. She slept more and more.

My role during this last year is still something of a blur. I drove down to Raleigh every other weekend, sometimes staying overnight with my brother and his family, but more frequently spending an hour or two with my mother, then driving the four hours back. I would wait until she woke up, and we would usually have about an hour of time together before she nodded off again. She was under Hospice care for nearly a year. Her doctors expected her to die before the Christmas holidays, but she rallied and continued to do so repeatedly. Katie's first child was born in October, and she brought him to Raleigh so his great-grandmother could meet him. Family came and went, saying goodbye again and again.

I began going to Raleigh every weekend, and I usually managed to talk, hold her hand, rub her feet, and tell her I loved her. In March, she began not waking up. The last time I saw my mother, I talked to her, but I have no idea what she might have heard. She did not appear to know that I was there. My husband and I had planned to go during Spring Break to Greece. Would we go or not? After talking to my brother, we decided to go ahead. So we left on the long flight. My mother died during the night as we were flying over the Atlantic.

Mom died over two years ago. She was 92. I said goodbye to her many times during those last years, each time thinking I would not see her again. My mother didn't die as she would have wished. She had spent more time than most of us thinking about her own death—together, we planned her funeral, picked the music and the musicians. In her last years, none of her children were able to take her into our homes. None of us were at her side for her last breath. We all did what we could, given the circumstances of our lives. True enough, but hard.

My own relationship with my mother was conflicted. She wished for a girly, musical, quiet child. I was athletic, bookish, and outgoing—not to mention stubborn, noisy, and argumentative. I never knew what to do with my hair; she never got used to my jeans. As I was growing up, her ideas about what it meant to be a woman seemed archaic to me; we argued over everything. But I loved her, as she did me, and I appreciated even then the gifts she gave me—music, intelligence, dignity, an awareness of beauty in the everyday, and a sense of worth.

She still appears in my dreams. And I have moments when her physical presence is unmistakable. When I was diagnosed recently with diabetes, a disease she lived with for most of her life, I heard her say to me that it would be okay, that she would show me how to live with it. I hear her behind the notes of a piano sonata, and in my attempts to put flowers in one of her old vases. I hear her urge me to express my gratitude more, my cynicism less. My mother's voice these days is that of my mother at her best. The old arguments are gone; she's not interested any more in how I wear my hair or whether I am wearing makeup. I do have a deep and profound sense that our relationship will continue and will help me as I make my own transitions into whatever the future holds. Her pervasive sense of her own mortality and her acceptance of it have been unexpected gifts. I've said goodbye to some aspects of my mother only to find, through her journals and my dreams, a mother I am only beginning to know.

Beth Harrison *taught philosophy and religion at Northern Virginia Community College for forty years before retiring in 2010. She established the Women's Center there and is currently Co-chair with Dr. Jill Biden of the Women's Mentoring Project. Beth serves as writer and Associate Editor for* Reading Between the Lines, *a journal that incorporates a Jungian perspective in the exploration of scriptures.*

Patricia Ann Auernhammer Matthews

Patricia a year before her death

The Last Winter

by Madeline Rugh

It's early December, the season of drifting gray smoke and crisp quiet in East Liverpool, Ohio. With little work available since the steel mills closed in nearby areas, the city is "depressed." She casts her forlorn reflection of tattered and sooty brick buildings onto the dark waters of the Ohio River. Her vacant eyes stare at the rusty barges loaded with coal bringing food to the always-hungry power plants upriver.

This is where my husband grew up, and I am staying at his parents' house situated on the banks of this great waterway. They live in a rambling, solid brick, three-story house with a long open porch across the back, overlooking the river. The porch boards are sturdy, though uneven in spots, and slant slightly downward away from the house. The brown paint on them is chipped and worn.

It is dusk when I walk onto the back porch, the rusty screen door creaking shut behind me. I am hoping to watch the sunset scatter some much-needed color into the sky and across the rippling gray water. There is an old, large maple tree that umbrellas much of the backyard and, when in leaf, obscures a view of the river. But this evening, she stands with midnight arms spread, holding a pale canopy of winter sky. A gentle breeze whispers through her up-stretched crooked fingers that suddenly begin a frenzied tapping and snapping, clicking, ticking, clacking, cracking…I am catapulted into an altered state. The peach-tinted clouds, having joined the staccato dance, are scuttling across the sky, rapidly changing shape like images in time-lapse photography. And then the mad tango of branch and cloud ends abruptly; everything is normal. Nothing is stirring. I stand there for a few more moments uncertain of what I have experienced. I know it is an omen, but of what I cannot guess.

As darkness descends, I return to the house and to a fitful sleep.

The next morning there is a phone call for me. I take it in the filled waiting room of my father-in-law's medical practice. It is my sister. Without introduction she says, "Mom is dead." Before I can speak or respond, some wild being surges forward and a cry spills from a place deeper and more ancient than anything I have known. She howls a loud, long, deep, and piercing cry. Embarrassed, my mother-in-law grabs me and shuttles me upstairs. The waiting patients stir like a small herd of animals looking nervously toward one another in alarm, unable to move.

I have been given a hefty dose of tranquilizer, and I sleep, dreamless and heavy.

The next day my husband and I drive home to Michigan, numb and disbelieving. I meet with my sister, father, and brothers and hear the story of my mother's death. It occurred the night before, around sunset; the snapping tree tango suddenly makes shocking sense.

My mother committed suicide. Her body was found by a maid at a nearby hotel she had chosen for this final dramatic act. The day before her death, she told my father she was going to Lansing for a Rosicrucian conference and would be staying overnight. She never left town. In fact, she was just down the street about one mile away. The coroner said he had never seen such a well-prepared suicide. My mother had covered the bed with a plastic drop cloth, knowing the body evacuates upon death. She had on a favorite dress with a note pinned to it that said, "Do Not Resuscitate." On the bedside table were all of her tablets and pills used to help control the pain and swelling of her very severe case of rheumatoid arthritis. From these, she had created a deadly alchemical brew. Cause of death: drug overdose.

Several months before, she had been hospitalized with what appeared to be a reaction to one of her medications. Too late, my father realized she must have tried to commit suicide at that time and failed. My mother would not fail again. She was 52, and I was 30.

My mother was a member of the Hemlock Society and a supporter of Jack Kevorkian and his efforts to assist people with honorable end-of-life strategies. She didn't believe in extending life when there was extreme pain, crippling illness, or a disabling accident. Because of her arthritis, she found herself crippled, often in a wheelchair, with an expectancy of continued deterioration, pain, and humiliation. She was of proud and severe German heritage and could hardly tolerate people looking down at her when she was in a wheelchair. She hated the idea of being taken care of and loathed her appearance, bloated and puffy from steroids.

We asked ourselves, was this an act of courage or despair or some incomprehensible combination? Why didn't we know she was considering taking her life? Did she drop hints that we all missed? The members of my family searched their memories, in the secret places of their hearts, for a word, image, or action that had been missed and so made us unwitting accomplices to her death. One memory that haunted me was seeing my mom sitting in a chair, arms wrapped tightly around her body, rocking gently. This was several weeks before her death, and I realize too late that it was a missed opportunity to ask, "Are you okay, Mom?" Chances are she wouldn't have answered me with any depth. She felt she knew as much as any therapist and would not have sought help. My mother was very proud.

It was a closed casket. No one said anything about suicide; it was an "accidental drug overdose." I desperately (though secretly) asked people from the Rosicrucian group what their spiritual beliefs said about suicide. They told me the soul would realize what it had done immediately upon death and then would be rebirthed quickly to work on the situation again.

When I was in junior high school, my mother introduced me to the mystical Christian sect called the Rosicrucian Order. We sat once a week in front of her beautiful arched vanity mirror in a darkened room with one white candle and the drifting smoke from the exotic rose incense so unique to this organization. We studied esoteric material that included metaphysical practices such as seeing auric fields or moving objects with thought. And yet, despite the beauty and depth of these practices, my mother was unable to apply them to her place of deepest wounding.

It was to these incongruities that I directed my own expressive works, poetry and paintings, in an effort to try to understand the paradoxical combination of her deep wisdom and an inability to see her own beauty. I wrote a poem to accompany the picture of her that the funeral home featured along with her favorite flower, the iris:

> *She was like a single flower, delicate, loved, and admired.*
> *But, like a flower, she could not see her own beauty.*
> *Trembling in winds that ripple our lives,*
> *though outwardly strong,*
> *her fragile insides could no longer survive.*
> *Now, in great pain, all we can do is cry.*
> *Yet her loving, caring spirit will,*
> *from our hearts and minds,*
> *never die.*

My mother had always wanted to be cremated. She viewed the fire as cleansing and purifying. So it was that my sister and I took turns caring for the cigar box-size ash container until things began to unravel even more. There were whisperings that my mother had left a note—not the one on her dress, but a why-I-committed-suicide note. I have never seen such a letter. My older brother claimed there was one and that it said she took her own life to try to get my sister away from an abusive relationship. He and my sister-in-law turned against my sister and isolated her. My sister was beside herself with grief and confusion and called me every day to talk. At one point, my husband (thinking he was protecting me) told her to stop calling. That was the last straw for her, and our family fragmented into guilt and accusation. My sister refused to speak to me after that, though I was desperately trying to let her know that my husband's feelings were not mine. Ten years passed before she was willing to communicate with me. I was as devastated by the loss of my sister as I was by the loss of my mother.

Approximately two weeks after Mom's death, everyone received a Christmas card from her. I don't know how she orchestrated this mailing.

Clearly, the cards had been addressed and perhaps given to someone to mail at a designated time. Imagine our shock when receiving a note from the grave, as it were. When my mother selected cards, she was careful and thoughtful with regard to imagery and sentiment. They had to be meaningful and appropriate symbols. My card had the statue of liberty on the front. I took this to be a message from her about freedom, that her death represented freedom for her. There was a note on the back telling me she had rejoined the Rosicrucians and that they would be having a Christmas party, which she would like me to attend with her. This note seemed to tell me that she hadn't been entirely sure of her suicidal plans when she prepared the card. I don't know what transpired that pushed her to a final and deadly decision and will never know. That is part of the pain and endless mystery of suicide.

Probably the hardest aspect for me was not getting to say goodbye. I am now very careful to always say goodbye to loved ones and friends and to tell them how I value their presence in my life. Our family never spoke openly of love or caring and showed few signs of affection, so this has been a practice of some difficulty for me, but it is a form of remembering and honoring my mother's act of courage and despair. (I think it was both.)

And then there was my Aunt Hattie, my mother's only surviving sister. She told me how angry my mother was at her father (a gypsy that my grandmother had become pregnant by, who had then been run out of town before he could marry her) and how she could not forgive him for making her illegitimate. My aunt said that she was out at the mailbox several yards away from the house on the day of my mother's death. She heard her phone ringing but was unable to get to the house fast enough to answer. The line was dead. Hattie said she could sense it was my mother, her sister, and was absolutely convinced she was calling for help. The thought that my mother may have suffered, panicked, and tried to reach out was profoundly disturbing.

After my mother's death, I asked her repeatedly to contact me, to let me know she was okay, to appear to me; nothing ever happened until about five years later. I had been going through some extraordinary measures to try and become pregnant, which included a procedure called a "cup insemination." A few weeks after receiving this treatment at a fertility clinic in Tulsa, I began having abdominal pain. I called the clinic to talk with my doctor, but he was on vacation. His substitute told me not to worry, that I couldn't possibly be pregnant, since the cup insemination almost never worked the first time. I reluctantly hung up the phone, still feeling apprehensive. The pain continued and increased. I called once more and received the same response.

That night I dreamed of my mother for the first time. I was riding my bicycle down a hill and saw her standing at the bottom, off to the side. I leapt off my bike and ran toward her with my arms spread wide open, shouting with joy to see her. I so wanted to hug her in a way we never did when she was alive. Instead, she held out her hand to stop me from touching her and said, "Not yet—but soon if you don't take care." I knew exactly what she meant. The pain.

The next morning I told my husband the dream and said that we had to go to Tulsa (about a two hour drive). My mother was telling me I would die if I didn't get assistance. We called the clinic one more time; my doctor was back from vacation. He was very alarmed and insisted that I come to Tulsa at once. We drove with me doubled over in pain. Upon arrival I went through a series of tests and was quickly prepped for surgery. I had an ectopic pregnancy that was about to burst. Had it burst en route, I would have bled to death. My mother saved my life—or was it just some part of me that used her image to guide me? Is my mother in two worlds at once? In spirit as an ancestor? Embodied in another incarnation? I don't know the answers to these questions, though I think about them often. I remain certain that my mother will come for me when it is time for me to leave. The moment when I can hug her will be the moment of my own passing.

Nearly twenty years after my mother's death, while listening to the struggle of a young student whose mother had just passed away, I felt compelled to revisit my own experience and create the responsive piece, "Sorrow of the Root Woman." I realized that much of my imagery and art-making was still attending to my mother's death. In the case of the Root

Woman image, it is the woman who is our root, the archetypal Mother; my sorrow was not only for my own loss and my student's loss, but the loss of the deep divine feminine, Sophia, the feminine face of God. Thus it is that my mother's death kept an underground stream flowing, which surfaced periodically, and now runs above ground and is reflected in my work in nature and spirituality. I'm only now coming to this realization and expressing my gratitude for being directed toward my own true nature and purpose for being here. This is my mother's gift from beyond the grave, sustaining in me what she could not find nor sustain within herself.

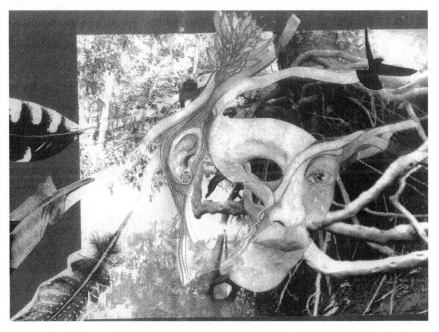

"Sorrow of the Root Woman," mixed-media photo montage,
12 x 18 inches, 1997

Madeline Rugh *is an artist, educator, and art therapist. A founder of the Imaginal Trackers Institute that provides arts-based courses in ecology and spirituality, she is currently a visiting professor of art and psychology at St. Gregory's University. Madeline's spiritual practice includes mixed media creation of ritual implements and contemplative walking with her dog Scully.*

Priscilla Watson Plautz

Mom and I playing in the backyard in Newport News, Virginia, 1982, when I was about six years old

Priscilla Plautz in Hampton, Virginia, 1998

Momma

by Jenny Watson Suh

My mother died on September 11th—but not that one. It was two years later, in 2003 on a Thursday. I was 26 and had just begun my first year of law school. So much of that day has stuck with me, details that, if the day had not ended as it did, wouldn't have been crystallized in my memory.

I was driving home from school when my friend stopped her car at the traffic light beside me. She asked if I wanted to go grab a quick dinner. "No," I said, "I'm not really feeling very well. I better get home." Strange, I thought to myself, I wasn't feeling ill until just now. Perhaps my body somehow knew what my mind could not yet, the news that was coming.

I got home to Ted. He was making plans with our friends to attend a concert that night in Boulder. It was Donna the Buffalo, one of my favorites. I told Ted that I wasn't feeling up to it and he should go on without me. Settling in, I pulled on some comfy clothes, my old Virginia shirt and pajama pants. I made myself dinner, tortilla chips with melted cheese. It was grad school, after all. As night came, the house was quiet, just Dixie and me. I was falling asleep in front of a movie when Dixie started barking. Her bark told me someone was outside. I got up and peeped out the front bedroom window. There was a police car in the driveway. I held my breath. Oh my god—Ted. The brain must have some mechanism that inhibits panic by flooding your mind with all the other reasons why a police car might materialize in your driveway at night. It's nothing, I said to myself, it's nothing.

The doorbell rang. More barking. I turned on a light and opened the door. Two women stood grimly on the porch, one wearing the uniform of the Lakewood police, the other in street clothes. "Is there a Jennifer Cox living here?"

I heard a voice say, "Yes."

"Do you know a Priscilla Plautz?"

The same voice conjured, "Yes, she is my mother."

They floated inside, up the steps and into the living room. "Your mother was in a car accident…The officer on scene did everything he could…"

The next moment I was transformed. I was a girl caught inside a dream. I looked down at my body—saw the Virginia shirt I knew I had worn to bed. I looked up and down the length of my arms—wiggled my toes—saw myself sitting on this couch. I felt awake, but I couldn't have been. I couldn't have been.

I came back to reality, back to that couch and into that moment. Then the tears began. The questions. The nausea. The crippling grief.

My mom had been at a memorial party for a friend of the family who was on the airplane that crashed into the Pentagon two years before. Driving home alone after dark, she swerved to avoid hitting some of those rubbery lane dividers. Her SUV struck the curb and flipped over. She wasn't wearing her seatbelt.

They explained that the police had been trying to contact my stepfather, but I learned later that he had gone to sleep with his cell phone off. He was out of state, visiting an aunt in Michigan. My mother did not have an "in case of emergency" in her phone contacts. They looked down inside her purse and found an old vaccinations book for a child called Jennifer. It must be her daughter, they thought. They then found my address in Colorado and sent these local officers to give me the news. I was there for her, if only my name on a tiny blue booklet. I was still there when she needed me.

What happened next was the hardest thing I have ever done in my life. At this moment I knew that this grief was not mine alone. I had to call my brother and tell him our mother was dead. I had to call my aunt and tell her that her sister was killed. And I had to call my stepfather and tell him that his wife was gone.

Momma

I never got the chance to say goodbye to my mother. But I do not wish it had been some other way. She and I were both terrible at goodbyes. Few were the occasions we parted for any length of time that did not involve a waterfall of tears and boo-hooing. You should have seen the day she dropped me off at college; people stared. If she had been diagnosed with a disease that took her slowly, I would have had to watch her die. My mother would have been tormented with grief every time we came to her bedside and wept with her. And what would have been worse is if somehow her body had held on, and my brother and I had been forced to decide to end her life. I tell myself this swift ending was the way she was meant to go.

My mother was strong and kind. The oldest of three children, she grew up in the middle class suburbs. Her mother had odd jobs, but mainly stayed home to raise her kids. Her father was in the navy and absent for long stretches. Despite more than her share of setbacks and heartbreaks, my mother stayed positive and was always looking forward. She was loved by many lifelong friends. She worked hard, achieving professional positions that no woman before her ever had. Nevertheless, her children, my brother and I, were the center of her life. She was there beside us, but never smothering. She allowed my brother and me to make our own decisions and mistakes. Our home was warm and safe and comfortable. I believe she gave us the ultimate gift, a foundation on which we could become the best version of ourselves.

I look for my mom everywhere. I place significance on things in her honor. The flock of pelicans that fly low over the surf are my mother and her friends. Every shooting star is a gift from her. The yellow butterfly that ushers in springtime is a sign that she is still with me. My daughter's sweetest embraces are somehow courtesy of my mother.

Sometimes I feel as if my mother sacrificed herself so that I didn't have to hear the policewoman tell me that Ted had died that night—so he could live to become my husband, my best friend, the father of my two extraordinary children. I know it doesn't make sense, but it could have been Ted's name uttered that night. And it wasn't.

One thing that losing a parent, or anyone whom you truly love, teaches you, is that life is so fragile. I know there will be another day when the doorbell will ring, or a diagnosis will be given, or another accident will happen. We all have an end date, even the people you swear you couldn't live without. You do, you live without them. And the pain, that cold searing pain, never really goes away—you just bury it deeper under layers of scar tissue. You put it in a box inside your heart.

When I talk about my mother, I still cry. The sting is still there. And I will go on crying, allowing myself to feel the pain of her death. I don't know any other way to deal with it. Suppressing the emotions feels like cheating myself. This tenderness is a part of who I am now. And to know me is to know this story of my mother.

I didn't say goodbye to my mother on our September 11th, nor have I said goodbye on any day since. How do you say goodbye to someone whom you see in the mirror every day? Someone whose voice you hear every time you speak? For some, saying goodbye is essential. They need one last expression of emotion or final utterance to close a special relationship. I am not one of those people. I can say with utmost certainty that my mother knew how much I loved her. She knew that I recognized and appreciated the sacrifices she made for my brother and me. She heard me say, over and over: I love you. That knowledge comforts me and gives me peace.

We only get one lifetime with our mothers, and sometimes that life is too short. My mom, who created, comforted, and protected me, was my first and purest blessing. She showed me that I was loveable and taught me how to love others. If I continue to see my mother in myself and feel her presence in life's beautiful moments, I don't ever have to say goodbye.

Jenny Watson Suh, *a graduate of the University of Virginia and the University of Denver Law School, lives in Truckee, California, with her husband Ted and their two amazing children, Tyson and Harper. She works at home as a mother and rental property manager. Enjoying the outdoor life of Tahoe, her family loves to ski, hike, bike, and wake surf.*

Roberta Ruth Eye Brewer Nesselrodt

My mother at age 20

A Daughter's Insight

by De'Onne Scott

My mother, Ruth, died of metastasized kidney cancer in May 2006. Her initial cancer was discovered only two years before. At the end, the cancer had spread to her lungs, lymph glands, breast, and finally her brain, which quickly caused her death. She died early on a Sunday morning, alone in her hospital room just a few days before her 74th birthday. I was at home when I got the call from my youngest brother. I was 52.

When Mom was a child, her grandmother appeared to her the night she died. Mom had not realized that what she had seen was an apparition until the next morning when her mother told her she couldn't have seen her grandmother because she had died the night before. So I'm sure she believed in life after death in some form. Certainly, she didn't want to die, but if she was afraid of dying she didn't tell me.

My mother was a strong person. She was a fighter and very positive about the treatment of her cancer. One of the effects of Mom's cancer that I couldn't get over was the loss of her hair, but she just seemed to take it in stride. I could never get used to seeing her look so different. My discomfort pushed me to crochet many types of hats for her to hide her baldness. I never admitted until now that I made the hats as much for myself as for her.

I was anxious during most of the time I spent with Mom during the days before she died, in part because I knew our time together was limited. I wanted to talk to her about our troubled mother-daughter relationship. I had tried to do so in the past, but we never seemed to have the kind of talk that could resolve some of my feelings. I also felt sad because I knew time was short, and all the questions I had about family history could not

253

be answered. Because the cancer was in her brain, she would sound completely normal one moment and then suddenly point out something that wasn't there.

I believe Mom was okay with her transition from life to death, although there was something that had caused her to cling to life for a while: her concern for my sister, Judie. It is hard for me to contemplate my mother's death without thinking of her. Judie was 18 months older than I was. She was born at home and premature, weighing very little, but the doctor was able to save her life. In retrospect, I realize she probably suffered brain damage. Judie was emotionally and financially dependent on Mom, who always protected her and helped her, so Mom must have known. Their bond became one of co-dependence; because Judie needed Mom so much, Mom felt powerful. Then I was born. It wasn't long before I felt like the unwanted child.

When Judie found out that our mother had cancer, she became increasingly self-destructive, smoking and drinking heavily. She had even stated to my sister-in-law that she wanted to die before Mom. When I got the call that Judie had died, stunned shock was all I could feel; tears quickly followed. Then I learned the surprising news that it was due to natural causes. I didn't know whether or not we should tell Mom that Judie had died to explain why she had not called or come to visit Mom in the hospital. The doctor's advice was that we should not.

When the hospital staff asked what we wanted done for Mom in the way of trying to extend her life, knowing she could not get well, we opted to only have her kept as comfortable as possible. When visiting Mom one day, I watched a nurse try to give her a drink. She kept choking, because the advancing brain cancer affected her muscle coordination. Wondering whether my judgment may have been cruel, I began to question my medical decisions on her behalf. Maybe we should have allowed Mom to be given the medical treatment. I had always heard that dying of dehydration was quick and fairly painless, and I couldn't stand the thought of her being pumped with so much morphine that she wouldn't even know she was alive anyway. Was I doing the right thing? Was she suffering more or was she suffering less because of my decisions? I prayed that she would die quickly; her inability to drink might be the quickest way this could happen. I feared I was taking the place of God.

Saying goodbye to Mom happened under these unusual circumstances. My goodbye was more a plea for her to let go and move on. She had no quality of life, and I knew she could not get well. I didn't want the doctors employing useless treatments to extend her life when there was no chance of reversing the damage to her brain or make her well. In the end, my brother, sister-in-law, and I finally told Mom that the reason Judie had not been to see her or call her was that she had died of a heart attack just a couple of weeks before. We told Mom that we loved her, that we would be okay, and that Judie had gone on and was waiting for her along with Dad, Grandma, and Granddad, so there was no reason for her to hang on to help Judie as she had always done. We hoped this would help her feel that she could let go and so be spared the inevitable suffering from a slow, painful cancer death. This was my goodbye.

Mom was not able to give us any verbal sign that she knew us, nor could she acknowledge what we had said. But I know she understood us because, instead of living six more months as we had been told she would, she died a day and a half later. When I last saw her, she was barely recognizable because of the ravages of chemotherapy and radiation. The fact that she didn't look like Mom anymore made it easier for me to see her dying.

Mom's funeral was unusual. Because my sister had died three weeks before, Mom's funeral became a double funeral in that our sister's ashes were placed in our mother's coffin. This seemed to be the appropriate thing to do, since in life the umbilical cord between Judie and Mom had never really been severed.

When my aunt asked if I was going to speak at Mom's funeral as I had done for my stepfather, I said no. Because my relationship with Mom had been so painful for so much of my life, I just couldn't bring myself to speak. I didn't think I was strong enough to hold back the bitterness I had always felt, especially since my thoughts and emotions were in such upheaval. I shed only one tear at her funeral.

I couldn't remember a time when I didn't feel emotionally guarded while in Mom's presence. Almost immediately after she died, I felt a kind of elation and freedom. For the first time, I felt safe when I thought of her because she couldn't hurt me anymore. However, I still wanted her near me when I was clearing out her house. In my mind I desperately asked for Mom's guidance so I could do what she would have done while I was dividing and giving her possessions to my remaining siblings, my sister's daughter, and myself. Throughout the months it took to clear out her house, sell it, and close her estate, I sensed that she was right at my shoulder helping me. I was comforted and confident that I was making the right choices.

After her funeral, there were two memorial services. At one of them, I heard many people, including important politicians and everyday humble folks, speak about Mom and the impact of her life on theirs. She had been the president of her homeowners' association, and through her efforts, she helped save the homes of hundreds of elderly and low-income families. I came to realize how differently my mother was seen by others.

Mom was the most talented person I've ever known. She taught me to cook, sew, crochet, and cross-stitch, to love history, and so much more. When she died, I completed her unfinished crocheted afghans, sewed her name labels on them, and distributed them to her offspring so her last efforts would not be wasted.

Mom had many collections. One of them was what she believed to be special Kennedy dollars. In reality, they are normal one dollar bills that have the letter K and four elevens on them (Kennedy was forty-four when he was assassinated). I save them now in memory of her, and this helps me feel that I am still connected to her in a small way.

She had a keen mind, and although she didn't finish high school, she was well read and especially loved history. When my first history book was published, she was so proud. Unfortunately, she had died by the time my second book came out. Because she was always involved in our family's histories and genealogies, I feel this responsibility has been left to me since her death. I have often wished that I could ask her why she had a certain photograph and how the people or places in the photographs were connected to her or to me.

I am now the family matriarch, a position that should have been my sister's. I am haunted by Judie and think of her almost obsessively. Because she died young, I can't help sensing that my life, too, could be short. Somehow because she and Mom were so bonded in life, and now in death, I feel excluded again. I also feel guilty because I expected my sister to be more than she could be.

When all has been said and done, I believe that Mom did the best she could, and I have no right to judge her or how she lived her life when I don't know all of her life's experiences. I loved Mom and miss her, but probably miss the Mom I needed more than the Mom I had.

De'Onne Scott *was the first person in her family to graduate from high school. After attending 21 years as a part-time student, she graduated from college. Married, with two daughters and two grandchildren, she has had two books on local history published and has written several biographies and history books, which she donated to her regional library.*

Rose Anne Cassidy Kearney

Mom walking home (photo taken early 1950s)

Mom and Dad with sunflower (photo taken sometime in the 1970s)

Goodbye in Stages

by Peter Joseph Kearney

When my wife Clare and I moved into our new home in Fredericksburg, Virginia, about five years ago, we unpacked our belongings, but there
were some things we never could find. One of them was a prayer book that
belonged to my mother, in which she had written that it was a Christmas
gift to her in 1923 at the convent school she attended in Ireland. She was
then about 17 years old. In time, the spine of the book deteriorated, and
my father repaired it by operating his sewing machine to put a new leather spine on the book. Thus it became for me a treasured keepsake of both
Mom and Dad, a symbol of their life together, and I lamented its loss.

Only a couple of weeks ago, Clare discovered it in a small box that
had been out in the open all these years, one in which I had never thought
to look. I was overjoyed to have it again as a tangible sign that Mom and
Dad are with me, both of them together. It confirms for me how much my
mother meant to me, a confirmation especially valuable when I reflect on
how devoid of emotion I was at my mother's death.

When my mother passed away almost ten years ago, Clare and I were
living in Falls Church, Virginia, and Mom was in Hayward, California.
She had gone there to be with my brother Johnny and his wife Nila, who
both wished to make Mom's declining years as pleasant as possible. Mom
was reluctant to leave her home in Brentwood, New York, and in time she
concocted the disturbing notion that my brothers Johnny and Tony had
maneuvered her transfer to California in order to take possession of her
Brentwood home. Johnny and Nila, on the contrary, were nothing but generous in their solicitous attention to her at a time when she was not able to

take care of herself. Eventually she insisted on moving out of their home. Johnny and Nila finally acceded to her wish and moved her to St. Regis Retirement Center in Hayward. Her physical problems had started with a fall and broken hip in Brentwood and were aggravated by a similar fall and break at the retirement center. She was now confined to a wheelchair. Her gradual physical decline was accompanied by a form of dementia that had her often living in the past. She would ask me and my two brothers, whether in person or on the phone, if we had heard from people of long ago whom we barely remembered or didn't even know.

During Mom's four and a half years in California, Clare and I visited with her three times. During our second visit, Mom sat quietly by herself in Johnny and Nila's home and didn't communicate in any sustained way. Though I said hello and kissed her in greeting, I spent almost no time in her company. I have since found myself wishing I had done otherwise, just sitting beside her for a while even if she said nothing. At that time, there didn't seem to be a point to it, but I have regretted that behavior.

By the time of our next visit, she had moved to the retirement center. I recall wheeling her about as we all toured the place, which was reassuring in its homey atmosphere and in the evident care given to the residents. I recall conversing with Mom as we went along. She was even alert enough to lodge a feisty complaint about my wearing a beard. I remember looking at her as we left the center and thinking that this might be the last time I would see her alive. It was. That our last meeting had some life to it and some sharing has been a comfort to me.

The call about Mom's death came some months later. Johnny and Nila made all the arrangements for the funeral mass in Hayward. Years before, Mom had told me that she wanted to be buried in St. Raymond's Cemetery in the Bronx, New York, next to Dad, who had died almost 20 years before Mom did. I told this to Johnny, who arranged for the air transport of Mom's body to a funeral home near the cemetery. We three brothers then had one of our all-too-rare meetings. Our emotions at that time were subdued. Perhaps that was because Mom's death was not unexpected. She had been failing for some years and had almost reached 94 years of age.

Nonetheless, I was somewhat surprised at my grieving so little over her passing. Later, at work, a counselor had told of his own lack of mourning until 6 months after his mother's death. A lady friend of his mother said simply what a lovely person his mother was, and he suddenly broke into uncontrolled weeping. I wondered whether the same would happen to me. It never did, and now, almost 10 years later, I doubt that it ever will.

Although I grieved little at the time of Mom's death, I can think of some earlier farewells to her and recall how emotion-laden they were, either for her or for me. I like to think of them as early stages of the final goodbye. My first long-term goodbye was a most exciting one for me, as I boarded the USS Constitution to sail over to Italy and spend my final four years of study before ordination to the priesthood. Mom had said to me a couple of days before I left, "How will I ever get along without you?" I was also very touched by her giving me a house key so that I would know I was always welcome to come back home if I ever changed my mind about the priesthood.

Then there was the time of one of her visits when I was teaching at Catholic University in Washington, DC. While she was there, I caught a severe cold, and she decided it was better that she leave rather than burden me with concern about her. I can see her smiling sweetly as she turned and waved to me on her way to catch the bus to the railway station. Suddenly I was a lonely little boy, and I wept and wept.

The third farewell that comes to mind occurred on my visit home to Mom before my leaving the priesthood and marrying Clare. I kissed Mom goodbye and walked several blocks with my suitcase to an elevated subway station in the Bronx. As I stood on the platform, I suddenly heard Mom calling my name, and there she was on the sidewalk below, hollering and waving her arms. She seemed unmindful of all around her and perhaps only then realized that I was really leaving. I waved back and called out goodbye to her, and then the train came between us. Later, my brother Tony told me she was utterly distraught for the rest of the day. I feel sure she was worried about the state of my soul, because I had not received permission from the Church to marry. Shortly after Clare and I were married, however, we received a lovely card from Mom wishing God's blessing on our marriage. Apart from that, we were not in contact with her until her anxious phone call on that fateful day in Washington when an airplane crashed into the 14th Street Bridge and a backing Metro train buckled, crushing two passengers to death.

Whether it was a matter of Mom's emotions or mine, these lesser farewells indicated to me how strong was the bond between us. The awareness of that love has stayed with me through the years. It seems to express itself occasionally when I dream. Even though Mom has appeared only sporadically in my dreams since her death, a couple of them in this past year have been reassuring. In one, we hugged each other, and Mom told me she was pleased with me. In the dream, I wondered how that could be so, because in fact I had been in frequent angry arguments with her during the several months before I left the priesthood and married. In another dream, she was seated doing some sewing, and she asked me to come and sit beside her. Might the dream have been telling me that some mending of our relationship was taking place because of those regrettable times in Hayward when I neglected to sit beside her?

For my part, I also initiate communication with Mom. I spend a little time in prayer thinking of both Mom and Dad almost every day. On my bureau, I have a photo of the gravesite where they both are buried. A psychic I visited years ago recommended that I have a cup of tea with my deceased Dad every now and then. But Mom and Dad always had their tea together, so I have my occasional cup with both of them at the table, asking them how they are, wishing them well, and requesting their help. As I do so, I face the possibility that I may be merely talking to myself. However, I also think that such a view has no greater claim to truth than the belief that interaction with them is possible, so I go along with my urge to commune with them as well as with God.

I think of Mom and Dad as a couple when I converse with them. The recent rediscovery of Mom's prayer book that Dad had mended only reinforced that notion. Accordingly, I like to think that my repeated communion with Mom and Dad together compensates for my not bidding farewell to Mom as she was dying. When she was buried on March 1, 1999, I offered to the small group of mourners at her graveside some reflections about her:

In the home of one of us three brothers, there is an old photograph of Mom from about 45 years ago. She is wearing a long coat and kerchief, coming home on Mapes Avenue, carrying a bag of groceries. She seems unaware that her picture is being taken. As one of my brothers said, "It's a great picture. It looks just like her."

What is it about that picture that is really "like her"? I think it suggests how she centered her life on home and family, providing for us from day to day. In this simple picture, you can see a lot of love. It was a love that expressed itself in different ways. Sometimes it was tender, with a hug and a kiss and an encouraging word. At other times, it was strong and fierce, even desperate. It could break into anger if someone hurt one of her sons; or, if one of us was seriously ill or hurting, she might say, "Why couldn't it have happened to me?"

But, while we recall her love gratefully, we have also a sense of sadness about Mom. She didn't carry just the light burden of groceries but also heavier burdens that wounded her deeply, expressing themselves in moods that took something away from her loving and kind disposition. These burdens were a sort of mystery. Perhaps they were remnants of her childhood, hurts and sadness from long ago. We brothers wondered what they were and, to her credit, Mom sometimes wondered too.

Whatever they were, now is the time for a special trust that God is good and that God does the right thing. In accord with God's own mysterious way and in God's own mysterious time, Mom can lay her burdens down and begin a new life of peace together with Dad. For this hope, I find another image, which I believe is in the homes of all three of us brothers: Mom and Dad seated side-by-side on lawn chairs in Tony and Rosalie's back yard. Dad looks contented, and Mom has a light, friendly smile. Above their heads is a huge sunflower that bends down toward them. The sunflower suggests the light of God's love looking down upon them and giving them new life and peace together.

Peter Kearney *was a priest and Bible teacher at Catholic University in Washington, DC. He eventually resigned from the priesthood, married, and worked at the Library of Congress as a cataloger of Jewish materials. After retirement, he continued to work there for several years as a volunteer. Peter spends his time enjoying his book groups, guitar lessons, and writing limericks for friends.*

Ruth Gardner Hardesty Brittle

Ruth Brittle with daughters Betsy and Nancy about 1950

Ruth in the Light

by Nancy Brittle

Becoming our mother's caregiver was not the shock or struggle that worries some sons and daughters of elderly or infirm parents. My sister Betsy and I had already moved, as adult children, back into our parents' home some fifteen years before my mother needed us as her daily companions. In fact, the precedent of taking care of the elderly was already established in our household. Our paternal grandmother had turned her "good front parlor" into a downstairs bedroom for her ailing father, and several decades later, my mother and father cared for his parents in our home.

Our grandmother, a paralyzed stroke victim, lived out nearly ten years of her life in that same "parlor." There she spent her days unable to speak or move but with her family around her attending to her needs. During this time our mother was also a key part of the care of several other elderly relatives and friends. There was no question or even much thought about our own parents' long-term needs. They did not have any insurance. They had us.

We needed to make no mental adjustment to take care of our mother; rather, we had to accept that our mother would die of a difficult disease. That was the hard part. Betsy and I suffered with this realization.

It was just after the Christmas Holiday 2001. My sister and I, both schoolteachers, were back at work. We taught within fifteen miles of home. Our mother's urologist and friend through long family association had called my sister and me at our schools and asked us to meet him as quickly as we could in his office. At our prodding, Mom had gone in to see him. She had not felt well all fall, but because her general practitioner had suddenly died in October, she was without a doctor and had not gotten around to finding a new one. Finally, Betsy and I had convinced her to go see her specialist, Dr. Datta.

He wasn't absolutely certain, he said, but he had seen so many of these cases over his long career that he was pretty sure Mom had ovarian cancer. She was 84. At that moment neither Mom nor Betsy nor I realized the gravity of this particular cancer, but the C word was enough to punch us each in the chest.

After some relatively frank discussion, Dr. Datta and his wife were on the phone to the local hospital, setting up the required tests and also making arrangements for Mom to see Dr. Peyton Taylor, a specialist in gynecological diseases at the University of Virginia. After many hugs and assurances of support from their office, Dr. and Mrs. Datta walked Mom, Betsy, and me to our cars. That was the beginning of the good things as well as the bad. We had fine medical help. We did not know it then, but during the next five years, along with some of the best of our days, came the realization of untold fears.

Certainly that winter afternoon heralded the beginning of our long, unplanned journey through what most told us would be a grueling illness. We were adult children who had made the decision to come home again. We had lived harmoniously with our parents until our father's death, and since then it had just been the three of us, Mom, Betsy, and me. We were all very close.

Until that afternoon, our mother had easily driven her car, shopped, cooked, been Senior Warden in our small church, gardened, enjoyed traveling, and lightly played the role of matriarch over a large array of cousins, nieces, nephews, and their children and grandchildren who seemed to love their "Aunt Ruth." She was an avid reader and loved a good game of bridge or Scrabble. She certainly did not look or act her age. In fact, she seemed ageless.

That afternoon put Betsy and me on the edge of the abyss. Mom was sick. We were devastated. Cancer did not run in our family. It caught us completely by surprise. As teachers, for decades we had run our lives by a lesson plan. But we quickly found that there are no lesson plans for dealing with cancer, particularly with the elderly. Through trial and error and some good advice from cancer experts, we found that we needed to be flexible, open to change, and willing to accept help.

The three of us talked about the importance of continuing to find beauty in each day and of quietly dealing with the unruly aspects of this disease. Mom worried that she would "be a burden" to us. Although Betsy and I wept in secret in our deep grief and insecurity, we also knew that, however the future was delivered, we had to be sure that our decisions on Mom's care were based on sound medical knowledge. We needed to continue our daily lives as normally as we could, supporting Mom but at the same time encouraging her to remain as independent as possible.

Several situations unfolded to make Mom's time filled with good living as opposed to fear and pain for her and for us. Dr. Datta's skill and compassion as a physician had introduced him to many first-rate doctors in the hospitals around us. Because of his close working relationship with the University of Virginia's Dr. Peyton Taylor, we found that excellent hospital and cancer center. From the moment Mom became Dr. Taylor's patient, we were all part of a shared plan. We knew that this gifted man's quick assessment of all aspects of our mother, his skillful surgery, and his advanced knowledge of ovarian cancer and its treatment enabled us to begin our journey with more confidence.

Actually, Mom enjoyed her trips to the cancer center. She loved the roll of the land as we drove up and down US Route 29 to Charlottesville. The road was familiar to her, and she delighted in being part of the changing seasons on those many trips. She responded to and was grateful for the deep commitment to the treatment we found at the cancer center. Dr. Taylor and his nurse Paula offered enormous and unflagging support for all three of us.

These two became part of our extended family as they kept in constant contact through e-mail and phone, easing our fear when they could and suggesting strategies for various aspects of Mom's care at home. Shortly after she became his patient, Dr. Taylor stopped by home to visit Mom. He saw the "lay of the land" and told Betsy and me that this house would work well for Mom as the disease progressed. Skilled and supportive, the doctors and nurses at the cancer center not only helped us forge a path through the complexities of aging and cancer but also showed us the importance of allowing others to help us.

The second condition that enabled us to navigate these difficult years was our mother's own good humor and her ability to repress the negative. The family joke for years had been that Mom was the "Queen of Denial." Sometimes we had wished she would be a bit more aware of our definition of reality. But in retrospect, her way of seeing the glass as half-full may have contributed more than one would imagine to her resilience in the face of her advancing age and condition. On the other hand, we suspect she had a much greater awareness of the gravity of her disease than we thought at the time but just was not going to give in. She was not raised to cave.

Born in 1918 at the end of World War I, our mother was part of that strong generation who grew up in the Great Depression. The daughter of a Methodist minister and his wife, she was in college by age sixteen and lost her father in an accident the spring of her freshman year. Shy but warm, Mom finished school and was teaching by the time she was twenty. Life for her after World War II—as the wife of a dairy farmer, raising two daughters, teaching, caring for two invalid in-laws in her home—did not provide an easy set of tasks. But her positive outlook and determination made it good for all of us in her family as well as for her students. She never complained, she never gave up, and in that respect, she set the tone for her own old age and illness. She was an easy patient for us to work with.

Mom's faith played a key role in her life. She was a quietly fervent believer. She always told us that God never asked us to do more than we could bear. When Betsy and I heard her cancer diagnosis, we wondered, not for the first time nor the last, if God had put us to a test we could not face, let alone pass.

Mom did not want to give up one iota of her independence. She had always loved pretty clothes and cared about her personal appearance. Every day Betsy and I helped in choosing something that "looked nice" in her favorite colors. We found sensibly priced and easily washed pants and tops in some of the local stores. As long as we had known Mom, neither Betsy nor I had ever seen her without her earrings or lipstick. Among her college buddies, she had been known to wear lipstick to bed "in case a flyer should parachute into my dorm room." When she was wheeled into the operating room for her cancer surgery, Mom's last words to me were "Is my hair okay and my lipstick straight?" Mom continued to dress, to wear earrings and her lipstick, but at great physical cost, until the last week of her life when she could no longer get out of bed.

Of course, she lost all her beautiful white hair in the first rounds of chemotherapy. She did not want a wig, so Betsy and I found attractive scarves and hats. She made wearing hats to church the thing to do again. She wore them to weddings. She wore them to lunch. When her hair grew out again, she traded her old bouffant style for a French gamine cut. We teased her about her Audrey Hepburn look. When Mom could no longer easily go out to the beauty shop, a hairdresser friend came to the house, and Betsy quickly learned how to wash and do little trims to Mom's hair.

By the time Mom's illness was diagnosed, she was a widow living in a very small town, almost a village really, where her career had been teaching children from town and the surrounding farms. Some of those children were now over 70, some in their late twenties. The town had changed considerably in the nearly 60 years she had been there. Most of her peer group had died. But through all those years, Mom had kept in contact with the many relatives in her own family and in our father's. And she never lost touch with her eight suitemates and roommate from college days.

Luckily for all of us, one of her college friends, Adelaide, two years older than Mom, had bought and moved into our great aunt's house next door. On the other side of us lived our cousin's war-bride wife, Simone. Both women, widows also, spent many mornings and afternoons, just as they had for years, sharing a cup of tea or glass of iced tea, depending on the season, joining her on the side porch, in the yard, or in the den, bringing in news from town or family, letting the dogs in and out for her, or watching the four o'clock news. They helped Mom keep her daily routines. Sisters in age, these three very different women gave each other solace and strength, and the two found purpose in supporting the third, physically and emotionally. Our mother often voiced her gratitude.

Dr. Taylor encouraged us to get a new puppy to replace the schnauzer that we had lost to old age the month before Mom's cancer surgery. I wondered how we would manage both a young dog and Mom's cancer, but Dr. Taylor said if she liked dogs and was used to having dogs then we should get her another dog. It was the best decision we made in the scope of her entire illness. Billybaggins, a 12-week-old puppy, joined our team in June of that year. He, along with our old terrier Lucy, and Adelaide's little Buttons were all three by Mom's chair each day. Sensing change and not wanting to leave her, they were in her room in their places on the foot of her bed where she wanted them the week of her death. These little animals gave us all much joy during Mom's life and have helped ease the grief since her death.

Almost every afternoon after I got home from school, I would put Mom and usually Adelaide and a dog or two in the car, and we would go for a ride. Over the back roads, through the woods, alongside the river, up into the foothills of the Blue Ridge, or down into the flatlands on the way to the Fall Line, we would take our drives. Mom often said that the worst thing about getting old was not being able to drive! Often quiet during these rides, the three of us communed in companionable silence, and the presence of these two strong women helped give me strength.

A couple of miles away, Mom's best teaching buddy Mary had retired with her husband. The two had been traveling partners with Mom and our father. Mary came to our house several times a week to play Scrabble. In the first years Mom's game was great, but as time went on and she began to fail in her last winter, Mary continued to come to play Scrabble, and gently, without Mom's knowledge, manipulated the game so that Mom's score was the higher one, or was close! It was with Mary that Mom first talked about death and her concern about her "girls," Betsy and me. Mary had lost a sister to ovarian cancer and understood every aspect of our grief.

Our cousin Sally from New York, our cousin Sue, a nurse who actually worked with Hospice during Mom's illness, our cousin Nonie from Atlanta, our cousin Bayne from Virginia Beach, all came in the early months of the illness to help Mom, Betsy, and me cope with the many challenges to our combined lives. These close relatives and friends made all the difference in the long run. Dropping in constantly was the second generation of cousins and often the "boy cousins," Bo, Nelson, and Ray, who assured her that they would take care of Betsy and me and the house. These fellows of few words offered much comfort to their "Aunt Ruth." The kindness of her sisters' and cousins' adult children made Mom's days rich. Betsy and I were grateful that they listened to us, hugged us, forgave us when we were sharp, and understood when we ran out of time and energy.

Mom suffered from macular degeneration before her cancer, and after her surgery and initial treatments, her vision deteriorated rapidly. She lost the sight of one eye completely and had only a bit of sight in the other. She wanted to write letters as she always had; she continued to listen to TV news and to watch the Olympics. Gradually, I began reading some magazine and newspaper articles to her as we waited each evening while my sister fixed supper, and together we would do her beloved *Washington Post* daily crossword puzzle. As time went on, she said she would be interested in my reading some of her favorite books to her. That began a routine that we both enjoyed every day. My sister would also read to her, as would various cousins and friends who came by to visit or help. But it was my sister's and my time every night, after we had her bathed and in bed, to read. I remember those years with Mom after she lost her sight as rich hours of companionship. We read and then asked her questions about the passages. Her memories and opinions would be sparked by an author's words, and we'd listen to our mother's experiences and views that were often revelations to us.

Mom had spent much of her teaching career as an elementary school reading teacher. Today she'd be called a reading specialist. She always loved reading as did our father, and they both passed that love of books, newspapers, and journals along to us. She relished a good mystery, but she also enjoyed biographies and history.

We reread all the James Herriot books several times. We read McCullough's *John Adams* and *1776*, Katherine Graham's biography, Tom

Brokaw's *The Greatest Generation*, and all the books of poetry that Caroline Kennedy collected. She loved hearing us read the books on the building of Skyline Drive (she never tired of telling us that she and her mother were there when Roosevelt opened the Drive). As a minister's daughter, she always enjoyed passages from the Bible, especially bits from Proverbs and the Psalms. (We asked three of our friends and relatives to read some of those favorite pieces at her memorial service.)

The hours shared in reading to Mom are some of my sister's and my most treasured memories. Ever the teacher, Mom used this time to continue to teach Betsy and me how to live, only now without her. She was older. We were older. She was able to pass on a mother's wisdom to her daughters, and we were grateful.

During that long week when Mom was dying, Betsy and I continued to read to her, almost nonstop, so that she would not only hear our voices, but also the author's words she had so enjoyed. We played many of her favorite classical CDs, and since the piano was in what became her downstairs bedroom, we each softly played some simple melodies that she had always enjoyed: our first recital pieces, hymns, folk songs, a little Schumann. We read her many children's poems—ones she knew by heart and had read to us and to her school children. Mom's "daytime companions," her three little dogs, were on the end of her bed when she died, and the *Child's Garden of Verses* was on the bed stand.

So much about Mom's long illness amazed us. That she lived with her cancer for five years surprised the doctors, as did her beating back a pulmonary embolism. Unable to cope with the full chemo cocktail, Mom began a second round of a less toxic drug. A volunteer at the UVA Cancer Center was one of my old high school pupils, herself a premed student interested in becoming a cancer specialist. Bonnie was often there when Mom went in for chemo. She, Dr. Taylor, and nurse Paula Rowan Page would all stop by and ease whatever anxieties we might be feeling. It wasn't just Mom who benefited from those circles of caring at home and at the cancer center, but Betsy and I also. As caretakers, intimately tied to the patient, we were on this journey through the unknown as well. Often, I think we were more frightened by all the unknowns than Mom. The medical teams, family, and friends who cared for our mother and lessened her fears did the same for us.

After a year, it seemed that the cancer had spread. With the counseling of Dr. Taylor and his good nurse Paula, we entered palliative care at UVA. Our local provider was Hospice of the Rapidan, and for six months Mom seemed to gradually fade before our eyes. This was a difficult time for Betsy and me; we were grief-stricken just at the thought of losing her. We would rush home after school to spend as much time with her as we could, continuing our routine of reading, listening to music, and allowing short visits of friends and relatives. As the summer began and wore on, both Bayne and Simone, wives of our father's close cousins, died. Their deaths affected us all deeply, as they had been a wonderful, long part of all three of our lives and, more immediately, had been so helpful in sitting with Mom and entertaining her in the dark weeks of her illness. Grief was almost overwhelming for all three of us.

As it happened, I became ill in the fall and required major surgery. Dr. Taylor was my doctor at this point. When Mom realized that I needed surgery, she seemed to rally. And, just after I returned home from the hospital, Hospice released Mom! She had begun to walk, get stronger, and play a sharp game of Scrabble. She lived another three good years. Mom seemed to have experienced several miracles during her long illness, and that was one of them.

Our town is too small to have large clubs, groups, or church congregations to help with runs to the doctor, chemo, and the like. But, through our family and a small circle of friends, we found comfort, relief, support, laughter, and food. In the last months when age and disease made it difficult for Mom to be alone during the day, and her old friend and neighbor Adelaide had left for a retirement home, we employed Mom's sitter, Mattie, who had been with us during the first Hospice experience, to stay a longer day again. For five days a week she would quietly be by Mom's side, helping her with her bath and meals, the dogs, the phone, and the visitors, from the time Betsy and I left for school in the morning till we got home in the afternoon. We managed by ourselves on weekends and holidays. It was Mattie and Cousin

Sue who came with the Hospice nurse LuAnn the night after Mom died to help us bathe and prepare our mother for the next part of the journey.

What were we learning on this journey? What have we learned since? A lot about cancer, diet, exercise, and chemo, of course. But also about the power of friendship and family. We discovered how to balance giving and taking better. We realized that people really want to help. Much of what I brought to the planning table I gathered from my teaching colleagues who had gone through similar situations. From special foods that would stay down when the stomach was queasy to how to access home health care, to clothes that were comfortable as well as stylish for Mom, to the store with the best price for patient-care items—these were just a few of the insights Betsy and I got from our friends.

It has been valuable knowing someone who has experienced the loss of a mother or has been intimately involved with that mother's care. These folks had "been there before us" and knew the importance of having choices and having somebody to listen or help in small ways. In the final analysis, we all travel this journey of the caregiver in our own way. Under the same roof and with the same loved mother, my sister and I handled the stress, the grief, the ups and downs in different ways. I gardened with more vengeance than joy sometimes. Betsy sometimes vacuumed the rugs for what seemed to be from sunup to sundown. I wrote long letters and painted many portraits of Mom. Betsy played the piano more loudly and longer. Our mother watched us and knew—and told us every night that she loved us and was thankful for this time with us.

She outlived her prognosis by sheer will and love. In the years since Mom's death, Betsy and I have continued many of the family traditions that were important to the three of us. And we have created some new ones. The boy cousins helped us move the bedroom furniture back upstairs. Mom's photos are off the walls of the front room and replaced by the paintings. The dogs have divided their time between Betsy's room and mine. I still write and Betsy still plays the piano. And we know that grief cannot be rushed. Life's rhythms continue, but some adjustments take time before new harmonies and new tempos move smoothly.

We feel privileged to have been able to care for our mother as she cared for us and for so many others.

"Ruth in the Light," 22 x 28 inches, oil on canvas
(As I saw Mom sitting at the kitchen table one September morning a few months before her death, she seemed to be in a cloud of light. I asked her if she could just sit there for a bit as I rushed to get my oil paints. To pass the time she wanted to do some darning. In the pose she is trying to thread a needle, even though she was nearly blind by that time.)

Nancy Brittle, *in middle age, returned to her childhood home and became an English teacher in the school she once attended. Fortunately, this allowed her to be with her mother in her declining years, following the path of her mother and grandmother before her in caring for the elderly at home. In her retirement, Nancy has returned to a first love, painting.*

Ruth Shauck Bannerman

My mother Ruth's wedding day in November 1935

The two of us (seventy years later) a few months before my mother's passage
at the age of ninety-seven

A Good Death

by Susan Thesenga

I had the great privilege of being with my mother at the time of her death and for most of the two weeks before she died, as well as tending to and sitting with her body for the two days following. The services of Hospice let us look after her at home, and another service helped us to care for her body after death. My mother's body lay in her bed until family members placed her in a casket, which we then accompanied to her burial.

Being with my mother in her dying and with her body afterwards was intimate, profound, and comforting. In every detail of her passing, I was given glimpses of the perfection of God's great design. And I felt the completion of a karmic cycle, knowing I had fully worked through my issues with her.

I was able to give my mother in her dying what she had not been able to give me in my birthing: physical intimacy, visceral reassurance, emotional warmth, and a feeling in the room of safety, fearlessness, and peace. In offering this deep connection as one of us transitioned from embodied awareness to non-embodied awareness, it hardly mattered who was mother and who was daughter, or whether the passage was into or out of the body. The transition at death out of the physical and into the *mystery* is no less wonderful than what occurs at birth.

The Hospice chaplain used exactly this metaphor with my mother, inviting her to consider that just as humans on "this side" welcome a soul into a new body, we might be welcomed also on the other side to a new state of consciousness, traveling through the tunnel of death, paralleling the journey through the birth canal. My mother, who was not religious, though always open and curious about life, liked the metaphor. And so I used it often in my attempts to reassure her and guide her in her passage.

Just outside the window of my mother's bedroom, in which she lay dying in her hospital bed, a mother duck sat on eleven eggs in a nest on the patio. Birth and death were that close. Two hours after my mother died, Michelle, the Hospice nurse who had beautifully guided us through every step of the dying process, came to visit (even though it was her birthday), saying that when she woke up with a dream of baby ducks, she knew my mother had passed.

I had incredible support in caring for my mother, not only from the Hospice staff—all of whom were terrific—but also from my sister Martha, who came regularly and was supportive, and from Maureen, who had become my mother's full-time caretaker. I could not have managed without everyone's assistance.

After my mother died, we had the service of Beth Knox, who helped us tend to her body—washing, dressing, and laying her out in her own bed. My mother was radiating the peace that I suspect comes from a good passing and subsequent loving care. Beth, whose services I found invaluable, runs an organization called Crossings: Caring for our Own at Death. Beth came to this work through her own personal tragedy of losing a young daughter to an airbag accident. She was in the hospital when her daughter died and fought the hospital's policy of sending the dead to funeral homes. She convinced them of her right to care for her own daughter's body at home.

It is perfectly legal for anyone to do this. Most of the myths and fears we have about death and dead bodies are fostered by the funeral industry. There were no smells, no decay, and no health hazards whatsoever in having my mother's body cared for at home, which, of course, is what families always used to do. It was also essential that we had Beth's help, because she knew exactly what we needed to do at each step. And she works with a funeral home that has a sympathetic staff who will provide only those services the family wants. We had a casket delivered to the house, into which we transferred my mother's body, and we had them provide a hearse and limo to the cemetery. And that was all. (Most funeral homes try to sell you on the false idea that embalming is necessary, and that they have to do everything. It isn't and they don't. Embalming only came into practice during the Civil War when bodies had to be shipped long distances after death; it is not necessary and is horribly invasive.)

Having the body at home was a great lesson for the grandchildren. My twenty-three-year-old daughter Pamela was at first scared to see her grandmother's body, but when she eventually chose to go into the bedroom, she fell into a state of reverence and amazement, commenting on how beautiful her grandmother looked, how peaceful and radiant her face was, and how evident it was that the Grandma Pam loved was no longer there. Pamela described going through a "wall" of fear of death and said that afterward, she felt more comfortable and grounded in her own body. She just wanted to know where Grandma had gone. Her unanswerable question gave us an opening to share as a family some important reflections about the mysteries of spirit.

Both dignity and kindness were evident in my mother's dying process and were reflected in her face at her death. As long as she could still talk, she always thanked us for everything we did for her. She graciously received the hymn-singing and prayers that were offered to her by friends from my church. She spent time with everyone she loved in the two weeks before she died, waiting until the last grandchild, who was finishing college exams, could come. Then she waited one more day to die until I returned from a quick trip, as she knew how much I wanted to be there.

My mother was intelligent and liked to know what was going on. She grilled the nurses on exactly what physical changes would take place, even though she didn't always like what she heard. She objectively described her observations of other realities as they began to appear, including a recurrent "dream" of a beautiful 1930s ballroom where many of her dead friends were dancing. Even the changing "pictures" she saw on the wall were reported with a curious and detached interest.

My mother's lifelong anxiety about everything—letting her children cross the street alone brought heart palpitations—lifted once she faced her ultimate fear: death. She was mostly relaxed and was even funny. When she told me that she had a vision of a man in a black suit coming to get her, she looked at me, winked, and added, "And he looks just like Elvis!" When I shared with her that my sister and I, who have not been close, agreed on every detail about the burial and memorial service, she quipped, "Well, that's worth dying for!"

My sister and I were blessed with a deep harmony during this time. We agreed on funeral and burial arrangements, the casket, and all the other choices one needs to make. I felt entirely supported as she let me take the lead in the emotional and spiritual arenas where I am strong, and I gladly followed her in the financial and legal realm, where I had complete trust that she would execute matters impeccably.

I have waited much of my life to be present for a conscious death. My father died suddenly; my stepson died prematurely; my childhood best friend was already unconscious when I sat with her until she passed; my first spiritual teacher was in denial until almost the moment of her death; and my first church leader died without warning. It is one of the great wonders of my life that my own mother became the vehicle through which I could experience dying consciously.

Sensing that her time was near, Maureen and I both spent the last night in the room with my mother. We all slept deeply and peacefully. When we awoke at 6:00 a.m. my mother was still breathing, but minutes later, as I sat on the bed holding her hand, she took her last breath. Maureen and I were fully present and well rested. Even in this detail my mother's consideration for others shone through.

In the moments after Mom's death, I wept—not so much in grief (that would come later) as in gratitude—because she had let me be so fully with her in this most profound of all passages we must each traverse. The personal love I felt for my mother carried me into a transpersonal realm where there is only love, one that transcends death and personalities. The two of us merged into one consciousness, melting into the inner reality of union behind our outer lives of apparent separation. Relaxing even deeper, the ground of all being became apparent—a space of compassionate awareness, of empty fullness, of vibrant nothingness—the place we come from and the place we return to.

I was flooded with the deepest peace I have ever known. It was my mother's final and greatest gift to me.

Thank you, Mom.

Susan Thesenga *co-founded Sevenoaks Retreat Center in Madison, Virginia, in 1972 with her husband Donovan, where they still live and work. She is author of* The Undefended Self *and of the memoir* Love Unbroken: From Addiction to Redemption, *co-authored with her daughter. She enjoys being an active grandmother.*

Sylvia Jessen Ott McGrath

Mom and I on Easter day in Livingston, New Jersey, 1951,
at my grandparents' house

My favorite photo of Mom—picking wild roses at the shore of
Spring Lake, New Jersey, sometime in the early '60s

Death by Poetry

by Carol Thayer Cox

There were a number of times when I thought I might have said good-bye to my mother for the last time. My brother Alden and I used to joke that our mother had nine lives, like her pet cat Katie. Mom almost left us so many times that we began to think she never really would, that she would be here forever. I think she might have believed that as well. For a span of about 15 years, she underwent multiple surgeries and a myriad of complications and setbacks. Each time she always managed to rally and return to some sort of equilibrium, but never quite the same as the one she had held before. It seemed as if we were all part of a surreal tragedy in which we kept experiencing crescendos of tension over and over without ever reaching the denouement. Peace is what I sought, perhaps for myself as much as for her.

I can look back now, though, and see that the beginning of the end started the morning of June 11, 1997, when Mom experienced her first ischemic stroke at the age of 81. She had already undergone and recuperated from two knee and two hip replacements during the previous seven years and had healed from complications following these surgeries, as well as fractured wrists and broken ribs that occurred as a result of several falls. But it was that morning in June that she lost all perception of time, never to be retrieved again. She could no longer keep track of the minutes or the weeks or the months. I had always imagined that my mother had a tiny implanted clock and compass that guided her from hour to hour, from place to place. No matter what was happening, I could always rely on Mom to provide a sense of being grounded in time and space. But without her internal polestar she was disoriented. She became disconnected from the predictable rhythms of life she knew so well: the waxing and waning of the moon, the swelling and ebbing of the tides, the lengthening and shortening of sunlight as the seasons came and went. This stroke stripped her of her anchor, and she slowly began to drift away from us. It was a subtle and sometimes imperceptible change, but we felt it nonetheless.

In November of that same year, Mom was diagnosed with colon cancer for which she had surgery. Although the cancer had broken through her intestinal wall, chemotherapy was not recommended. This last round of anesthesia and probable stroke while she was undergoing surgery, however, left us with a mother who no longer responded as she once had. It took a full year for her to begin to show signs of being the woman we once knew as our mom. But she never fully came back. We assumed that her cancer was what would take her in the end, so we began the process of trying to say goodbye. Thus, my mourning started long before Mom's actual departure eight years later.

She continued to have transient ischemic attacks and more surgeries during the remaining years that she lived in her apartment, which Alden had built onto the side of my husband's and my house. The issue at hand for me was how to have a relationship with someone who sometimes acted like the mother I had always known and other times confused me with either her mother or my daughter, who admittedly looks a lot like me. I decided my goal would be to assist her in maintaining a familiar routine to help orient her.

Holidays were always special to Mom, so they provided promising times to help her focus on the here and now. My husband Jerry and I would buy a perfectly shaped Frazier fir for her Christmas tree each year. She used a walker, so it was difficult for her to decorate her tree, but she would sit and carefully unwrap each antique ornament, and we followed her directions as much as we could. Sometimes her grandchildren would be available to help. We would make Christmas cookies together, a tradition she loved. And I sat alongside her, assisting with the task of signing and addressing cards to be sent to friends and family. In the early years I would push Mom in her wheelchair through busy malls to shop for presents. She always enjoyed watching the children lining up to sit on Santa's knee, and she loved to see everything looking so festive. During the latter years, I did all the preparations and shopping and would bring home for her approval the presents I bought. We wrapped the gifts together and she signed all the cards. She always insisted that I use her money to buy something for myself. I will never forget the year she signed two cards to put on my presents: "To Mom—With love from Sylvia." That was the first time I cried over the loss of my mother.

What was so strange about this is that Mom had experienced a strained and difficult relationship with her mother, who was nurturing in many ways but had also been critical and rejecting of her daughter. Mom always tried so hard to please her. The fact that she saw me as her mother called me up short! I came to realize, though, that since I was taking care of my mother, much as a nurse or mother might, Mom's confusion was understandable. And who knows, perhaps in a previous life I was her mother, and maybe, in her state of consciousness, she was closer to that reality. At any rate, I believe, in retrospect, that this was an opportunity for Mom to feel some acceptance from her mother and thus to experience some healing. I can only hope so.

My parents separated when I was five years old. At that time, I started feeling responsible for my mother's happiness. In a poem I wrote to her when I was quite young, I compared her to a sycamore tree that sheltered the birds living in her branches. As one of the birds, I promised to visit her forever and to care for her no matter how old she became. In my heart, somehow I had signed a contract to that effect. So I never questioned my situation. I will admit, however, that occasionally I resented it. There were times when I had to choose between her needs and those of other family members, and rarely was there a satisfactory solution. Also, my career path might have been different had I not resigned from my full-time job to take care of her. But I know I made the right choice to do so and ultimately am at peace with it.

It still embarrasses me to say that my mother spent the last four and a half years of her life in a nursing home. This is not a scenario she had wanted, nor did I like being in the position of making it so. But there was really no choice in the matter once it became impossible for her to put any weight on her legs. Her osteoporosis had gotten so severe that her femur crumbled between her two metal joints. She underwent complex surgery to repair her leg, but nothing could be done. After she had spent a month in the hospital, it was determined that she would never walk again, although true to her resilient spirit, Mom really did try. A healthcare facility was the only option for us. She was confined to a chair and needed a chairlift to put her into bed and take her out again. At this point she was also incontinent because of her strokes and was almost completely deaf. Her compromised awareness resulted in her mostly accepting her fate with little protest. It broke my heart, however, to see her there.

I am not happy with some of what my mother had to endure in the nursing home during her last few years of life. And when I recall it, I feel as I did then, helpless to do anything to change what happened but guilty about it, nonetheless. My mother deserved much, much better. No matter how hard one might search, there is no such thing as an ideal residential treatment facility. It's not the same as home, and no matter how many dedicated and caring people are employed at the place, there are always a few staff members who should never have the job of caring for the infirm. Fortunately, the good experiences outweighed the bad, but a really ugly one, of which there were several, can carry much weight. And since I could not be there all the time, I had to accept the fact that I had no control over what might happen in my absence. I wish I had been able to hire someone who could have been with my mother every day to monitor what went on and to protect her, but that was out of the question. So, I tried to find ways to make her life there as pleasant as was reasonably possible.

Mom's deafness created a problem. We had tried hearing aids while she was living in the apartment next to our house, but she kept losing them. Keeping track of them at a nursing home, where even her bottom dentures disappeared, was obviously impossible. My solution was to communicate with her by writing on an erasable board, and I provided several in her room for this purpose. I had posted a notice on the wall above her bed that explained the situation to the staff, and I wrote it in the form of a request from my mother. Without that sign, many of the staff members assumed, since she didn't respond to their words, that she must have severe dementia, so they treated her accordingly, not giving her choices and not acknowledging her as a person. Fortunately, some of the employees were appreciative of my note and actually took the time to use the erasable board with Mom. However, every time the state officials came to inspect the facility, they removed the notice. They said such a sign was demeaning and disrespectful to the patient! I never could convince them otherwise. As soon as they were done with their inspection, I would put it up again and stake my claim to do so, which always caused problems with the rule-abiding employees, those who couldn't understand that having the sign was indeed respectful of my mother's needs to be treated like a person who could think and communicate.

Even though Mom had stroke-induced dementia that fluctuated from day to day, there were times when she was quite coherent, and we communicated well, with her talking and my writing. Luckily she was able to read with her one good eye. She had been an avid reader all her life, and in the nursing home she used fiction to escape into a more appealing world than the one in which she was living. I tried to provide her with a steady supply of quality reading material. A flowering plant in her room, her favorite paintings on her walls, and a bird feeder outside her window were other ways Alden and I attempted to mitigate the harsh reality of her life away from family.

Because Mom had been an excellent cook, her primary complaint about her situation was the awful food she was given. She loved it when I brought her homemade food, though I did not do it as often as I would have liked. While Mom was there, my daughter Kim and I interviewed her and made a cookbook of her favorite recipes that also included commentary about her life and many photos of her from childhood through adulthood. At some point during her stay, the nurses and assistants began to borrow Mom's cookbook to copy some of her recipes, and then they would discuss with her the ones they had tried. I was told by the social worker that this cookbook was instrumental in my mother's establishing good relationships with many of the staff. Seeing and reading about her as a young, vibrant, creative woman helped them to view her differently, not just as an old woman who was deaf, crippled, and compromised.

MY BEST GINGERBREAD

$^1/_2$ c. sugar
$^1/_2$ c. butter
1 egg
1 c. molasses
$2^1/_2$ c. sifted flour
1 c. hot water
$1^1/_2$ tsp. baking soda
1 tsp. cinnamon
1 tsp. ginger
$^1/_2$ tsp. cloves
$^1/_2$ tsp. salt

Cream shortening and sugar. Add beaten egg and molasses, then dry ingredients which have been sifted together. Add hot water last and beat until smooth. The batter is soft, but it makes a fine cake. Bake in greased shallow pan for 35 minutes in a moderate oven (325° to 350°). Makes 15 generous portions. Good old-fashioned gingerbread. Serve warm with vanilla ice cream.

Sylvia & Alden in front of Cousin Ellen's
House in Westmoreland, NH, 1948

A page from *Sylvia's Favorite Recipes*

Death by Poetry

My mother generally preferred a positive approach to life, even during difficult times. The song "My Favorite Things," which Maria sings in *The Sound of Music*, could have been her theme song! She would rather be glad than be sad, so she would do what she could to make others happy, which in turn brought her delight. She was a natural nurturer, and people were drawn to her. For as long as I can remember, I would hear, "I wish she could have been my mother."

However, sometimes her love for my brother and me felt possessive and even suffocating, especially in our adolescence when we were trying to separate from family. Ours was a blended one that included our alcoholic stepfather. Coming from a need to feel loved and accepted, Mom was a classic enabler; like typical children of an alcoholic, my brother and I often sacrificed our own feelings to keep the peace for Mom's sake, out of our love for her. After all is said and done, though, we really were fortunate to have received Mom's love from our very first experience of her. As a mother, I understand this as much as I do as a daughter. It is a love beyond measure, fierce in its protectiveness and compassionate in its acceptance. It is a love that has remained, even in Mom's absence.

Although many of my mother's life circumstances were painful and distressing, she was a survivor, and her love for the beauty on this planet was her therapy. My brother and I were her apprentices. Every glorious sunrise or sunset was reason to rejoice. Taking time to listen, smell, touch, and see life with Mom was the best part of our childhood. Whether genetic or learned, Alden and I continue to have an appreciation for the aesthetic and a desire to help keep our world pleasing to the eye. This is a bond the three of us understood without words.

Like her beloved Tanta Anna, Mom seemed to embody the concept of *joie de vivre*. Each season and every holiday were a cause for celebration. She welcomed the first snowflake of winter as readily as she greeted the first daffodil of spring. Even during her early years at the nursing home, she would find things to be joyful about, whether something from a book she was reading or the memory of a dream. I distinctly remember one particular day when she recounted her happiness as she described an incident (she

291

presumably dreamed) that she was convinced had been real. She told me in precise detail how she had cooked a delicious roast chicken dinner for everybody there and had decorated the tables with flowers from her garden. She was so delighted that everyone liked her meal, especially her apple pie. Truly a Pollyanna at heart, if her reality was not to her liking, she fantasized one to suit her. This approach had always worked for her, and it sufficed off and on for the first couple of years in the nursing home.

One's world shrinks considerably, however, in a residential care facility. My mother's friends of her age were experiencing their own health problems, so it was rare that any of them went to see her. Family members, as well as friends, visited less frequently the longer Mom was there. Although at the time it was hurtful, I do understand that people's lives are busy, and I, too, have been remiss in visiting infirm or ill people I have cared for deeply. And, granted, nursing homes are not pleasant places to spend time, and maybe my mother's diminished state was hard for friends and family members to accept. There was one notable exception, however. Mom's weaving instructor and good friend Rita Brown went to see her once a week for at least ten years, which included drives that took Rita over an hour from her home. For the last two years of Mom's life when she was the most compromised, Rita and I were her primary visitors. It meant a lot to my mother, and I am forever grateful.

Although Mom's health steadily declined during her final years, she astonished doctors and nurses with her sheer will to survive. She continued to bounce back from every infection and flu she contracted. I would get calls that she was quite sick, but one round of medication and back she would come. Eighteen months before Mom died, however, she became very ill with a skin condition that for over a year was diagnosed incorrectly by her physician and dermatologist. Their treatment exacerbated her problem, which resulted in her being hospitalized with severe complications. Her high fever brought on hallucinations, and she conversed with her father, whom she dearly loved, as if he were standing right there in the room. I wondered if he was there to comfort her, and I thought perhaps her time had come, but she maintained her indomitable resolve to live.

Although Mom recuperated from this ordeal, she had lost a lot of weight and her spirit seemed beaten down. I tried to talk with her about how concerned we all had been and how we thought she might not have recovered. But as was her pattern, she would have nothing to do with the thought of death. While she was still perfectly cogent, before the year of her stroke and cancer, I tried to assess whether she had given much thought to what happens beyond death. But I simply couldn't engage her to talk about it. She surprised me one day by saying that she thought death was the absolute end, that there would be nothing afterwards. This was sad and perplexing to me. She had stopped going to church years before but never would say why. (I learned later that a minister had told her that she was a sinner in God's eyes because of her divorce.) Thinking that perhaps she might entertain the idea of reincarnation, I offered her the book, *Start the Conversation*, but she didn't like it and just didn't want to think about dying. I tried again to bring up the topic of death on other occasions to no avail. Her grandfather and Tanta Anna had both lived into their late nineties, so Mom assumed that she would probably do so as well. Only once did she say to me, "When the time comes, I will be ready."

About six months before Mom died, Jerry and I moved from our house (the one with Mom's apartment) to a one-level rambler. The first day there, I sat exhausted in my rocking chair late into the night, and I suddenly began to sob because I could not share my new home with my mom. I couldn't even tell her we had moved, as she continued to imagine that she still had a home that she could return to when she recuperated. She was no longer able to realistically assess her situation. That evening as I sat alone in my cluttered living room, I was aware of missing my mom's aesthetic yet practical advice. I realized it was the first time I had moved into a new place without her being present—scrubbing and unpacking alongside of me, sewing curtains for our windows, suggesting landscaping ideas. She always enjoyed every moment of assisting me. I was struck with how much I missed her. Though she had not yet died, I realized that I had been mourning the loss of her in my life for some time. I was grieving the loss of our relationship. Her actual death did not bring the sense of finality I felt that night.

During our move in the process of downsizing, I was trying to consolidate some of my mother's belongings. Drawn to open a particular box of hers, I discovered six poems I had never seen that she had written while in high school. I decided to take them to her. It happened to be a good day for Mom: She enjoyed the homemade soup Jerry had made for her, and then she took her poems and began to read them one by one. When I asked her if she remembered writing them, she nodded and smiled. She continued to read and re-read each one, carefully and intently. At one point I said to her that I thought her poems were beautiful, and she looked at me with a smile I hadn't seen for some time, and the sparkle that had been missing for a long while returned to her eyes. She must have read each poem at least thirty times, as if in an effort not to forget. Once she was finished, she folded them in half as they had been and handed them back to me. I told her that I would take good care of her poems, and she said thank you. She was tired then, so she closed her eyes, and I kissed her goodbye.

Most of these poems were about Mom's ideas concerning God, nature, and the afterlife, concepts that adolescents often struggle to understand. Here is one, written by 16-year-old Sylvia Jessen Ott in 1931:

I Have Communed With God

As I sit with half shut eyes
And listen to the music surge
From soft smooths
To turbulent stacatto
And back again,
I but dimly see the players.
They are but phantoms
Playing the will of the composer –
Playing the will of their own souls,
As they live a life,
Empty of all but melody.

With the surge of the bows
As they rise in frenzied unison,
Thought turns to life –
Ever vital, never languid.
Then as the melody turns pensive,
I see lambs
Grazing in pasture –
Deep pools,
Reflective and therein mystic.
But as the theme radiates in splendor,
Then it is
That I commune with my God.
Brief
But, Oh, what a cherished vision –
A thrilling moment
For my soul alone.

The sound life ends.
The dim light is replaced
By a brighter.
But melody has already turned to thought,
And thought cannot be lost
Amongst other things.
I shall not forget –
I have communed with God.

Within three days my mother contracted the flu, a common occurrence in nursing homes during the winter months. My expectation was that she would rally as she always had in the past. So I did not change my plans to drive with Jerry to New York State for the 50th birthday party of Alden's lifetime partner, Eddie. When I told Mom where I would be for the weekend, she said she didn't feel well and only wanted to sleep, so I didn't stay long. At the time I did not realize that those would be her final words to me. And I have often wondered in retrospect whether she felt abandoned by me those last few days of her life. With a heavy heart I have often questioned why I didn't listen to my inner self and stay home. While I was in New York, I talked with my family about the poetry experience and about my intuition that, because of the connection she made with her poems, Mom might not be with us much longer. I somehow knew that her ninth life hung in the balance, but I was banking on more time than she had.

Saturday night I received a call from a nurse that my mother had a bladder infection for which she ordered an antibiotic. That, in itself, was not unusual. I replied I'd be home from New York the next evening. Early Monday morning, February 28th, a nurse called to tell me that my mother's vital signs had dropped overnight and that I needed to come as soon as possible. I asked if my brother could get there in time if he could catch a flight, but she said my mother probably had only a few hours left. It was snowing hard, and it took me about an hour to make the 25-mile drive to the healthcare facility from my home.

When I arrived, Mom's eyes were closed and she was not responsive. I sat next to her and held her hand. Two certified nurse assistants showed up, and together they tenderly washed my mother's body, applied lotion, brushed her hair, and dressed her in a clean nightgown. I put her soft bedroom socks on that I had recently gotten for her. These two women seemed like angels as they supported me through this process. I have a recollection of the room being filled with light while they were there. And then I sat alone with Mom for the next four hours, which seemed like an eternity. I so wished that I could have played music for her or sung her a lullaby, but I knew she couldn't hear. I just said the words in my mind that I wanted to say to her, trusting she would somehow be able to receive them. I asked for her forgiveness, and I also forgave her for the things I had resented. Mostly, I thanked her for loving me and prayed for a gentle passing. I kept saying in my mind, "Go toward the light, Mom. It will be okay."

During that time by her side, I recalled her joyful story of my birth. She always took great delight in telling me what a wonderful day it was for her. She woke up in labor on a sunny spring day and telephoned her family friend, Dr. Starr. He arrived in his red convertible, and the two of them rode fast in his car with the top down, going through traffic lights with the horn blaring. When they arrived at the hospital, Dr. Starr got Mom on a gurney and went to put on his scrubs. The nurse called to him that I was on the way. Dr. Starr ran into the room, became aware of the immediacy of the moment, and walked toward Mom to assist in the childbirth. He had not had chance to tie his scrubs, and they fell to his ankles. Mom said he had on plaid undershorts and argyle socks with garters. She laughed out loud and out I came, completely in the caul. As I thought about my birth, I wished I could help make her transition as gentle as she had made mine.

Eventually Mom began the death rattle. I had been with my stepfather when he died, so I recognized this moment. At this point, I felt her spirit leave her body. In another five minutes, she breathed her last breath.

It was clear to me that Mom had made a decision not to struggle anymore to beat the odds, as she had so many times before. At the age of 89, eight days after she read her poems, Mom died of pneumonia, peacefully and quietly with me at her side. I believe the experience of reading her own poetry helped her to reconnect with a part of herself that she may have lost along the way. And I'm convinced that something shifted to allow her to cross the threshold she had been on for so very long.

Five days later we had a memorial service for Mom and read four of her poems. She was cremated, and some of her ashes were divided among family and close friends who had gardens and wanted to have some of Mom's green-thumb energy sprinkled on their flowers. We put some on our roses but saved most for later.

On my 60th birthday in April of that year, I drove to the yard of my childhood home in New Jersey, left a few of her ashes on the dogwoods and Japanese maples she loved so much, and then met Alden and Eddie at the shore. We walked across the sand and dodged the waves of an incoming tide to get to the end of the rock jetty. We tossed Mom's ashes and the petals of two-dozen pink roses high into the air on a clear and cloudless day, where a whirling wind whisked them away over the deep cerulean sea. It couldn't have been choreographed better. The light petals sparkling in the sun floated like iridescent jewels on the dark surface. Wet with ocean spray, we cried and hugged and laughed, feeling we had metaphorically set Mom's spirit free at last. At that poetic moment I felt liberated as well, as if I had been relieved of a weight I had been carrying around with me for years. Mom always loved to travel, so Alden quipped, "She should be in Portugal by tomorrow!"

Five years later, our roses are flourishing. During their season, I try to keep a vase of pink roses near a framed photo of Mom. It feels a little like an altar to her and brings me joy.

I have dreamed a lot about my mother. Often I would awaken agitated, fearing that I had forgotten to do something for her or trying desperately to get to her when she was in need of help. But then finally I had a comforting dream. She was probably in her early 70s, certainly not as frail as she was during her last years. Mom, Alden, and I were on a road trip to a place I had never been before. We drove through lovely scenery that reminded me of southwestern Ireland. The clouds obscured the sunshine most of the time, although we did occasionally glimpse a ray or two as well as a rainbow. The three of us were in silent awe over every exquisite moment, driving around bends that suddenly offered up wildflowers along rocky walls and then around another curve that opened to vast vistas of misty shoreline. We saw fewer and fewer homes along the way, and at one point I thought that we were surely lost. But as we drove up a steep hill, we saw our destination: a large white inn with a wrap-around porch. Alden and I took Mom upstairs into her cozy room that had a pitcher filled with fragrant summer roses, and we helped her unpack. Then we went into town to eat together in a charming cafe, where we enjoyed our meal and one another's company. When we returned to her room at the inn, we helped Mom get into her favorite nightgown, tucked her into bed, and gently kissed her goodbye. She seemed resigned yet happy. I had a faint memory that this is where we had witnessed others come to their final rest. Somehow we knew Mom was lying down to die and that we would not be seeing her again. It all seemed predetermined and natural, as if we were sending her on her final journey with love in our hearts. I awakened feeling a sense of bittersweet calm, resolution, and peace.

Perhaps my unconscious was offering me a more pleasing final scene to this tragedy than the one we were given. I prefer to believe that Mom came to visit me in my dream to provide a beautiful way to say goodbye to her for the last time.

*Inspired by the creativity of her family, friends, students, and clients, **Carol Thayer Cox** has devoted much of her career as an art therapist to teaching, supervising, researching, theorizing, collaborating with colleagues, and writing. Encouraged by her mother's words, "try to leave the world a better place," Carol passionately advocates for peace, social justice, and a greener environment. She enjoys poetry and art.*

Viola Johnson Hicks

My mother and father in Tuckahoe, New York, in 1943

Mother at about 72 years old

My Mother

by Johnny P. Johnson

My father died when I was only 16 years old, and my mother died 34 years later. During those 34 years, Mother and I became very close. My sister was six years older than I, and she left for college in 1947 and was never at our home for more than three months during the time between 1947 and 1951. The bond of love and respect between Mother and me was strong. The only change in that wonderful relationship came about during the last six months of her life. The love and respect remained, but Mother's dementia was challenging.

Viola Johnson Hicks was born March 2, 1909, and she died June 28, 1986. The cause of her death was congestive heart failure. Mother struggled with high blood pressure for at least 25 years before she passed. It could have been an even longer period, but since she had not been seeing doctors regularly, it probably went undiagnosed.

My mother began periodic doctor visits when she was in her late fifties. Before then, she only went to the doctor when she felt it was absolutely necessary. Even after she began routine check-ups, she did not always do what they said. She often listened to her friends who did not necessarily embrace the concept of "following the doctor's orders."

During the spring of 1986, Mother's ailments began to take their toll. She had difficulty moving with the degree of confidence that she had before. She accepted it with some reluctance. The situation was serious enough that I hired a woman who lived next door to be her daily caregiver. My mother did not like the idea of having someone outside of the home doing the things that she had always been able to do for herself.

For nearly sixty years of her life, my mother was a domestic worker, and being a "country girl," her work ethic was exemplary. So when she was unable to do for herself and my stepfather, it was extremely difficult for her. Her fear of having to go to a nursing home did not help her emotional state.

Our hometown of Henderson, North Carolina, was approximately 160 miles from Fredericksburg, Virginia, where I live. Because my sister had her own health problems and lived in Michigan, it was left up to me to be the family caregiver. I was able to go to Henderson for two or three days twice monthly for at least nine months, since I had accumulated quite a few days of leave as a teacher. Once those visits started, I was able to observe Mother's slow decline in health until her death.

My visits focused on grocery shopping, cooking, housekeeping chores, doctor appointments, and any other necessary business. Mother began to be more stubborn than ever. We had always had a very, very close relationship, and sometimes it was extremely hard to accept Mother's negative attitude towards me. Dementia was one of the reasons for her mood changes. Mother was the kind of person who was always in charge, and not being able to maintain that status had to have been devastating for her.

It always seemed odd to me that Mother talked about death more than the average person. In the late forties, she went to the funeral home two blocks from our house and viewed a corpse in a casket that showed the whole body. From then on she talked about having the same kind of casket for her burial. It seemed to me that Mother spoke of dying far too much. At least twenty years before she died, she told my sister and me what dresser drawer her burial gown was in.

In the late thirties, following my brother's death at birth, Mother had a very serious operation. After that surgical procedure, she seemed to think that she was living on borrowed time. As a devout Christian, Mother prayed that she would live long enough to see the day when my sister and I could take care of ourselves. Once that happened, the subject of death was often in her conversations. My mother's faith had a lot to do with how well she accepted the inevitability of physical death. She was such a giving person, and quite often she was more concerned about not being able to help others as she once did. Mother's gratitude for God's blessing was foremost in her mind, and even small blessings were not taken for granted.

On my last trip before Mother died, her dementia was more obvious, but there were still times when she was quite lucid. It was a very hot spell in June. As I was about to leave, I told her that I was getting her an air conditioner the next week. There had been much talk on television about the adverse effects of heat on the elderly. But she and my stepfather had the opinion that air conditioners did more harm than good, an attitude shared by many of the elderly people in our neighborhood. When Mother said it was okay, I was pleasantly surprised—and being pleasantly surprised was a big thing for me, because Mother, during the last few months of her life, was not usually agreeable to my suggestions. I gave her a kiss and told her that I loved her. She said "I love you, too," and we said our goodbyes. It was the last time we would say "I love you" to one another.

During the trip back to Fredericksburg, I felt more gratified than I had on most of my return trips. During the last three months of her life, Mother's dementia and her circumstances had caused her to view me as a "thorn in her side" rather than a dutiful son. It did hurt a little bit, but after talking to other people about their experiences with their parents, I found that Mother's reaction to me was rather mild, comparatively speaking.

Three hours after I arrived in Fredericksburg the phone rang, and my stepsister told me that Mother was being rushed to the hospital. As the rescue squad crew was taking Mother out of her room, I could hear her say, "Lord have mercy, Jesus." An hour and a half later, I received another call and was told that she had died. It made me feel almost numb, and a few tears came.

Later, I was bombarded with all kinds of thoughts. Mother had only finished what is now called middle school but was very smart when it came to the things that really mattered in life. She was hardworking, caring, and always reaching out to people in need. Without a doubt, she was the most respected and best loved woman in our neighborhood. Those thoughts overshadowed my experience of her as an unusually stubborn, uncooperative, and sometimes verbally abusive woman on whom dementia had taken its toll. I thanked God that my last moments with Mother were positive ones.

Mother had talked with my sister and me about her wishes regarding her funeral arrangements, which made most of the decisions quite easy. Even though it was a sad time, we had some occasions to laugh as we were making preparations. First of all, the shroud (nightgown) was not in the drawer that she had told me for the last three or four years it would be in. A neighbor was in the house at the time, and she informed me that Mother had changed the drawers in recent months. It was funny to me that almost all the neighbors who visited knew where the nightgown was kept. When I mentioned it to the mortician, a man our whole family knew from birth, even he was aware of the correct location. He said Mother had told him on one of his visits. Mother had discussed death with my sister and me, but not until after she died did I learn that she talked about it with anyone who would listen. This took place over a period of many years.

The funeral, though sad for me, was really a celebration of Mother's life. It was held at the church she attended when she was a child. After her marriage to my father, she moved her membership to a church in town. Later she went back to her original church and was a member there for the last 35 years of her life. The eulogy was given by her pastor, and it was heartwarming to hear him acknowledge my mother's finest qualities. Other people spoke about how generous and caring she was; they mentioned that in spite of her not being able to come to church during her illness, she always sent her offering. Her funeral was very much the way I thought it should be.

There have been many times since Mother's death when I tried to make some contact with her. Each time I have gone to the gravesite, I have shared things with her and Dad about their grandchildren and great-grandchildren. Even though she remarried after my father's death, she told my stepfather that she wanted to be buried beside my father. My stepfather accepted that desire of Mother's. Talking to both of my parents at the same time when I am at the cemetery has been therapeutic. Sometimes I sense that my parents are aware of events that relate to our family. I probably have dreamed about Mother over 25 times since her death. I often think about those dreams but have not been able to come to any conclusions.

I always thought that my mother's prayers really made a difference in my life. Therefore, my sense of security suffered because Mother was no longer there to pray for me. For a time, it was a hot issue for me. But after a few years, I realized that God does not erase the prayers of people after they die, especially if these prayers were for those who are still living.

I still miss my mother, but I have the assurance that she appreciated what I did for her, and I know my gratitude for her is tremendous. In most of the speeches I have made during the last forty years or more, I mention that among all the people who have influenced me, my mother has made the greatest impact on my life.

Although the public schools did not offer art education in Henderson, North Carolina, where **Johnny Johnson** *grew up, his interest in art led him to become a practicing artist. He taught art for over 40 years in the Fredericksburg, Virginia, schools, where he mentored many young people. Johnny is proud of his teaching experience and continues to paint and exhibit his works.*

Virginia Harrison Hews

Mom and I sharing chi in 1958

Mother Chi

by Melinda L. Hews

The First Day

Pulling my chair close to Mom's bed in the ICU, I take her hand, an eczema-scabbed version of my own, and hold it in love and prayer. "God, I am not asking you to save Mom's life. Let her life go where it needs to go now. It's okay." Her hand warms; it is my chi and my mother's chi combining and flowing back and forth. It is her real hand and her real life energy, not well, but still very much alive. My conscious mom would dismiss the idea of sharing energy in this way, let alone calling the concept by its Chinese name, "chi." But her spirit feels otherwise. I pray for my mother's life and for mine; I am thankful for her caretaking of me, her mothering, her hands-on care in my life. I feel myself letting go of her while she fills me with her life force.

I lay my head on a pillow on the rail by her bed, cuddling as close as I can. My silent tears flow freely as I finally let down the I'm-ready-for-my-Mom-to-die guard. In this moment I don't have to be the brave daughter trying to figure out the right thing to do for her. I experience the kind of comfort I feel when I hold my own daughter as she falls asleep at night.

The Second Day

My mother, unconscious because she is sedated, struggles and gags against the tubes pulling bile from her body. She tries to breathe in spite of the machine doing it for her. Someone has scrawled "3-14-07 #7.5" on the white tape under her nose. The nurse looks gently at her, swabbing the dried blood out of her nostrils with a Q-tip and Bacitracin. She still believes

Mom is a person worth caring for, worth receiving the small gifts that keep us human. She cleans her face and heats a shower cap for a fake shampoo to remove EEG goop from her hair. I love the kindness of this woman.

I don't get Mom's chi today when I pray for the right outcome. As I cry on the toilet in the stuffy, overused bathroom for visitors, I feel the ancestral and generational pain of maternal loss. I feel my mother losing her mother when she was just thirteen. I feel my grandmother losing her mother when my mother was three. I feel my sister losing her baby minutes after the child's birth. The mother energy of generations of women connected to me through blood and psyche sweeps over me, and my chi courses and hums with the presence of these mothers in my life.

The Third Day

The nurse brings Mom out of sedation with all four of her daughters and her longtime family doctor around her bed. She was last fully conscious when she arrived at her Monday bridge game where she had a seizure. She looks around at us, blinking, trying to comprehend where she is and why we are all there. As she sees each one of her girls, she gives a small smile of recognition that says, "and you're here too?" Nothing brings more pleasure to my mother than to have all of her daughters together with her. None of us live in her town or even in her state. So I imagine her realizing that lying in a hospital bed with all of us present means something serious is happening.

Her doctor asks the life and death question, "Do you want us to stop what we are doing? You are on life support."

Mom looks surprised at the question and her eyes widen in fear. She shakes her head deliberately, "No!" Perhaps she is even still wondering why she is here rather than at her bridge game. Her "advance directives" instruct otherwise, but the directives are not available in the emergency room when Mom is brought in after suffering the seizure. Mom's friend, who follows the ambulance to the hospital, calls Julie first. Julie then calls each of us to tell us the news. Jennifer, the youngest sister, immediately calls the ER and reaches a doctor who asks if she wants Mom to be intubated.

"Is this the normal thing you do in this situation?" my non-medically trained little sister asks.

The doctor says, "Yes it is; she will die if we do not put her on a ventilator to help her breathe." Hearing this, Jennifer consents. Beth, the eldest sister who is a doctor and has Mom's medical power of attorney, is on another line demanding that she not be put on a ventilator. She is interpreting Mom's advance directives and knows the longer-term medical consequences of intubation. With two opposing instructions from the family, the ER staff chooses the immediate life-saving course of action.

We four daughters have not been able to agree about what to do since. Unsure about her mental capacity, we decide to ask her what she wants. After Mom's vehement "no" to the doctor's question, we confer outside of her room. The doctor voices our struggle between hope and reality. "I don't think she'll live through this," he says, "but it's too soon to take her off life support, and she has now said to stay the course."

"How much can she really understand about this?" I ask my sister the doctor. Beth looks anguished under the burden of multiple roles: oldest sister with medical power of attorney, physician, and frightened daughter of a critically ill woman.

"We can't really know," she answers, her blue eyes filled with pain and the blank look of doubt that all of her medical training does not overcome. She is first a daughter, not a doctor.

Later, only lightly sedated, Mom becomes agitated, as she feels more congested. "Do you want to sit up?" I ask.

"Yes," she nods. Julie and I, the middle two sisters, each hold one of Mom's shoulders as we raise the hospital bed.

"Hello, Mom!" Julie says, through tears. Mom brightens and smiles at her, then turns her head to me and gives me a cold one-eyed stare, as if she blames me for forcing her to decide whether or not she should live.

I look into her eyes and say, "I love you, Mom. I'm sorry you're here with all this going on that you did not want." She closes her eyes and turns away, then rolls her head back toward me and repeats the "stink eye." I try to let go of the icy feeling that comes over me with this harsh look. She has never looked at me in this way in all my 49 years, so why now, I wonder. As the nurse comes in to put her back under with the sedating drugs, I wonder if Mom will ever look at me or nod in my direction again. I don't want this to be the last look shared between us.

After a Week

I need to fly home. My family and my employer need me. My sisters understand and encourage me to go. Mom isn't off the ventilator yet, and in order for her to live, she will have to come off of it in the next two days. And I have to leave.

Julie, who does not like medical situations, helps the nurse move Mom in the bed. She washes her tenderly as if she were caring for a baby and dries her off to make her more comfortable. Mom's tense face relaxes. I realize as I watch Julie care for Mom that she is the one for the job.

"I have already let you go, so I can't deal with your visceral needs anymore. But I am glad for both of you that Julie can do it," I think to myself. *"I can tell you I love you, which doesn't seem to matter at this point,"* although I know it has mattered completely.

"Goodbye, Momma. I have to go home," I say. "I love you. My sisters are still here for you, and I'll call you every day." Mom's eyes are closed, and she is drugged. She does not even give me a stinkeye of acknowledgement to leave with as I turn to go. The machine hisses on, filling her lungs. I won't ever know if she has heard my voice. I can't look back. I have to go out into my life.

Two Days Later

My daughter Claire is so happy to have her Mommy back. Wednesday school ends early, and I am working at home so I can pick her up and enjoy a treat of lunch-out at the Nordstrom Grill. Glasses clink and conversation hums as ladies lunch, silver shopping bags at their feet. I barely hear the cell phone ringing in my purse.

I can tell by her voice that Julie is anxious. "You need to talk to Mom right now. They're going to disconnect the ventilator and see if she can breathe on her own!"

"Does she know what is going on? That this may be it?" I ask her. Julie replies that she believes Mom understands the situation, and she will put the phone next to Mom's ear now. "I love you, Mom. I'll be praying for you and thinking of you. Know that I love you very much. 'Bye." I hear the ventilator's hiss over the noise of the restaurant, but my mother's voice is silent.

Julie says that Mom smiled hearing my words and that she will call me and tell me what is happening when she can. Click, the phone goes dead, and the hubbub of the restaurant continues.

"I may have just said goodbye to your Grandma for the last time," I explain to Claire when she asks why I've stopped eating my lunch. Suddenly, she too is no longer hungry.

"Let's go home, Mom," she says.

The Twelfth Day

The phone rings early that morning. Julie tells me Mom has died, and we talk for a moment. Patricia, Julie's daughter, had taken the night shift at the hospital and was dozing in a chair by her side when the EKG alarm woke her announcing Mom's death. I feel calm and breathe deeply as I make breakfast for Claire. Then I look up and see Mom's college-graduation-portrait face smiling serenely across the room at me, and I burst into tears.

Claire comes down the stairs, ready for school, and I tell her that Mom died a few hours ago. Her sweet countenance falls for a moment as the news strikes her. We had planned on spending spring break at Grandma's the following week. "Well, I guess I won't get to show her how to use her computer now," Claire ponders, living in the practical immediate world of an eleven-year-old. "Grandma would have said, 'the things you kids know how to do!'" as she munches her cereal.

"Go brush your teeth, honey. We don't want you to be late for school." I encourage her to move along.

As I sit at the table absorbing my life without my mother in it, Claire runs halfway up the stairs, only to turn around and run back down to give me a hug. I ask her if she is okay, and she pulls away from me, cradles my face in her hands, her own face inches from mine. "No, Mom. The point is, are you okay?" I feel the empathy of my mother through this question from my daughter. I am grateful that my mother has taught me the value of kindness that I now see in my young girl. I am pleased to be both daughter and mother at this moment.

Over a Year Later

I see evidence of my mother in everyday events and exchanges as my family moves on with their lives. My sisters and I share the small kindnesses and the wry sense of humor we learned from our mother. Sometimes I hear her sharp, critical tongue and the Depression-era sayings coming unbidden from my mouth in conversation.

My daughter tells me that she actually has seen her grandmother when we first returned to her house in the week after her death. "She was in the driveway when we left the last time, Mom," she tells me. "And she looked so happy. It made me feel sad that we can't be with her anymore." I see that it comforts my girl to have seen her grandmother, and I believe her.

My mother is with me in my dreams: I clean up old houses that feel like hers, but not exactly. This cleaning activity, this creating my own psychic home, pleases her. Seeing that I am coming into my own creativity, she knows I can mother myself more completely now.

My hand sometimes reaches for my cell phone on my commute home from work. Her number, the home phone of my childhood that belongs to someone else now, is still filed under "M" for Mom. I'd like to tell her about some workplace drama or small triumph that happened in my day. Lately I've noticed her in my rear view mirror, waiting. I tell her about my day and I know she is listening.

Melinda Hews *is the third of four daughters of a respected judge and his supportive wife. Her father died suddenly of a heart attack in 1989. Melinda pursued a career in healthcare management, married later in life, and had her only daughter at age 38. She continues to work in healthcare, raise her teenage daughter with her husband, and write.*

Acknowledgments

We are grateful to all the authors of this volume who were willing to grapple with the questions we asked of them, never retreating once they had committed to delving into their memories to write their stories. Their honesty and trust in us during the editing process has been humbling and deeply gratifying.

As dedicated editors, we were aware that our weekly scheduled meetings sometimes demanded sacrifices by our families. But we were fortunate that our spouses, Jerry and Beth, as well as our closest friends, were staunch supporters and never lost faith in our mission.

We appreciate Kimberly Cox's meticulous proofreading of our manuscript as well as Wendy Miller's reliable mentoring, especially during the publication process. We also thank Helaine Patterson, a long-time friend and public relations specialist, who valued our concept so highly from the start that she has worked diligently on multi-leveled ideas for publicity.

Last, but certainly not least, we offer our enduring and heartfelt gratitude to Lisa Hagan, who lovingly held our vision from the beginning, never giving up hope that it would indeed someday be a reality, and to her colleagues, Beth Wareham and Laura Smyth, who also contributed their wisdom and believed in what this book could offer.

Biographies of the Editors

Carol Thayer Cox *has been on the faculty of the graduate art therapy programs of George Washington University, Vermont College of Norwich University, and Pratt Institute's School of Art & Design. Co-author of* Telling Without Talking: Art as a Window into the World of Multiple Personality *(W.W. Norton, 1995) and co-editor of* Portrait of the Artist as Poet *(Magnolia Street Publishers, 2006), she has written numerous professional journal articles and book chapters. Carol is also founder and director of MUSE, a performing arts troupe that teaches psychological theory through the arts.*

William A. Harrison, III *taught English for forty years at Northern Virginia Community College. During that time he marked and graded—edited—tens of thousands of student essays. He wrote occasional commentary for* The Washington Post *and edited the college's 2000–01 self-study, a five-hundred page analysis of the institution required for re-accreditation by the Southern Association of Colleges and Schools. He retired in 2009 and since then has embarked on a new career as an artist and novelist.*

Made in the USA
Middletown, DE
23 March 2017